THE RELIGIOUS VOCATION

THE RELIGIOUS VOCATION

BY

RICHARD MEUX BENSON

Formerly Student of Christ Church, Oxford
Founder and first Superior of the Society of the Mission
Priests of St. John the Evangelist, Oxford

EDITED ON BEHALF OF THE SOCIETY BY THE

Rev. H. P. BULL, S.S.J.E.

Sometime Superior General

WITH AN INTRODUCTION BY THE

Rev. LUCIUS CARY, S.S.J.E.

WIPF & STOCK · Eugene, Oregon

Wipf and Stock Publishers
199 W 8th Ave, Suite 3
Eugene, OR 97401

The Religious Vocation
By Benson, Richard Meux, S.S.J.E
Softcover ISBN-13: 978-1-7252-6516-5
Hardcover ISBN-13: 978-1-7252-6517-2
eBook ISBN-13: 978-1-7252-6518-9
Publication date 2/3/2020
Previously published by A. R. Mowbray & Co., 1939

Instructions upon the Rule of Life given to the members of the Society of St. John the Evangelist in the Mission House Chapel, Oxford, by the Rev. Richard Meux Benson, Founder and first Superior of the Society, during the years 1874 and 1875.

PREFACE

THE Society of St. John the Evangelist was founded on St. John the Evangelist's day, 1866, when Father Benson, Father Grafton, and Father O'Neill, who had been living together for a year previously under the guidance of Father Benson, took the vows of their Religious Profession, in one another's presence, to live in perpetual observance of Poverty, Chastity, and Obedience. The present parish of Cowley St. John, Oxford, in which the Mother House of the Society is situated, was then a part of the parish of Cowley, and the Society has been given its common appellation of the 'Cowley Fathers' from this circumstance.

At first there was but the Rule of the Society, drawn up by Father Benson as its Founder and Superior. The Constitution of the Society as an organized body, with its appropriate Statutes, did not take place till 1884, when the Statutes and Rule of Life were formally approved by Bishop Mackarness, then Bishop of Oxford, in his chapel at Cuddesdon.

The Rule of Life was fashioned gradually, and took its more complete form when the Society was thus firmly established; and from time to time alterations have been made in accordance with the provisions laid down in the Statutes, but the spirit of the Society is that which was impressed upon it by the Father Founder. The quotations from the Rule that occur in the following pages are from its present form, and are such as have a general application to any form of the Religious life. The instructions, which are now printed for the first time, were given to the members of the Society in the chapel of the Mission House, during the years 1874 and 1875. They were taken down in shorthand, but were not copied out and circulated in the houses of the Society until 1883. They were not intended as a complete exposition of the principles of the Religious life; but they exhibit fully the meaning of the Religious vocation. They are instructions on the main principles of a Religious Rule, and on the fundamental spiritual exercises of the Religious life.

In the present edition only such alterations have been made as seemed necessary for a printed edition, or were required to make the meaning clear. In certain places obscurities, arising from the origin of the text, have been interpreted in the light of the Father Founder's other teachings, but the general character of the instructions, as oral and largely extempore addresses, has been preserved, and with this the Father Founder's characteristic definiteness and fullness of utterance.

In a few instances the life of the Society externally has somewhat changed in emphasis from the original strict asceticism of the Father Founder's vision. It has been thought well, however, not to modify his statements, but rather to indicate, where necessary, in the Notes added to this edition the later developments of the Society. The instructions represent the ideal which fashioned its early years, and laid the foundation of its stability. They represent principles that cannot be laid aside, however much they may have been found to need the balance of the later practical experience of the Society's extended life and work in the Church.

The best guide to the Father Founder's utterances is to be found in the Holy Scriptures themselves. He used familiarly their language, and it is generally possible to parallel what appear at first sight to be difficulties in his statements, with similar difficulties in the Bible itself. He learned from that sacred source, and was ever content to await the solution of all mysteries in the revelation of the final manifestation of Christ. But as in Holy Scripture one passage must often be taken in connection with another, if the full truth is to be apprehended, so it is with some of the Father Founder's words, and attention is called to this in the Notes, where necessary.

A brief analysis of each paragraph has been given, and the instructions themselves have been broken into sections, in order that the sequence of thought may be more clearly apprehended, and their devotional use made easier. The Father Founder speaks out his whole soul in these pages, and his words bear the impress of intense conviction, born of deep personal experience, and sustained and nourished by constant meditation on the great Christian truths. He had trodden a new path, and almost alone, in the circumstances of the Church of his day. But to-day his followers and disciples are many, beyond the ranks of the Society which he founded. To them as to ourselves, no words, perhaps, could more fittingly introduce this record of his early teaching than the tender longing appeal of St. Francis to his sons and brethren:

O DILECTISSIMI FRATRES, ET IN AETERNUM BENEDICTI FILII, AUDITE ME, AUDITE VOCEM PATRIS VESTRI.

CONTENTS

CHAPTER		PAGE
	PREFACE - - - -	7
	INTRODUCTION : THE SPIRIT OF FATHER BENSON - - -	13
I.	OF THE OBJECTS OF THE SOCIETY -	37
	NOTE A—The work of our sanctification.	
II.	OF THE CALL OF GOD - -	48
III.	OF OUR VOCATION AS SUBORDINATED TO THE LIFE OF THE CHURCH -	56
	NOTE B—The forfeiture of a vocation.	
IV.	OF THE CALL OF GOD, CONTINUOUS, ABIDING, AND PROGRESSIVE -	69
V.	OF LIFE IN COMMUNITY - -	80
	NOTE C—The rise of Religious Communities. NOTE D—Natural unfitness.	
VI.	OF THE THREE VOWS - -	90
	NOTE E—This nature of sin. NOTE F—The cost and blessing of obedience.	
VII.	OF LIVING UNDER RULE - -	103
	NOTE G—The grace of the Society.	
VIII.	OF OBEDIENCE - - -	108
IX.	OF CHASTITY - - -	119
X.	OF POVERTY - - -	131
	NOTE H—The infection of wealth.	
XI.	OF CONFESSION - - -	145
XII.	OF COMMUNION - - -	153
XIII.	OF THE DIVINE OFFICE—ITS NATURE AND DIGNITY - - -	164
	NOTE I—The mutual life of the Spirit. NOTE J—The Jewish use of the Psalter.	

CHAPTER		PAGE
XIV.	OF THE DIVINE OFFICE—THE SPIRIT OF CHOIR - - - -	175
XV.	OF THE USE OF THE PSALTER -	182
XVI.	OF MENTAL PRAYER - -	190
	NOTE K—Revelations in the ordinary Christian Life.	
XVII.	OF THE DAILY MEDITATION -	200
	NOTE L—Common meditation on the same truths	
XVIII.	OF FASTING AND MORTIFICATION -	208
	NOTE M—The *Spolia Opima*.	
XIX.	OF INTERIOR MORTIFICATION -	221
XX.	OF THE BURIED LIFE OF THE RELIGIOUS	229
	NOTE N—The joy of Jesus upon earth. NOTE O—The Religious and the world.	
XXI.	OF DEMEANOUR - - -	241
	NOTE P—Contact with the world.	
XXII.	OF SPIRITUAL INSTRUCTION—THE WITNESS OF A RELIGIOUS COMMUNITY IN THE CHURCH - - -	258
XXIII.	OF SPIRITUAL INSTRUCTION—WITH SPECIAL REFERENCE TO HOLY SCRIPTURE - - - -	271
XXIV.	OF CONVERSATION—THE LAW OF SILENCE AND THE LAW OF SPEECH -	281
XXV.	OF CONVERSATION—THE SANCTITY OF THE GIFT OF SPEECH - -	292
	NOTE Q—The truth of our interior life. NOTE R—The word of God.	
XXVI.	OF CONVERSATION — OUR SPEECH ONE WITH ANOTHER - -	306

INTRODUCTION

THE SPIRIT OF FATHER BENSON
By the Rev. Lucius Cary, S.S.J.E.

NEARLY a quarter of a century has passed since the warrior spirit of Richard Meux Benson passed to its rest triumphantly in the first catastrophic months of the Great War. Since then a new generation has arisen, intensely preoccupied with its own problems, and to a large extent disposed to discredit the values and even the principles of the preceding age. To the old order, pregnant as it was with the seed of disorder, there has succeeded an era striving after order, yet actually more chaotic by reason of the domination of fantastic theories and of false lights. Alone in the conflicting shadows the Catholic Church remains faithful to her age-long witness, and it is in her constant teaching alone that ultimate security will be found. But in her case also, the diversity of interpretation introduces a spirit of uncertainty. If not she herself, at least multitudes of her children are infected with intellectual and moral restlessness.

At such a time it may well be opportune to recur to the teaching of one not unworthy to be called the last of the prophets of the old order, and like all prophets, gifted with a vision that belongs to the order of Eternity and true reality illuminating the events of time. The spirit of Father Benson can only be apprehended when it is recognized as prophetic spirit, illuminated by a light that is supernatural and charged with creative energy of life. In that recognition the means will be found for resolving the difficulties of those who find themselves dismayed by the austerity of his asceticism, or perplexed by seeming anomalies in his doctrinal outlook. Whatever memory may preserve or legend have transmitted of the amazing activities of his ministerial and Religious life, can be accounted for by the spiritual energy of the mystical life which found its overflow of Charity in unwearying action.

The number of those who cherish personal memories of Father Benson, gathered in the years between 1866 and 1890 while he was in England as Superior of the Religious Society which he had founded, is becoming small. But among them are those who are most deeply convinced that the true nature and the essential greatness of the Father's character have never been sufficiently realized. His career of creative activity, coming in succession after the first tide of the Oxford Movement, and at a period when the worst of the troubles that followed the Movement had subsided, did not share the arresting quality which the Movement itself possessed. Yet none the less it was in the strictest sense a continuation and a spiritual application of the deepest life-energy of the Movement, and it is from that point of view and not in detachment from it that it should be regarded. It neither swerved in the direction of Liberalism, nor reacted towards Mediaevalism, but maintained the direction which the Movement originated, while eliciting and developing the inmost spiritual elements which gave to the Movement its true survival energy.

But if the witnesses of the earlier period are becoming few, there remain those who watched the last fifteen years at Oxford. There, with external activity increasingly precluded, those around him could see the constant spirit undistracted in its fixity on God. And they knew that as it was in the declining years of physical weakness, so and not otherwise it had been through the long years of his consecrated life.

Now after a lapse of years, it has seemed fitting to offer to a wider circle that which has been the peculiar treasure of the Society which he founded—the exposition and spiritual commentary upon the Rule. The commentary itself is incomplete; but there is enough available to enable those who approach it in a serious and sympathetic spirit not only to gather instruction for themselves in details, but also to see the field of the spiritual and Religious life illuminated with the light derived from a clearly manifested vision, and again in that light of vision to discern at least something of the spirit of the Seer.

For it may be observed that these instructions, together with the letters already published, and especially those addressed to Father O'Neill, are in a different category from the books of spiritual commentaries and meditations published by him.

self in his lifetime. The latter, offered to all and sundry for instruction and edification, though instinct with a lofty spirituality, are to a certain degree accommodated to the need they are intended to supply. The former, addressed to men whom he had formed or was forming for participation in a common life which was to be the concrete presentation of the content of his own vision, have no such accommodation. They represent the spontaneous and free outpouring of his own spiritual perceptions concerning the vital themes of which he was concerned to treat. Trained in the school of the Psalmists and of the Beloved Disciple, intellectually and spiritually tutored by St. Paul, deeply influenced by the Fathers of the earliest centuries, he poured out of the fullness of his own spiritual attainment interpretations and counsels of penetrating sagacity and wisdom, in language and with imagery often baffling to the ordinary mind.

I

The words 'prophetic' and 'mystical' have been already used, and it is in such connection as this that their use may be justified. For though the terms are not synonymous, they, together with the word 'contemplation,' are descriptive of different qualities or functions of a life that has a specific relation to the supreme Reality of God. That which is common to all is immediacy. The contemplative is immediately percipient. From beneath and through the multiplicity of thought and mental activity of various kinds, the spirit perceives, however dimly, and gazes towards the uncreated light. The mystic is immediately vital in that he lives in a world of far greater reality than the world of sense. While the natural faculties are normally engaged with the events and circumstances of natural life and the manifold interests, social, intellectual, aesthetic, arising from them, he is in himself borne upon a tide of life of another order. He is conscious of himself as one who (if he be a Christian) has his true life hid with Christ in God. And because that life is known by him as the true life, it supplies the interpretation of common life according to a different scale of values. The prophet is immediately recipient and declaratory. It is his function to receive directly the truth which the divine Wisdom would have him deliver, with its specific bearing upon the problems and the conduct of those to whom its message is addressed. 'That which we have seen and heard declare we unto you.'

But neither prophet, mystic, nor contemplative is stripped of his own personality; and in the contact which he has with those who would profit by his immediacy, that personality has to be taken into consideration. If we are accustomed to consider various schools of mysticism they will usually be found to be grouped in the first instance locally or racially, though the original local characteristics may tend to be diffused abroad by personal discipleship, and through the greater Religious Orders with their wide dissemination. A comparative study of spiritual life strictly from this point of view would be of interest. For the moment we are only concerned with the suggestion that as the main distinctive quality of the prophet, mystic, or contemplative is his immediacy, when he becomes an intermediary for others, his personality and the influences bearing on its development should be taken into account.[1] The words of the prophet, the life lived by the mystic, the prayer of the contemplative belong to his condition and his circumstances; but the utterance, the essential life, and the vision belong to the supernatural order and to the eternal.

The origin of the distinctive spirituality of Father Benson may then be confidently sought in the whole-hearted devotion with which from his birth he had been given by his mother's piety to God. Such evidence as is available would seem to show that from his first awareness of this dedication, he had not only acquiesced but had corresponded with the general tenor of its demands. Accordingly, when he found himself at Oxford at the time when the learning and spiritual power of Dr. Pusey had secured his ascendancy among the promoters of the Catholic Revival, not the spirit only, but the whole soul of Richard Benson was ready to receive the formative influence of one whose authority he reverenced till his life's end. His spirit was ready to observe and assimilate, but it owned no other master in the full sense of the word than the Spirit of God and of Christ. His

[1] An example of this may be seen in the very interesting study of St. Teresa of Avila by the Abbé Hoornaert, *Sainte Thérèse Ecrivain* (English translation, *St. Teresa in her writings*).

reasonable soul was ready to give its intellectual powers to be instructed, and its will to be directed, by one who was reopening old avenues of approach to that knowledge for which his whole self had come to thirst increasingly; but he was more than a receptive disciple. *Sitivit in Te anima mea*, was already the aspiration of his life; henceforth all his powers were to be devoted to the quest.

But that did not mean that the young man with his great natural abilities was indifferent to the interests which his education and station offered. It belongs to the study of his spirituality to recognize that he could make use of his intellectual and social opportunities for the enrichment of the personality which, according to the spirit of his original dedication, he purposed to offer. And this enrichment was to have further use in the fulfilment of the vocation, still unrevealed, in obedience to which the creative spirit would be specifically exercised. What we would observe is that the spirit-life within taught him to preserve the necessary balance, so that he could use without abusing, acquire without possessing, could learn to see all things in God, and to use all as means through which to pass to Him.

Meanwhile, for his more immediate study the influence of Dr. Pusey and the main appeal of the Revival had turned the student to the Hebrew Scriptures and to the authority of Patristic literature. In them he found that which formed two at least of the main motives of his spiritual life and teaching, the transcendental glory of God and His eternal purpose, and the riches of the mystery of the Incarnate Word.

It may be worth while at this point to note that in the opinion of some theologians and of philosophical students of religion of such authority as Dr. C. C. J. Webb, the intellectual powers which Father Benson consecrated to the service of his spiritual vision and message were of no mean order. Platonist rather than Aristotelian in his outlook, he would hardly have been touched by the great revival of Scholasticism even had it come when his intellectual powers were at their height. He used his gifts for the assimilation of the vital truth attained through his Scriptural and Patristic studies, in order that he might himself worship more perfectly in spirit and in truth, and might also be the better enabled to help others to be partakers of the same sanctification which he had been inspired and taught to seek. His counsel in the opening chapter of *The Followers of the Lamb* may be taken as a faithful portraiture of his own intellectual life and its methods. 'By intellectual study,' he writes, 'we must follow up the teachings of past ages in the fullness of its scope. We have not to maintain truth, but to live in the truth so that it maintains us. . . . We are not called to deal with theology in the way of massive learning, but we have to handle it effectively as a living power.'

II

But, to return to our main theme, it would probably be true to say that in the spiritual order a profound sense of God and of the divine holiness was antecedent to the ever-increasing knowledge gained through devotion to the Incarnate Word, the Exalted Christ. For him the fear of the Lord was indeed the beginning of wisdom. That which came to St. Augustine in a blinding flash of revelation—*in ictu trepidantis aspectus*—might seem, perhaps by virtue of his original dedication accepted, to have grown upon him with his growth.

Historical instances have made us aware of the formative influence of vision. The two most familiar perhaps are those of St. Paul and St. Augustine. To each of these there came a great converting revelation from which the subsequent transformation of life and character began. But the vision that wrought the conversion remained as normative. The glory of the moment faded, but the truth revealed and the power conveyed did not change or wane. For in such divine interventions a factor is introduced, and that of sovereign value, into all life's calculations and estimates, and from its first incidence and acceptance the process of transformation begins.

But Father Benson, with his life devoted from infancy, needed, in the providence of God, no catastrophic conversion. His vision, no less clear, no less compelling, presented itself spiritually without the psychic disturbance incurred by a great conversion. It may perhaps be said that conformation rather than transformation could describe the process of his growth, though the ultimate mystical transformation in God would still be the goal of attainment.

But if we eliminate the factor of conversion, it may be said that the path of approach to formative vision in the Father's case was rather that of St. Paul than of St. Augustine. St. Augustine had been disillusioned by the bankruptcy of the philosophies with which he had been preoccupied, though he had been brought to the crisis of his conversion by the Neoplatonic conception of the absolute Being and Majesty of God and the insignificance of creatures. St. Paul, a Pharisee of the Pharisees, deeply impregnated with the teaching of the Sacred Scriptures, needed a spiritual illumination no less catastrophic than that of St. Augustine, but his revelation was the vision of the exalted Christ. For the former it is the attainment of the one, true, holy, personal God; for the latter it is the interpretation of that already known. The trained philosophic mind of St. Augustine, confronted in his new vision of God with the inevitable problems raised by the relations between the holiness, justice, and mercy of God and His creation as we observe and know it, finds his guide in the teaching of St. Paul. And in the problem that is most inscrutable of all concerning the freedom of men and divine predestination, both alike are constrained to fall back upon the unsearchable and essential justice which belongs to the infinite Holiness of God.

This particular point is adduced because there are recurrent passages in Father Benson's teaching which have been interpreted as involving him in Calvinism. And it may well be that his early Evangelical training affected the language in which his thought is clothed. But there can be no doubt that had he been pressed for explanations he would have given the same answer which to the mystic and contemplative suffices—*neminem damnat nisi aequissima veritate ; aequitate occultissima et ab humanis sensibus remotissima judicat.* For it is not only in what are familiarly known as mystical experiences, whether in or outside the actual domain of prayer, but in all the conduct of life, moral alike and intellectual, that the soul which is converted and illuminated is conscious that it is in relation, not with another soul like to itself though immeasurably greater in every conceivable regard, but with One who is absolute and transcendent, and who yet condescends to intercourse with the reasonable soul which is His creature.

Herein we may find the key to the spirituality of Father Benson. For a soul that is not only convinced of such truth, but is penetrated by it and immersed in it, sees the drama of history in the light of eternal purpose. And in that wide conspectus of Creation and its story seen in the light of eternal purpose, it reads the story of the activity of redemptive Love. Confident in the Love and Justice of the Eternal, it claims its right to relegate to the realm of supra-rational mystery the paradoxes with which the would-be believer is confronted. There is even a kind of ecstasy in the agnosticism which exclaims with St. Paul, 'How unsearchable are his judgements, and his ways past finding out!'

If, then, we find the root of Father Benson's

spirituality in his original devotion, it will be in this atmosphere and with this light that we shall see its growth to be maintained. From every side there comes the witness in more or less homely language borne by those who remember their first contact with him. 'He spoke, he taught, as one who saw everything from the other side.' And this represents not the resourcefulness of an intellectual, suggesting new points of view, but the wholly other aspect of one who sees the object, not from below or from its own level, but from above, that is, in the light of God.

III

But there is yet another essential influence to be recorded before the spirituality of Father Benson can be understood. If we are right in giving a certain priority to his perception of the divine transcendence, the holiness of God, and the eternal purpose, we must hasten to remember that the light in which he sees is that 'Light which lighteth every man, coming into the world.' Here he becomes at once the pupil of St. John, and under his tutelage the constructive work of his spiritual life goes forward. Not light alone, but life of God invading His creation—life that creates a wholly new relation between man and God—becomes the transforming factor in the experience of human spirit. And this accordingly appears as a predominant element in the spiritual life and teaching of Father Benson.

In the school of St. John his own deep personal devotion to the Incarnate Word was ever increasingly enriched and matured. From the Beloved Disciple he not only gained that penetrating insight which his teaching displays into the demands of discipleship and the privileges of fellowship; but he learned to enter deeply into the mystery of communion with the divine life through incorporation into Christ. For him the actual development of character is gained not so much by the discipline of moral precepts, as by ceaseless endeavour to rise up to the demands of the life that has been received. Whatever he may gain of dogmatic definition from St. Paul, it is always the Incarnate Word Himself, as interpreted by St. John, who gives to him the word of life. That which he thus receives becomes to him the interpretation of an otherwise ineffable experience. To this no doubt we may trace the amazing vitality of his teaching. It is the mystic charged with life who assumes the role of prophet, and speaks of things human according to the values of a wholly supernatural light.

The same conjunction of mystic and prophet has marked influence in another aspect in the spiritual outlook and in the constant teaching of the Father. So thoroughly does the Evangelist impregnate his disciple with his own understanding and interpretation of the Incarnate Word, that the pupil passes on to share something at least of the spirit of his teacher. There is notably in these intimate instructions, but also recurrently in his teaching, a strong apocalyptic strain. He cannot rest content with the richness of Christ as it is here and now received in the life of the redeemed. He must seek and find and know for himself all that the spirit here may know of the glory of the heavenly City and the life of its citizens. Stimulated by St. John's vision of that heavenly City, he describes in his own language the life in love as lived by the Saints in glory. And his words are not to be taken as a preacher's oratorical rhapsody; they represent part at least of the content of the seer's vision, and as such they make their contribution to the wholeness of the spiritual life as lived and taught by him.

IV

We have described Father Benson as the last of the prophets of the old order, and have sought to substantiate the claim. As representative of the old order he stands apart from the modern schools which have come into being in the present century. On the spiritual side there has been a remarkable revival of the study of mysticism and the mystic states. On the secular there has been an even greater and more subversive activity in the study of psychological phenomena, in the course of which not a few eminent secular psychologists have invaded the realm of spiritual phenomena and religious experience. Though these two movements have been contemporaneous and have very important interactions, yet it may be safe to say that they are independent in their origins, and that in fact the revival of the study of mysticism was due to a quickening of the experience of mystical life under the inspiration of the Holy Spirit.

The mystical experience has at no time been absent from the life of the Church, for the simple reason that the essential life of the Christian is fundamentally mystical, since it is the participation in the life of that fellowship which is the mystical Body of the Lord. But there have been tides of recognition, as there have been tides of secularism, of humanism, and of rationalism; and we may well believe that the quickening of the mystical and purely spiritual vitality has been the action of the Holy Spirit in practical witness against the movements of the merely human intelligence and will.

Be these things as they may, what we are concerned to note is that Father Benson, though a great master of the spiritual life, stands in his own great simplicity outside the region of these more modern questions and controversies, whether of principles or of details. The devout reader would look in vain in his teaching for definitions of contemplation, whether infused or acquired, or for instruction on states of prayer. It was not that he was unfamiliar with the writings of the great masters, from St. Bernard to the Spanish golden age and to the *École Française*; but in the intense energy of his own spiritual life and its vivid immediacy, he was not concerned to pause in order to analyse and rationalize. Had he been led to do so, we may perhaps hazard the conjecture that he would have found a place between St. Bernard and St. John of the Cross. With the latter he would share the profound mistrust of the natural and human elements which yielded the asceticism that offends the susceptibilities of so many critics. Like the former, he is deeply moved and guided by intense personal devotion to our Lord. But his own immediacy is too strong, his evangelical confidence too secure, to allow him to become the pupil of any later master than the Beloved Disciple. St. John's counsel, 'Love not the world, neither the things that are in the world,' and his pronouncement that 'the whole world lieth in the evil one,' are sufficient authority for him to justify the demands he makes on those who would seek their own apprehension of the vision that had been granted to himself.

Here we may find a clue to that which may have impressed many as an outstanding feature of the spiritual doctrine of the Father. It is the characteristic which leads those who knew him to think of him as animated by a warrior spirit. The perspective of his vision showed him not only the holiness and majesty of God the Eternal, but also the sovereignty of the Divine Will and the might of God. As against these he saw, in human history and in the story of salvation, the challenge of evil uttering itself in innumerable forms. The primal sin of fallen angels, the subtle suasion that involved man in their fall, were for him the cause of all the forms of evil in creation, as well as of the 'sin that doth so easily beset' the human soul. 'The whole world lieth in the evil one,' and though through the great Redemption the power of the prince of this world has been broken, his domination is not yet abolished, and he can use the natural order as a means to suggest and convey the spirit that is evil.

This does not involve the Father in the Manichaean doctrine which would regard evil as having absolute being of its own. Nor does he regard Nature as being evil in itself. But it does throw light on his conception of the relation between the human spirit and the world around it by reason of the endless suggestion and solicitation conveyed through nature and the sense life to the human soul. 'The whole world lieth in the evil one,' writes St. John. 'Mortify therefore your members which are upon the earth,' says St. Paul. Father Benson's insistence on mortification is in strict harmony with these apostolic counsels. His teaching is not the result of a faulty metaphysic; it is rather of the nature of a call to meet the enemy of God on the field which he has chosen for the conflict. It is not fear which impels, but the spirit of victory which inspires the warrior of God. In connection with this it is significant to note the great influence which the *Spiritual Exercises* of St. Ignatius Loyola, the warrior saint, seem to have had on the retreats of a month's duration given by the Father in the early days of the Society.

As with mortification, so also it is with discipline, though in a somewhat different category. In the forefront of the vision of the Divine Glory there is seen the figure of the victorious and exalted Christ. It is He who has broken the power of evil. It is He who through the Holy Spirit pours life into the redeemed. In

Him, and strictly in Him, 'we are more than conquerors.' The discipline, as distinct from the mortification, which is imposed, is so ordered as to make the soul in the first place more attentive by minimizing distractions, and thereafter more amenable by its fitness to meet the demands of the grace that is given. No one who has been accustomed to listen to the oral teaching of the Father will forget the refrain that recurred so constantly, 'We must see that we really are rising up to' this or that privilege or call. It is in the last degree characteristic of his spiritual teaching that he leaves behind mere moralism and cold duty, and calls for response to the upward calling of an imparted life. Seen in this light, his ascetic teaching is not, as many seem to think, repressive and restrictive; it is essentially liberating. If we are to die it is that we may really live.

V

The influences which contributed to mould the spirit of Father Benson have been suggested, and it will have been observed that they were to a very large extent characteristic of the spirit of the Oxford Movement. In all that pertains to personal sanctification, in the conflict with sin, and in communion with God in and through Christ, he was deeply imbued with the sacramental teaching of the Catholic Church as propagated by the leaders of the Revival who immediately preceded him. But a spirit so strong and vital could not be content to profit by the fruits of other men's labours. He had his own distinctive contribution to make. His sacramental faith gave him a deep sense both of the dignity and authority of the Priesthood, as it taught him the meaning and value of Absolution, and showed him the depth of the mystery of the Eucharistic Sacrifice and the richness of the Blessed Sacrament. These spiritual convictions in due course inspired him to be a leader in the ministerial activities of parochial Missions and Retreats. But in the meanwhile there was a specific call awaiting him which not only demanded a full and final self-consecration, but also evoked and directed the creative energy of his spiritual life. This was his Vocation to be a leader and himself a Founder in the newly recovered state of Religious life.

The task divinely imposed on Richard Meux Benson was creative in the truest sense. Others, such as Dr. Pusey, had preceded him in making foundations of Communities; but their work had been that of stimulating, guiding, and legislating for others while they themselves remained in the secular estate. Father Benson was a pioneer in the sense that he in person led and inspired those whom he gathered round him, asking of them, imposing on them, nothing that did not represent the fruit of his own spiritual experience. In the Rule he delivered and in the instructions in which he expounded it, there is nothing that is merely theorizing or speculative. However exalted the teaching, however searching the demand, there is apparent throughout the vital and quickening quality that belongs to clearly apprehended vision, and to the experience derived from an unhesitating response. From this there is derived also a coherence which enables those who receive his teaching in its wholeness to gain something at least of its spiritual power of transformation.

It is characteristic of Father Benson that he claimed nothing for himself, everything for the vision. He was wholly free from any lust of domination. Indeed he had pungent criticism for those who thought they had vocation to be Superiors. But he knew himself entrusted with a commission; and as steward of that particular mystery committed to him, he was resolutely faithful to the charge. He was therefore in no wise concerned merely to organize a Community, leaving it to develop according to the changing demands of circumstance. For adaptation in contingent matters he was prepared, provided there were no forfeiture of the essential spiritual demand imposed by the vision, nor relaxation of the means by which the realization of the ideal was to be sought.

The nature of this tenacity may be realized by a comparison of the teaching given in the original instructions now being presented, and that of *The Followers of the Lamb* produced nearly thirty years later, long after he had committed the guidance of the Society to other hands. This later book was originally intended for the same Society, but it is addressed to a later generation, and it is not, like the earlier, an explicit commentary on the Rule. If there is a mellowing of expression in the treatment of the subjects common to both series of addresses, there is at least no loss in the clarity of vision, no diminution of the comprehensiveness of the integral demand. The same adoring contemplation of the Divine Majesty and Holiness, the same overwhelming consciousness of the eternal purpose, pervade both alike. In both there is the same call to the realization of the transforming power of the indwelling Christ, the same demand for conflict, and the same confidence in victory against the ancient enemy of God. The spirit of Father Benson is continually rising, and would have others rise in daily life, from preoccupation with things temporal to the full measure of the 'upward calling of God in Christ Jesus.'

Yet it is easy for those who never knew him to misunderstand the true character of such a life. If one who was so close a friend and fellow disciple of their common master as Dr. Liddon could speak of 'Benson's odd severity,' it is not surprising that strangers should be repelled by a self-discipline to which they do not possess the clue. It is easy for those who know only the record of his immense missionary and evangelistic labours, to think of him chiefly as a great master of activity, but they do not take account of the hours and even nights of prayer from which the seemingly spontaneous outflow of his energy was derived. And the same is true with regard to that which is his special creation and the embodiment of his spirit; it is easy to think of the Society, framed by his Rule and trained by his instructions, as one among many active Communities, by reason of the manifold and varied occupations on which its members are engaged. If ever it should come to merit such an estimate, it would be because it had lost the spirit of its Founder, and deserted the principles on which he willed that it should be sustained. The Rule is not a mere code of regulations for the ordering of conduct and controlling of relations, but the concrete expression of a mode of life dictated by the content of the vision. It is by virtue of this integrity, and the essentially spiritual quality which informs it, that it is capable not only of inspiring, directing, and controlling the activity of the missionary, but also of providing a true spiritual home for those whose personal vocation would lead them more definitely on the way of the contemplative life.

Let any who would understand, consider the time allotted daily to mental prayer, and the instruction as to how that time should be employed ; let them take into account the silence which rules for the greater part of the day, except on the call of charity or duty, the reasons for which that silence is appointed, and the way in which it is to be used. Let them reflect on the prescriptions and instructions that regulate conversation with externs, and even that among the members of the Society, in order that they may realize the extent and the manner in which the spirit of Father Benson requires not separation from the world only, but a continual renewal of life energy from unbroken union and intercourse with Christ. A life so ordered, whatever the wealth of its overflow in action, is not a mere active life, but one of evangelical energy surcharged with light and charity from the exercise of contemplation, purified in its natural part by penitence and penance, illuminated by unremitting study of the ways of God and of the divine revelation, sustained by abandonment to the eternal purpose of God in Christ Jesus. Such was the life that the Father sought to propagate in the family of his spiritual generation. Such was the life of his own spirit as he lived and taught.

THE RELIGIOUS VOCATION

CHAPTER I

OF THE OBJECTS OF THE SOCIETY

WE must seek to realize increasingly the purposes for which our Society is called together—to live for God, to live by rule, to work for God under those vows by which He has given special blessings to all our work. And we must bear in mind that our Society, being called by the name of St. John, must have its special honour to the Incarnate Word. The great purpose of our life must be to realize the life of the Incarnate Word; and the great purpose of our work must be to do the work of the Incarnate Word. To understand the Incarnate Word, and His working in all our acts, we must seek to live by those three vows which we take. We must understand that they really do bind us to the Incarnate Word, as being the life which He led upon the earth. There must be a continual reference of our whole being to the Incarnate Word. Whenever we are in any doubt, our one thought must be, What is the way in which the life of the Incarnate Word will

<small>The purpose of our life, the manifestation of the life of the Incarnate Word.</small>

be most truly manifested in me? This is that for which we are set apart, to rest thus, as it were, upon the bosom of the Incarnate Word, and to learn the will of God from that fellowship of heart with Him; to rest in the fullness of that love with which He will always welcome those who do really seek to rest upon Him.

'In the beginning was the Word, who being Himself one with God by indissoluble unity of life, called into existence the whole universe of creation in accordance with the will of the Father.'

<small>The Word, the source of the old creation and of the new.</small>

We must remember that the present creation is derived from the Word, just as truly as the system of grace is derived from the Incarnate Word, and so the outer creation is a preparation for the inner; the spiritual world is but the development, the carrying on, of that which had begun before. They are both by the same Person. 'By Him all things were made' (*St. John* i. 3), and by Him all things were renewed, and all according to the will of the eternal Father; and as the old creation is the work of the Son as much as the new, so the new creation is as truly according to the will of the Father as was the old. It is the Word of the Father, by whom the mind of the eternal Father is made known to us, and if we have to honour the Son we must be careful to honour Him as the Son, careful to honour the glory of the Father in Him, not resting in Him as a separate end, but resting in Him as being the image of the eternal Father, who is the fount of Godhead, the creator of heaven and earth.

'*And the Word of God having become incarnate for our salvation, sanctified His humanity by the discipline of a life of suffering in obedience to God, in order that He might bring the fallen world back again to be sanctified through the Truth.*'

He created the original world by a single act of power, but He has sanctified the new world by a process of self-discipline, uniting Himself to the world. Taking upon Himself our nature, He has begun the work of our sanctification by the sanctification of Himself, bringing the energies of His own created being into perfect unity of action with His own eternal Life; glorifying our own created nature in Himself; taking upon Himself a human will, but bringing that will into perfect identity with the divine will which He had eternally. So He glorified our humanity, not merely by an act of transcendent power transfiguring it, but by an act of moral dignity elevating it.

The Word incarnate glorifying our humanity.

'*It is the object of the Society of St. John the Evangelist, in adoration of this Divine Mystery to seek that sanctification to which God in His mercy calls us, and in so doing to seek, as far as God may permit, to be instrumental in bringing others to be partakers of the same sanctification; bearing always in mind, that above all things it is necessary for those who would carry out the work of missions to abide in Christ, apart from whom we can do nothing, and that if we abide in Him the life which we have must show itself in us in acts of love to all mankind. For as Christ loved us, so must we also love one another; and we must be ready to lay down our lives for the brethren, if we would be true to that eternal life which is in the Son of God.'*

<small>Sanctification our first object.</small> As He sanctified Himself, so it is for us to sanctify ourselves by the continual surrender of our will to the will of the Father, in whatever way it is manifested, whether it be the will of God in all the circumstances of His external Providence, or the will of God in all the appointments of our Society. We have to realize that the will of God is that to which we must conform ourselves, and in which we have to seek for sanctification. This is our first object, to sanctify ourselves through the truth, to sanctify ourselves in union with the incarnate Saviour, to sanctify ourselves in conformity with the will of God. Whatever else we leave undone, the culture of ourselves must be the constant aim of our life. There will never be any period of our life in which we have not something to do, because we have at all times to bring our own nature up to this requirement of divine sanctification. This is what we have to seek; and since God in His mercy is pleased to call us, we may be quite sure that He will enable us to find what we seek. We cannot be more desirous to have than God is to give.

<small>Sanctification by the Word of God.</small> Nothing can restrain the power of His divine holiness. God desires to sanctify everything in union with Himself. The Holy Ghost seems, as it were, to burst the bonds of the divine nature, the bonds of infinity, in order to sanctify us fallen creatures. And if we realize what it is to be sanctified, we shall understand that our sins are no hindrance to our sanctification. If we

could be as pure as the highest of the Angel host, yet we should need to be sanctified by the power of the Holy Ghost. So the Word of God does come to us, calling us to this divine sanctity. 'He called them gods, unto whom the word of God came' (*St. John* x. 35), and so we are called into the divine nature to be sanctified in the truth of God. This, then, is what we have to seek, and we are to seek it with a real confidence; but while we are thus confident, we must always remember that God does nothing for us without our seeking. We must seek, though it be God's desire to give.[1]

Sanctification is a self-communicating principle. We cannot be holy, and have a self-contained righteousness, just rejoicing in the contemplation of our own holiness before Almighty God. We cannot be sanctified except upon the condition that that same blessed Spirit which we receive goes forth through us to the sanctification of others. There is no limit to this. It has been said that the great proof that the philosopher's stone did not exist is that, if it did, everything would have been turned into gold long ago. It is just so with the life of the Holy Ghost in the soul. It must communicate itself to everything round about: but one soul really and truly sanctified is capable of transmuting a whole world into newness of life. Nothing resists the power of the Holy Ghost but the will of man. It is a power which triumphs over all possible circumstances, and therefore, however incompetent we may be

Sanctification self - communicating, and all-prevailing.

[1] See Note A at the end of the chapter.

for our work by reason of our own incapacity, if we are sanctified we can do everything.

<small>Sanctification in accordance with the law of Christ, wrought out in love.</small>

The work of sanctification, then, is no mere uncertain work; it is a work carried on according to the law of Christ, that same law by which Christ lived. 'As He is, so are we in this world' (1 *St. John* iv. 17). We can do nothing without Him. We are in Him, and that not except by working, except as we work the work of love, even the love of Christ; a love far stronger than that of any mere man to man, a love which is indeed the strongest that man knows: and yet it is beyond that; for while it is truly the love of man, it is also the love of God. The love of God shines out in the love of man, which we must have if we are to be truly sanctified. 'The love of Christ constraineth us' (2 *Cor.* v. 14). This is that twofold love, the love which belongs to us as men, and the love given to us of God.

<small>The infinity of love.</small>

There can be no limit to this love. We cannot say, 'I will love to such a degree'; the infinity is gone. Once say, 'I shrink from such and such a work; it is beyond me,' and in that moment we fall away from Christ. We have, therefore, to rise to the call of Christ in all the fullness of the power of God. It is not enough that we are merely an association of men anxious to do good in the world; it is the work of God we have to carry on. Herein is manifested the love of God towards us, that 'while we were yet sinners, Christ died for us' (*Rom.* v. 8; cf. 1 *St. John* iv. 9 ff.). Herein is the love of God manifested by us, in that we are ready to 'lay down our lives for the brethren' (1 *St. John* iii. 16). If we do not attain to that, the love of God is denied. We may attain very near to it, we may go very far beyond the love with which men ordinarily love, but that would only show how unapproachable is the love of God. Nothing must be the limit of our love. Whatever we are called to do in the love of the brethren, we must be ready to do, however great the suffering, toil, danger, reproach, weariness, however much against our natural tastes, or our own immediate conception of what might have been expected. We are to watch for the calls of the love of God, and be ready to rise up to them in all the fullness of power. The more truly we do this, the more shall we find the love of God working with us.

We must be very careful not to think, 'I am ready to lay down my life for the brethren,' unless we can say, 'I am doing to-day what the love of the brethren demands' — the common duties, wearisome perhaps, and yet not far removed from what is ordinary. In our studies, in our prayers, in our pastoral work, in any preparation for other work that may belong to us, in all things we must realize 'the love of Christ constraineth us' (2 *Cor.* v. 14). We must feel within ourselves the impulse of the unchangeable love which knows no limit. It does not act spasmodically and come forth in great energies, and then relapse into idleness; it comes forth in one continual flow of divine power, like the law of gravitation. As the attractive power is constant, free from all jerk, binding all together in its mysterious grasp, so

<small>The love of the brethren flows forth from the love of God.</small>

the love of God is both attractive and expansive. It binds us all together in a solidity of being, which nothing can break. It operates upon us under all circumstances. It controls every motion. Whatever other motion may be communicated to us, this force of divine love must never lose its power upon the soul.

Our life and work sustained by the vision of the life and work of the Incarnate Word. So must we be always watching to live in the power of that divine love, reproducing, or rather not reproducing but actually proving continually that calm, dignified life of the Incarnate Word of God. 'I live; yet not I, but Christ liveth in me' (*Gal.* ii. 20). So spake St. Paul, and St. John delights to tell us of the abiding unction of the Holy One within us (cf. 1 *St. John* ii. 27), of the fullness of the divine light which shines within us, of the communication of the heavenly life into which we are gathered by union with the Son of God. Our outer life in the world must always be the manifestation of this divine life: self-forgetful, ever remembering God; self-distrustful, ever trusting God; blind to all the suggestions of self, heeding not the wars and tumults of the outer life, but abiding continually in the vision of the eternal peace. Our outer life and our work are one. We cannot live except we work, and we cannot work except we live. Our life is the life of God; our work is the work of God; the life and work of God incarnate. We must repose in the bosom of Jesus—not merely as our great Patron reposed on the night of the Last Supper, but rather in that higher repose, in which he rejoices to live, in the glory of Him who loved

OF THE OBJECTS OF THE SOCIETY

him. So must we now learn in the fullness of Pentecostal power, in the power of the Holy Ghost, in the bosom of Him who is invisible. There we must learn tranquillity, there learn strength, there learn light, there learn love.

'*The Society shall consist of Priests in communion with the Church of England, and none except Priests shall have any voice in the Chapter. Lay Brothers also may be united with the Mission Priests in dedication to God in the Religious State, and shall assist in whatever way they are able in the works of the Society, whose life they have been called to share, but the government of the Society shall rest with the Professed Fathers only.*'

Our life is primarily the life, the continual life of the great High Priest in all the fullness of its mystical perfection, and those who are associated with us as laymen must remember that it is an association with the great High Priest. They are called into the Society, not merely that they may be with us, but with Him. It is He who must be continually remembered in every one of the Fathers of this Society, and whatever faults any may see in any one of us, nevertheless they must look through our faults to the glory of Him who is the true centre, nucleus, head, and life of this Society. All who are associated with us must behold Jesus in us; and it must be a special incentive to us to live worthy of Christ, to know that others are thus to watch us. Whether they see Christ in us or no, it will help us very much to humble ourselves for our faults, it will strengthen us very much to be watchful, if we know that

We are called into the fellowship of the great High Priest.

eyes are upon us to see whether we are living in the fellowship, in the power, in the love, in the likeness of Christ.

NOTE A

'*If we realize what it is to be sanctified, we shall understand that our sins are no hindrance to our sanctification.*'

Father Benson is here stressing the fact that our sanctification is the fruit of our union with God in Jesus Christ, and is His work within us by the communication of the Holy Ghost to us, not the result of our possessing powers or goodness of our own. The Holy Angels, even those that bear up the throne of His glory, veil their faces, and cannot know Him as He is. They too learn to see the glory of God 'in the face of Jesus Christ,' and will at last share thereby in a new glory themselves, the end for which they too are created. Much more then is man, the sinner for whose redemption the Incarnate Word came in the likeness of sinful flesh, wholly dependent upon the work of grace within him. 'Our sins,' therefore, 'are no hindrance to our sanctification,' if we yield ourselves up to the call of God, when it sounds within our hearts.

And as it is in the beginning, so it will continue to be during our life. We are not perfected by a single act. We remain subject to temptation. If, when we fall, we turn again at the call of God with renewed penitence, we can find the unfathomable riches of God's grace still awaiting us. Only penitence must deepen as the knowledge of God and of sin deepens. Nothing, Father Benson taught, can hinder our sanctification but the resting in ourselves. If we give ourselves to God, and in proportion as we give ourselves to God, His will will be wrought in us, 'even our sanctification.' 'It is this giving ourselves up to God which constitutes progress, and it is a very real thing.' 'No sin need keep us from a blessing, if only we draw near to God in true and loving penitence' (*S.S.J.E. Retreat*, 1875). 'There is nothing whatever that He can hold back from us, if we do not hold ourselves back from Him. There is nothing that He cannot accomplish in us, if we only look simply to Him for the accomplishment of His purpose' (*S.S.J.E. Retreat*, 1876).

CHAPTER II

OF THE CALL OF GOD

AS many as receive the Word of God become the sons of God by participation of His grace. It is on this grace of the divine call that we must rely for the accomplishment of any work that we undertake. No one, therefore, can be eligible into our Society unless there be sufficient evidence that he has received a call from God to this life and work, nor is any one to be rejected because some one particular gift may be wanting to him; God is abundantly able to supply every defect in those to whom His Word comes.'

Hearing the voice of God.

We must praise God for our vocation in so far as we have received it. In whatever measure the vocation has come, we must accept it as a gift from God leading us onward. There is the primary vocation towards the Society, and there is the vocation in the Society, and then there is the vocation still going on throughout life. We live by the call of God. It is not because He has called us, but because He is calling us; and we need to hear that voice speaking in us constantly, and with increasing power. We cannot fail of our vocation if we are listening for that voice, but we may fail of our vocation by neglecting to hear that voice. That voice spake to us when we were outside, and perhaps we followed it a little way; but that voice has gone on speaking, and the question is—Are we following it still? So that it is not enough for us to examine ourselves beforehand, whether we have a vocation, or afterwards whether we had it, but it is for us to examine ourselves whether we are following still, constantly, perseveringly, diligently, triumphantly. Oh, the joy of the divine vocation! Who can tell it? Whatever it be to which God calls any one, the hearing of that call is the very anticipation of heaven. Whether it be a secular or a Religious calling, and to whatsoever work in Religion, if we hear the voice of God calling us, that voice fills the heart with an intense rapture. Abraham heard that voice, and that voice has not grown dumb, has not lost its power, since Abraham's time. That voice has become flesh, has become flesh in order that by so doing He may call us more closely after His example. 'My sheep hear my voice'; I call, and 'they follow me' (*St. John* x. 27).

Great is the joy of hearing this voice, as it calls. And if God has begun to call us, and we want to hear His voice calling us to the end, we must abide steadfast in this voice. We must be constantly listening, and yielding ourselves up to it. Whatever other solicitations there may be in the world, we must always try and recollect ourselves, always try and retire into the inward peace and silence of the soul, and there learn what the Lord God will say concerning us (cf. *Ps.* lxxxv. 8). So try and listen for this voice of Jesus. Many there are who have had a vocation of God, and have been

<small>Following the voice of God.</small>

true to its original instincts, but then after a while they have been content to think that now their lot in life is determined. No, our Profession does not determine our lot in life. That is not determined until we stand upon the threshold of another world. We must go on following the voice that calls us.

The voice of God in our Society. We ought to praise God, then, for having received whatever calls we have received; and we ought to be diligent in cherishing those calls; and we ought to praise God for all to whom He gives the call. We ought surely to rejoice one in the other; and, therefore, whenever God calls any of us and gives us grace to obey the call, we ought to find intense joy, whether it be the calling of fresh members into the Society, or the determination of vocation by Profession, or the calling of any to some special work of toil, or difficulty, or care. In all these ways we ought to find a real joy in the consciousness of the voice of God speaking in the midst of our Society, and calling us on. We ought as truly to hear the voice of God in our Society as Adam heard it among the trees of the garden; only not to shrink from it, but to praise Him whose voice it is.

The sufficiency of the supernatural call of God. True we are sinners, and we are not worthy that God should thus speak with us; but sinners as we are, nevertheless the very fact that we hear this voice is a token that Jesus has come to deliver us from our sins. He does not come to reproach us, but to save us, and the voice is the voice of the Saviour; it is the voice which gives power, it is the voice that calls us to new life, it is the voice that communicates fresh faculties continually. Oh, we must give ourselves up in all our weakness to this vocation; and be sure that He will lead us on, not to that which we can anticipate, but to very much more. We know not what He is calling us to yet. The future is dark, and we follow on, and He reveals it to us step by step only. If we hang back from any one step only, then it is so difficult to catch up. If we have once lost sight of the voice that speaks to us, it is so difficult for us to regain the sight of the voice again (cf. *Rev.* i. 12). It requires much self-discipline to rise up to the call of Jesus, when we have once drawn back. It is supernatural, the original yielding; but the return, when we have once drawn back, is not only a work of supernatural grace, but it is a work of the greatest pain and difficulty to nature. So then, let us consider how truly the call of God has brought us together. Let us realize our own sufficiency for whatever we have to do, because God calls us, and let us realize the sufficiency of others because God calls them.

We must, then, find our whole stay and support in the call of God. And if at any time we are sick and weakly, we must remember still it is God's call. And so sick and weakly persons are to be acknowledged as having a true call from God. Sickness is a very special vocation. Sick and weakly persons are not to be admitted as members of the Society, if their infirmity is of such a nature as to render them habitually incapable of observ-

The call of God in sickness.

ing the ordinary rules of the Society; but the mere weakness which may incapacitate for some of the more urgent works, this we must not regard as any impediment from God. We must look upon the sick and suffering as pleading before Almighty God. If at any time we are sick and weakly, we must learn the great blessing of presenting our sufferings before God, not merely as the punishment of our own sins, but as an offering to Him in union with the Society. Sickness is a very special call of God. In other calls of God we are very apt to be mistaken; if we are really sick and suffering there can be no doubt. It is God's forcible hand laid upon us. We ought not to despise God's hand because it is visible; we ought to praise Him for making it plain what He would have us to be.

It is enough that we obey the call of God.

And we must be very careful not to think that we are thus unable to do as much for God as elsewhere. We must learn that those do most who obey most truly. It is not those who have most energy, or learning, or wealth, or skill, who do most for God; but those who give themselves up most truly to do His will. This, then, must be our endeavour, to give ourselves up simply to the will of God, to watch for His call, to entreat Him to make His call more and more manifest, to ask Him to lead us onward.

The purposes of God's call gradually revealed.

Whatever God calls us to is not the resting-place, but only a step of our pilgrimage. We must always remember that God has purposes for us, and very real purposes, which are still hidden from us. If we could but know the future of God's predestination for us, how marvellously it would invigorate us! We cannot conceive it for ourselves. It seems to us as if we were giving mere play to our imagination when we think of it, but we ought to remember that our imagination does not rise up nearly to the call of God. All that we can imagine God calling us to do is far short of the real call of God. We have but to discipline ourselves according to the measure of God's grace, to discipline ourselves and rise up to His call as it is manifest, and then it shall go on revealing itself more and more.

The wondrous call of God! God calls us sometimes to study, sometimes to prayer, sometimes to suffering, sometimes to ministrations, sometimes to retirement. The call of God is ever onward. The atmosphere into which we are called is no mere vacancy; it is no more a vacancy to the intelligent soul than the atmosphere is a physical vacancy. We are called onward into the thick throng of spiritual intelligences. They crowd round about us, but yet do not press upon us, so as to weary or oppress us, but rather so as to fill us with the sympathy of their own actions. We are gathered into this mysterious ocean of intelligent life, which surrounds the still greater mystery of God's own infinite being. God is calling us onward, and oftentimes it seems as if we were just left alone. No, we are being called into these higher regions of heaven. It is for us to realize our communion with all the Saints, and Angels that wait upon the Saints: our communion

The call of God onward into the consciousness of the spiritual world.

in the Body of Christ, and our communion in the fellowship of those attendant powers which surround the Body of Christ. God calls us on, and the heavenly host makes way for us to enter in, makes way as the water makes way for the keel of the vessel, closing round about us, and as it were rejoicing with a rippling as we pass through.

The joy of receiving the call of God.

Oh, the joy of the intelligences, while each soul is led onward! We ought to lose all sight therein of the mere things of earth, and of the lower physical nature; we ought to realize the call of God mysteriously guiding us, if we will but follow it. Oh, the glow of the divine life, the ripple of the heavenly light, the murmur of the joyous sound, the thrill of spiritual consciousness into which the soul is welcomed as it yields to the call of God! Thus, indeed, to be gathered into the spiritual world, and to lose sight of earthly things, is a great joy!

We must be indifferent to all but the call of God.

Our vocation, then, whatever it be, ought to be full of joy, for it matters not to us what the earthly circumstances may be, if we only have this divine fellowship, this spiritual exultation. Oh, we must be quite indifferent to what God may outwardly call us to, as long as we hear this inward calling, filling our souls with a divine tranquillity. So let us think that God is indeed calling us onward. In every time of darkness and of outward difficulty, let us seek to close our ears to outward sounds, to the turmoil of earthly discord, and to listen for this voice of God.

OF THE CALL OF GOD

O Blessed Jesus, speak Thou evermore in our hearts. Let us hear Thy voice, guiding us in that way which we know not, but which is known of Thee from all eternity. Let Thy voice speak in the ear of our soul, filling us with an abundance of delight. Call us nearer and nearer unto Thyself; enable us so to correspond with Thy call, that we may indeed have all the virtues of the heavenly host attendant upon us, that we may be enabled to act according to Thy power, that we may be transformed according to Thy will, that we may be enabled to gaze upon Thy likeness. Yea, Lord Jesus, Thou art calling us onward. Thou, the Word made flesh, art ever speaking, saying to us, Follow Me. Let us now fix our eyes by faith on Thee, and follow Thee according to the law of Thine earthly life, that so we may be enabled to behold Thee hereafter in Thy glory, and attain to the joy of Thy heavenly life, wherein Thine elect are called to live for evermore with Thee.

A prayer that we may hear and correspond with the voice of God.

CHAPTER III

OF OUR VOCATION AS SUBORDINATED TO THE LIFE OF THE CHURCH

The intense unity of life in the city of God.

OUR vocation is subordinated to the general call of Christ in His Church. This is true of all, dear brethren, whether priests or laymen, secular or Religious. We have our special vocation, but it is really only part of the great vocation which God has for His Church. It is measured off to us. We are not to think of it as a mere private treasure, an individual gratification, a selfish enjoyment to which we are called. Remember the highest call of any of the Saints in heaven, the call by which the Apostles themselves are raised, is not concentrated in their persons so as to draw them away from the rest of Christendom; but it is centred in their persons to be from them diffused, so as to spread its lustre, its glory, and its life throughout the whole city of God. And as it is with these twelve foundations of the city, so it is with individual Christians. We are not called into the city of God merely that we may enjoy ourselves there. It is not merely that we must not think of eternity as a never ending enjoyment, perpetuating in itself the selfishness of earthly life; the thought of eternity is intense unification of life. Eternity is the manifestation of marvellous unification of life. No one can possess anything in eternity, and have it simply as his own property; each one has it for the well-being of the whole. No individual can be a partaker of that life, and live within the sphere of his own simple thought. The life of heaven is a self-communicating life; it is the life of God. And as the Father gives the fullness of life to the Son, and the Father and the Son give the fullness of their life to the Holy Ghost, so each one of us dwelling in the power of the same Spirit must be continually giving forth that life: we cannot live in it upon any other terms.

So then all the glory that God has in store for us, is a glory in which the whole Body of Christ shall really and truly rejoice. And this we ought to bear in mind here upon earth, while we have to work out our vocation. We ought to remember that we are not merely labouring for a gift, which, if we do receive it, will be of the greatest blessing to ourselves; but we are to labour in the consciousness that we are cultivating our own selves, cherishing our own spiritual life, with a view to the sanctification and glorification of all that are around. 'For their sakes I sanctify myself,' said our Lord (*St. John* xvii. 19), and in the same manner we must in our own degree sanctify ourselves, that we in Him may be centres of sanctification. We are not to think that this is assuming to ourselves more than we have a right to; we have a right to it, because sanctification cannot exist upon any other principle. There is no sanctification but the sanctification of Christ,

[margin:] The sanctification of each is for the sanctification of all, for it is a participation in the sanctification of Christ.

and that sanctification of Christ is a radiating self-communicating power. We might as well imagine that a piece of metal could become thoroughly hot without diffusing any heat around, as imagine that we can be sanctified in Christ without diffusing that sanctity, just as truly as Jesus Christ Himself did, for it is the very same thing in us as in Him; it is from Him that we derive all that we have. What we derive from Him does not change its character by being given to us. It does not grow cold upon the way. It does not forfeit its fragrance. It loses none of its power. The sanctification which is in Christ is given to us just as truly as it exists in Him, and must work in us the same results as in Him, proportionate to the amount of communication we have received.

Each has his predestined place in the city of God. Consider, then, that God has a special calling for each one of you in His glorious city. Think of that special point in the walls of the heavenly Jerusalem, where already you begin to get a glimpse of your own name written by predestinating love. Think of the special predestination which God has for each one of us, that special predestination to which we are called each one of us; a fact just as real in the heavenly city, as our presence in this chapel now. Consider the glory of that predestination, how necessary it is to the well-being of the city of God. Yes, indeed! it is this which holds back the Kingdom of Christ, because the Kingdom of Christ cannot come until each of those predestinations has been achieved: the Kingdom of Christ cannot come while there is any glory which God has marked for His elect, which has not been appropriated to some successful conqueror. We are called to it, but we must win it, and until it be won the glory of the heavenly Jerusalem cannot be seen.

Therefore, the cultivation of our spiritual life is no selfish work. It is a work of far greater benefit to all around, than the cultivation of any merely natural faculties. We may cultivate the powers of science and language and the like, for the various purposes and interests of pleasure and business, or for recreation, or for intercourse of various kinds of heart and mind in the world; but all these various things come to an end. The cultivation of the life of the Spirit, the cultivation of the Holy Spirit of God, as a power of holiness dwelling in the soul, is the cultivation of a power which is to be manifested, and which is to endure, eternally. People often spend a great deal of time and toil in carrying out earthly purposes, but, even if they achieve them, it often happens that they cannot turn them to any account. A man may be anxious to get into some position in which he thinks he will be able to advance the well-being of his neighbours; but when he has acquired it, he may find that he is hindered by some circumstance. There are countless circumstances which stand in the way of our really using these things of the earth, but in the city of God it is not so. There, whatever we acquire becomes necessarily effective. It is powerful, and wide-spreading in its consequences, and nothing can possibly hinder it. There is no darkness there

The cultivation of the spiritual life, not selfish, but effective eternally.

which can stand in the way of any ray of light from any of the storeys of that heavenly city; there is no impediment there which can check the energy of any power with which that city lives; all the powers of the holy city work, radiate, shine out, mingle themselves in manifold consequences of marvellous beauty. Yes, they all shine out with a splendour which we cannot conceive, and they continue in various forms of delight, each equally beyond our present thought.

<small>In the city of God will be seen the resultant of all spiritual effort in this world.</small> Try, then, and think how every gift of God by which you are to attain your sanctification is to have its value and proper effect in the glory of that Kingdom. Here you may often seem to be shut up, unable to effect anything. Then you will see how all the accumulated energy of the divine life which God has been treasuring up within some hermit soul shall burst forth. Then you will see that not one moment of those blessed devotions has been lost. Then you will see that in all the progress of the earthly life there has been a gradual intensification of the divine power, which is at last to be revealed. How this ought to make us indifferent to the circumstances under which we may have to labour in this world! Our glory in that heavenly city is not dependent upon our natural gifts or position, but every glory depends upon our cultivation of the supernatural life, serving and glorifying God in all circumstances, and living in His power. Yes, we bear along with ourselves the resultant of all those various exercises of devotion which God at any time has permitted us to cultivate, and they shall

take their place in the joy of that heavenly city.

See, then, how thoroughly the inmost secrets of your hearts are to be disclosed, not merely to be seen by others, but that the whole multitude may rejoice in them. For there is no limitation in that blessed city to the glorious fellowship in which all are combined. There we cannot say that one is nearer to another than some one else; for in that city, in the truth of its life, there is no such thing as locality or nearness, for all is perfect union and perfect interpenetration of being. To the human eye it is revealed under forms which imply the ordinary measures of man and lines of space; but, in the revelation of the Spirit, it is not so. In the revelation of the Spirit there is that perfect identity of being, so that all are really and truly one. No distance of separation, of climate, or of age; no distance which may have separated us upon earth; no distance of perfection to which we may have attained, is between ourselves and the great apostolic Saints. No distance has any reality, for all are perfectly one; one undivided act of love thrilling through all. Each individual is a centre of spiritual emanations, while yet that Spirit which emanates from each, is an undivided Spirit; for there is the perfect indwelling of the Holy Ghost, dwelling in each according to measure, yet suffering no division while He communicates His powers to each. We must, then, dwell upon the thought of our special vocation in the Body of Christ, to live with the power of the Holy Ghost in the unity of this

In the city of God is a perfect fellowship of life, derived from the indwelling of the Holy Ghost.

E

glorious life; to realize then, as now we cannot, the marvel of the unity in which the Father, Son, and Holy Ghost dwell for evermore; to realize that same unity accomplished in ourselves, the glory of the redeemed to be made for evermore to be one with Christ Jesus.

Each individual has his place in the perfect number of the elect.

And if there is no distance which can separate, so also no multiplicity can bewilder. The number of the Saints is perfect, according to the fixed purpose of the mind of God, the mysterious hundred and fifty and three—the marvellous development of that mysterious number, until man cannot number it, yet it is numbered by God. Man cannot number it now, but when man is exalted into the fullness of the life of God, then shall we know the number of the elect; then shall we know that not one is wanting, and we shall have as intimate a knowledge of each one, as if that one were the only one we had to know. Consider this multiplicity of the manifestation of God in all the perfections of His Saints; a multiplicity without bewilderment, just as there is individuality without distance. Thou thyself hast to maintain thine individual character in the midst of this glory; the glory of God has to shine forth from thee; thou hast to carry on in it, in that glorious life, all the results of thine earthly pilgrimage.

The necessity of sanctification.

Oh, consider well how we, who have this hope, ought to 'purify ourselves, even as He is pure' (1 *St. John* iii. 3); nothing can enter into that city 'that defileth' (*Rev.* xxi. 27). From this we must be purged, and every soul must be purged, by the fire of the Last Day, ere it can enter into that city (cf. 1 *Cor.* iii. 13). If the soul had within itself any taint of earth, then it would be a principle of disintegration to that city. It would be like casting a stone into the fire instead of coal, which instead of adding to the heat would only split, and shoot out its sparks with destruction. Our whole nature must be purged. We are not to imagine that by rising up to some lower vocation we can perhaps take some lower place. We are not to think that God would allow His light and heat to shine through our imperfections. They must be wholly purged away.

Let us think, then, of having to take our place in the heavenly city with our own individuality, with the result of our earthly life! Think what it is to leave this world with a vocation carefully striven for! Think what it is to leave this world with a vocation slighted! It is not merely that we, whether priests or laymen, whether secular or Religious, shall lose something, if we have not done all that we might. We leave the world to become principles of glory in the city of God, and if we are not able to take our place thus, then we become principles of injury to the city of God, and the city of God cannot rise to its perfection until some one else has been found to attain to that which we had forfeited. We cannot take up with something lower; we must be cast away.¹ A vocation slighted is a vocation forfeited.

Meditate, therefore, upon the subordination of your own vocation to the general glory of the city of God, and consider that your own spiritual life The life of Christ in each the glory of the communion of Saints.

¹ See Note B at the end of the chapter.

is not your own; it is part of the common possession of the Saints. 'I believe in the communion of Saints'; that is to say, I believe that I am as necessary to them as Christ is to myself. Christ is the foundation, and I have the gift of Christ by which the city of God is to be perfected. We must realize the immensity of this divine life. It is not a mere individual, selfish treasure; it is a possession which we hold in common. It is not our own, it is not ours, it is the common possession of the people of God; it is, though in us, the life of Christ. Consider, then, whether you can indeed say that Christ is living in you, for the glorification of His people. Christ must be living in us. 'I live,' said the Apostle, 'yet not I, but Christ liveth in me' (*Gal.* ii. 20). All that we can do for others is not our own. Although we had all the zeal and all the intelligence of the great Apostle of the Gentiles, yet without this all would be valueless. It is Christ within the very humblest of us, which is the true building, perfecting power, by which the multitude of the Saints are to attain to their joy. Meditate upon your vocation, and see whether you are rising up to this, whether you are allowing Christ to speak within you, whether you are allowing Christ to minister within you. Is the life of Christ really restraining your own natural impetuosity, the impulse, of whatever kind, to which you are apt to be drawn? Is the life of Christ within you really making the glory of God to shine forth on all around? Are you careful to look to Christ within you? not to look to yourself, but to look to Him? not to think that you can pare off from yourself this or that infirmity, but that He can burn off all imperfections from you by the glory of His indwelling Spirit?

Then go on to consider how in the city of God the various radiations of light are to be mingled in the marvellous light of the divine revelation. Oh, the wondrous light of that city! In that city, it is not as in some city of the earth, where each light shines by itself in the midst of the surrounding darkness; multitudes, multitudes, forming lines of beauty in the midst of the darkness. It is not so there, for there is no darkness there; no intervening darkness to separate one Saint from another, for all are built up in the being of Christ, and the light of each individual Saint shines forth, mingling itself in the fullness of the eternal light with the light which shines from the thousands and thousands that are around. There is distinction without distance, there is multiplicity without bewilderment, and there is mingling without confusion. Yes, there is a marvellous reciprocity of joy there with which all the Saints give forth their lustre, and rejoice in the manifestation of their own experience of the divine love, while they rejoice equally in the manifestation of the divine love as it has been experienced, realized, and exhibited by all around. And as the pure white light is a combination of many rays of colour, so in the purity of the city of God there is a combination of manifold rays of colour. As there is the threefold Personality of the eternal Trinity, which is the basis of the heavenly light, so there is the marvellous multi-

The pure and manifold light of the city of God.

plicity of all the Saints, in whom this light shines forth reflected: and as it shines forth reflected, it shines forth in perfect unity.

<small>Joy in the vision of perfected fellowship in the love of God.</small> Try, then, and think of your proper vocation, your calling, your inheritance in the Saints; God's vocation for you to rejoice, not in some isolated glory of selfish magnificence, but, with an individuality indeed which abides for ever, to rejoice in all the fullness of the life of God, whether experienced by yourself, or by any other of the Saints. We must thus learn to rejoice in one another's life: if one member rejoice, all the members rejoice with it (cf. 1 *Cor.* xii. 26). We must learn to work out our vocation in constant submission to the inspiration of the Holy Ghost, and with a constant sense of the allegiance which is due to the communion of Saints, the city, the Church of the living God; that there we may be enabled to take our place, and shine in the glory of that heavenly city, living for evermore in the perfect revelation of that love, which while we were upon earth we were striving after, and exulting in that blessed vision of the eternal light, which flickered so dimly upon our eyes in this outer world of darkness.

Note B

'*We cannot take up with something lower; we must be cast away.*'

There can be no question of the need and value of the warning given by Father Benson of the seriousness of any deliberate, or even careless, slighting of vocation, as being not only a failure of the love to God in such a soul, but a failure also to realize the end for which that soul was created. It is, however, the more commonly received opinion that the Evangelical Counsels must be regarded as counsels of perfection, and not as precepts of salvation; and that there would therefore still remain a place for repentance for those who have turned aside, even when they had been previously convinced of the reality of their vocation. But such authorities agree that there would be grave danger of presumption, and consequently grave peril of salvation, in drawing back from such a call.

Father Benson's thought seems to be more closely allied to that of the author of the Epistle to the Hebrews, when he writes of those who 'draw back unto perdition' after having received the clear vision of faith (cf. *Heb.* vi. 4; x. 39). His teaching on vocation is based on a vision of the divine action, as regulated by and declaratory of an eternal purpose, revealed to the individual soul in an act of personal love, the rejection of which would be the rejection of God Himself. In the realization of vocation the soul is brought face to face with God, but the individual soul can never be conceived of as alone. The vocation of the individual soul is part of the working out of an universal purpose of wisdom and of love, and each individual is saved as he finds his place in the divinely-ordered whole. While then it may be right that we should refuse to limit the resources of infinite wisdom, justice, and mercy towards those who fail and yet turn again to their God, it is well that we should give heed to Father Benson's words, emphasizing the Apostolic warning, 'Give diligence to make your calling and election sure' (2 *St. Pet.* i. 10) and echoing the twice repeated warning of our Lord, 'For many are called, but few chosen' (*St. Matt.* xx. 16 and xxii. 14).

In the volume of meditations called *Benedictus Dominus* there is a meditation on predestination, in relation to the birth of John the Baptist, in which Father Benson writes, 'The will must choose what God has marked out; we cannot exchange our predestinated glory for any other. It is set before us from childhood as the end for which our discipline shall fit us' (op. cit., p. 403); and in a succeeding meditation on correspondence with vocation he writes, 'The vocation once forfeited never wholly returns. At the very best a vocation when regained will have the sad colouring of penitence instead of the brightness of purity.' But if we are true to God, 'The divine authority which calls us forth accompanies us, and makes us triumphant' (ibid., p. 407).

CHAPTER IV

OF THE CALL OF GOD, CONTINUOUS, ABIDING, AND PROGRESSIVE

IT is important for us to remember that not only is our original vocation of God, but the voice of God speaking in the depths of our soul is the foundation of our Religious life; and as our Religious life is to go on to perfection, it must be by the power of that voice making itself recognized more and more. Our Religious life is not a supernatural plant which afterwards is to grow with a natural growth. It is supernatural in its origin, and it is supernatural in its development. That same voice of God which called us at the first is ever calling us on, and we must ever be listening for that voice, yielding ourselves to that voice, obeying that voice, acting in the strength of that voice. *The call of God the foundation of the Religious life.*

The continual growth of the soul is then by a continual utterance of the voice of God. God never ceases to speak; our life therefore ought to be one uninterrupted course of increase of sanctification. The routine of our daily life may be just the same, but it is as when in traversing the ocean we see round about us for many days the same circle of water, and yet it is not the same; we are moving onward. So from day to day the *The voice of God a continuous utterance.*

routine of life may seem to be the same, but it must not be the same; we must be really drawing onward.

The voice of God calls us to Himself unchangingly. The voice of God is ever calling us nearer to Himself. There is no cessation, there is no change; it is continuous, and its course is straight. In the works of the world we have to resort to various experiments, by which at one time to effect one thing and at another time another thing, because the world is so varied that what is suitable in one age is not suitable in another, and what is suitable in one country is not suitable in another. But in dealing with God, our life must be the simple drinking in of the life of God.

The voice of God speaking within in ever fresh accents. And as God calls us, He makes His voice to speak within our ear. And that voice which has spoken within our ear, speaks not only for a time, but for the whole eternity of our lifetime; it is one, it is true, it is never to die away. From day to day some fresh sound comes; it is all the development of that original sound. It is not a sound that can clash with, or that can require the stopping of that earlier call.

The harmonious development of the call of God. But the call of God is not only continuous, it is ever-abiding. That which has been remains, and that which is to be is only the development of that which has been. And so we must understand the harmony of our spiritual life, how homogeneous our spiritual life must be, how self-unfolding our spiritual life must be; the life of God unfolding itself more and more within our souls, until at last the fullness of the divine likeness is attained. There is no oscillation, there is no uncertainty, but the continuous unfolding of that life of God which has been treasured up within the soul.

We must thus listen for the voice of God continually to speak afresh, and while He speaks afresh we must still keep our ear alive to that which He has already spoken, never forgetting it as ever-living in its power. Not, indeed, so looking back as to be over-careful as to what we ourselves have done in the way of corresponding, but listening for it. For however long ago it spoke, it is speaking still. All the past voices of God live on with an eternal echo within the soul, ring on with a sound never to die out. We are, then, to listen to all the past calls of God in all their fullness of abiding power. And it is our delight to understand the harmony which binds them to those calls which we receive from day to day. *The constant duty of recollection.*

And as God speaks, He requires us to listen. The voice is of no value to those who are deaf. And God speaks, to how many, alas, who never hear Him! We have put the world aside—for what purpose? In order to come and hear this voice of God. We are come here in order to listen to God speaking in our souls. We must take care, then, that we really listen attentively, listen devoutly, listen obediently, listen gratefully. The voice of God has called us apart in order that He may speak within us, and we must say, 'Speak, Lord, for Thy servant heareth' (1 *Sam.* iii. 9). When God finds us really listening for His voice, then does He take great delight in us; but if we *The necessity of listening for the voice of God.*

have come apart and failed to listen for that voice of God, then indeed we are but mocking God. Our divine life has no reality about it, unless we are listening for the supernatural voice, unless we are really saying, 'Speak, Lord, for Thy servant heareth.' Oh, how many there are who have come into Religion in the various ages of Christendom, driven in by outward circumstances, and yet when they have come in they have never cared to listen for this voice of God. Let us then be watchful. Let us listen attentively, devoutly, thankfully. God will surely speak. God will not keep us waiting. God does not wait to speak any longer than until He sees us ready to listen. He does not hold back His voice from any fitful waywardness on His part. God waits to speak until we can bear the voice. He wants our nature to get strong in correspondence with the voice that has been, and then He will speak again.

The strain of the call of God. The voice of God is a very trying voice, a very straining voice to the soul. The soul that listens to the voice of God finds God calling it to actions which seem to be impossible. It would be of no use for God to call us, unless the actions were impossible. God calls us to something more than we are. What we undertake because it comes within the reach of our own measure, this is not the call of God, strictly speaking. The call of God is to something beyond our own selves. God's call is not simply to illuminate us as to various things that may be chosen to be done in the world, but it is a call to something that is beyond the world, to something that is beyond our own selves.

OF THE CALL OF GOD

It is a call that creates, for it is the voice of the Creator. So, then, there always must be a straining in the call of God.

Yet although there is a straining, nevertheless there is an intense repose. Yes, the soul that is not carried on by the call of God is hurried hither and thither. It is shaking as it goes, like a train that is passing over uncertain lines. It shakes because of the insecurity of that by which it is borne on; it is knocked to pieces by the strain of its own littleness; whereas the strain of the divine power does indeed carry it out of itself, but also strengthens it to accomplish that for which it is carried out. We are carried out of ourselves in the fullness of the power of God. *The security of the call of God.*

We must, then, be listening to this voice of God speaking in our own souls, leading us onward. We must bear in mind the strain, but we must rest assured in the strength. The strain we must feel; the strength we must exercise. The call of God is thus strengthening us by means of new power. It is not merely like the strength of an Angel, or the strengthening of any natural faculty; that is to repair strength which already existed, or at most to supply nourishment that the strength may find its natural growth. But the call of God supplies strength that is beyond the mere natural growth. It is not merely the supply of material by which the strength of any habit may be perfected, but it is a new strength, over and above that which could be attained by any merely natural exercise of that which had been supernaturally given. We must go on, then, really *The enabling power of the call of God.*

relying upon this power, really feeling its strain, really doing our utmost, really feeling that it is beyond ourselves, and yet going on without fear, for we 'know whom we have believed' (2 *Tim.* i. 12).

The call of God creative and progressive, in ever fresh forms of experience, And then, as God thus calls us on, there is no limit to what He will call us to. We are not to think of God's future calls as if they were merely the exaggeration of something we have already experienced. The call of God is like the creating of a new sense from day to day. Though we have but five senses to our natural body, there is nevertheless no limit to the powers of perception which God is able to awaken within the soul. He is able to fill the soul with manifold powers of perception, to develop the soul with a fresh faculty of perception for every special excellence of His own divine nature. He is able to create within the soul a fresh instrument, by which to take it unto Himself. So we are not to think that what past sweetness we have enjoyed is just a small earnest of what is to be, or that the future is never more than a multiplication of that. Oh, no! as well might one who had gazed upon pure white light imagine he could understand the various colours of the prism, as we imagine we could anticipate those gifts which should be developed by those new faculties of development. As in geometry, there are various forms of dimensions, plane, spherical, cubical, so is it when the soul is taken *and of new knowledge of Himself.* up into the being of God. It may be that we think of gazing upon God merely as a picture;

OF THE CALL OF GOD 75

then we come to know further the solidity of God, the depth of the divine being; then we come to know the variety of form in which God reveals Himself to the soul. This is what the Apostle sets before us, in that mysterious 'length, and depth, and breadth, and height, that passeth knowledge' (*Eph.* iii. 18, 19). So in music, there is the enjoyment of the melody, and there is the enjoyment of the harmony; and then there are the various enjoyments of the various voiced instruments, of those that are vocal, and those that are stringed. Thus also it is in the enjoyment of the being of God. We shall find how the being of God unfolds itself, and develops within us fresh capacities of apprehension; or the old capacities assume forms altogether new. And as we may gaze upon an object, and admire the beauty of its form and colour, and then come to know the beauty of its taste or fragrance, so must it be with our knowledge of God. As God calls us nearer to Himself, it is not merely that we may know Him more perfectly according to that manner of knowledge, or that manner of fellowship, which He has vouchsafed to us already, but He would teach us to know Him in new ways. We are to seek, and find it, from day to day.

And so, in our meditations, we ought to look for God constantly thus to be making Himself freshly known to us. Not that we are to expect with each meditation to have any very startling freshness of conception as to God. Silently, imperceptibly, the rays of the sun fall on the atmosphere until all is light; and so God, as He

<small>We attain progress in the knowledge of God, as He makes His light to shine within us.</small>

rises from behind the mountains of our ignorance, makes the light of His glory to shine through the soul. We cannot tell how, but by degrees we are able to measure it, because we find that it does really enable us to do things which we could not do before. As the sun rises, we do not yet see the sun, but we begin to find that we can read the page of a book which but an hour before was altogether dim. So it is with the revelation of God. It is not that we catch any startling or dazzling perceptions of God, which give our nature a shock, even though it be a shock of delight, as we pass into the new conception; but as the light of God streams more and more upon the soul, we are able to read, to see clearly in that light, things which before were hidden. So we can take some measure of progress. What before was a difficulty, whether in abstract theology, or in the reading of divine Providence, or in the understanding of the dispensations of Christ, stands out now clearly. Things which seemed awhile ago contradictory, are now seen to be counterbalancing parts of the same sentence.

The revelation of God brings light and life. It is for us to live thus in the continual leading onward of God, shining out more and more in the soul, making one thing after another clear to us, developing within us the faculties of perception. The objects we have gazed upon for a long time assume new forms, their flatness is changed into solidity, and those beauties we have noticed begin to have other beauties of varied kinds mingling along with them. It may be that they have seemed to us things of death. It seems to us, it may be, as if we were gazing upon a mere stone by the roadside; we do not see that it is some living animal. But it rises up in the daylight to our view, and we see it bound off in the elasticity of life. So many things seem to us in the darkness to be objects of the dead world, but as the light advances they assume form. We watch them; we understand them; we begin to catch an idea that there is more than this dead world about them. At last we see them rise, corresponding to that life which has filled our own soul; we see them wake, and rise, and go forth in the fullness of the supernatural life which God has given them.

It is for us to be living in constant watchfulness of the progress of the divine life within our souls, and not to imagine, when we seem to see things clearly, that 'Now there is no more for me to see.' When does the noonday come for the true Religious? When does the Novitiate end? Only with this world's life. Yes, as long as we are in this world we have to go on learning and learning, watching and watching, receiving and receiving, as from time to time God gives us more and more. However bright things may seem, we are not to mistake the harshness of our clearest intellectual sight for the glorious vision of that which we are to see eventually. When the whole being is filled with the Holy Ghost, how marvellously shall we then look back upon this world, and our clearest sight shall seem to us as nothing. This, the noontide, cannot be in this world. We have to wait for that. We have to wait for God

The noontide of the true Religious.

indeed to reveal Himself in all His glory; but, meanwhile, we are to be progressing on towards that.

The death of the outer nature in the vision of God,

Oh, the intensity of that delight which thrills through the frame when the first bit of the golden orb lifts itself up above the horizon at sunrise! Ah, there is a shock in that delight! And so there must be in our nature, as it comes to see God. It is calm and tranquil, as the fullness of that light which fills the sky ever increases, until the soul beholds its God. But when the soul comes to the beholding of God, oh, then there is a shock through the nature! The outer nature dies in this shock. 'Thou canst not see my face, . . . and live' (*Exod.* xxxiii. 20). The light of God purifies thee, that thou mayest be able to bear that revelation, but, when that revelation comes, all thoughts of earth will fall away. Oh, if we have been living in the delight of the continual progressive revelation of God drawing us on to Himself, what shall be the joy of shaking off the form of earth to behold Him! To stand as it were transfixed,

while we await the taking up of the body into the glory of God.

to gaze upon Him! To gaze upon His glory, not seeing it indeed fully, but to gaze, and wait until we take up the body. Then to take up the body, no longer to be a veil, hiding God from the sight; to take up the body, trembling indeed as it comes into that presence, trembling as the ray of that dazzling presence searches it through and through, and burns out of it all the impurities of its earthly life! Yes, as the soul takes up the body, it finds the body now no longer binding it down to earth, but in that very body it rises up to be absorbed into the glory which it has been so long contemplating. It is for us to dwell in the contemplation of the divine glory, until we be indeed absorbed into it, looking forward to that great reality, the end of our being.

And we must meanwhile be constantly listening for God's continual voice, listening for God to speak, not with any jar upon our nature, but with continual imperceptible revelations of Himself. Yet however tender those fresh revelations, the sensitive soul knows them, rejoices in them, lives in them, becomes transformed thereby; learns in the light of that morning to glow with the joy of divine life. Self melts away and the new life takes possession of it. It lives, yet no longer is itself, for it is taken quite into this divine life and joy. *The gradual transformation of the soul.*

O blessed Jesus, Word and Wisdom of the Father, speak Thou more and more in our hearts, giving us ears to listen. Shine forth more and more in our hearts, giving us eyes to see. Purify our lives more and more with Thy presence. Stablish us in Thy glory. Enable us to contemplate Thee now by faith, so that in the end we may have the fruition of Thy glorious Godhead. *A prayer for the contemplation of faith.*

CHAPTER V

OF LIFE IN COMMUNITY

The Church the focus of our life.

WE need to realize that we are called by God to be gathered up in His Church as in a focus; that we are called to exercise towards one another that love which ought to animate the whole body.

Our need of one another.

The Religious life to which we are called is not perfect, but it is one of common sympathies. The mind of man is by nature so constituted that it requires to be sustained by sympathies akin to itself. Some persons there are who are able to be content in the consciousness of the communion of Saints and in the company of Jesus; but most of us, though we do not want all our earthly neighbours as friends, do want a few who may live near us, and help us on to rise to the height to which God calls us. And so our life is not the life of solitaries, but a life in community.

Our recognition of the communion of Saints.

Nor is our Society a society drawn out of the Church, but drawn together within the Church. And it is not drawn together as supplying something wanting in the communion of Saints, but as the means to arrive at the recognition of that communion. The object of all Religious societies is to gather up, and, as it were, focus the love which ought to animate the whole body of the

Church Catholic. The existence of smaller communities than the whole Church certainly implies something wanting, some imperfection, in the state of Christendom, but the infirmities of human nature necessarily obscure the divine glory which belongs to the Church. So it was that in early times such communities rose up, in which that love might be more perfectly attained.[1]

But it is important for us to remember that the love which animates any society of this kind is derived from the great body of Christendom at large. There are special gifts of God indeed to the Society, but only as it is a society within the Church. The small body is to realize and intensify the gifts, to realize the energies, belonging to the whole Church. The life of a Religious community is not a breaking away from the rest of Christendom, from the Church, to lead a better and a purer life, but it is a breaking away from the world; and this, not that we may take refuge in some special shelter of our own building, but that we may enter into the shelter of those divine graces which are derived from God and are common to the whole body of the Church. We must realize then, first, the relationship of the Society to the Church, and then the internal relationship of the members of the Society one to another arising from God's call.

<small>The life of a Religious society drawn from the Church.</small>

God has called us not from the Church, but in the Church, to a special mode of life. No one can have this, except it be given him

<small>The call of God the origination of our Society.</small>

[1] See Note C at the end of the chapter.

from above. We must recognize, then, that the existence of the Society is a manifestation of the voice of God in His Church. We are not gathered here because God was not with us before the Society was formed, but rather because He was. We are called; why, we know not. We are called to take some position in the Society, we know not what, but yet we are called to something He has in store for us. We need constantly to meditate upon the divine vocation as the origin of the Society, and as its guide for the future. Our Society was not called by human wisdom. If it had been formed by ourselves to meet some special emergency, then we should be continually downcast, constantly watching and speculating upon success. But we feel that God has gathered us, and that there is no occasion to give way. Our life in obedience to the divine call is our success, our own ample reward. It is enough that He has joined us together; we can leave the result and all the future to Him, content to be simply living in the divine will. We need not to look for external indications of success; the less we look for them the more God will give us, the more likely we shall be to find them. If we were to look to find them, we might very likely be deceived; then, if we did see results, we should fear lest God should be displeased with us. So, then, look to this divine vocation as the origination of our Society.

<small>The call of God the security of our Society.</small> And as the divine vocation is the origination of the Society, so also is it the security for our permanent growth. God does not speak merely

for the moment. When He calls into being a thing, He will preserve it. He calls for the purpose of continuance, provided that the sins of those who found, or of those who carry out the life, do not cause God to withdraw His call. But if God calls us, He does not tell us what He calls us for. He tells us to do some little thing in which we must be faithful. He is preparing us for some greater thing all the while, and if we are faithful in that which is small, He will lead us on to the greater. We must not despise the day of small things.

Thus must we recognize this call of God as the security for the future. As we look to the future, we see great troubles coming both upon the world and upon the Church, 'distress of nations, with perplexity' (*St. Luke* xxi. 25), but we know not our part in it. We say, 'Here am I, send me' (*Isa.* vi. 8). What for? Whither? we know not. But this entire readiness is a sufficient call to bring down the fullness of the divine mission. God may have called our Society for purposes of which we are altogether unaware, but we have only to be true to our divine vocation. If we are to take any part in the future of Christendom, it is because we are true to this divine vocation, not because of this or that earthly affection. God delights to employ those in His work who are naturally unfitted for it. Natural unfitness is really an advantage, for God chooses the weak things of the world to confound the mighty (cf. 1 *Cor.* i. 27). We have only to be ready to do His will. There is no room then for pride, rather it is a subject

God calls for His own purposes; we have but to be faithful.

for humility; God perfects our work. So let us recognize this call, and this divine purpose for our Society; ready, without any stay in the world, but leaning on Him, all our strength in the will of God.[1]

As individuals, it is the call of God that has brought us into the Society.

And we must recognize the divine vocation for each, individually. We come into the Society, not because it suits us, because it takes our fancy, or agrees with our judgements, because our tastes are satisfied, or because it enables us to get on well and happily,—none of these, but simply because God calls us. This is what we have to search for in preparation, before our Postulancy, during it and during our Novitiate, to look for the manifestation of the divine vocation. For this we must lay aside our own likings and tastes, all things individual to ourselves, for they prevent the truth of our Religious life. We are called out of self, with all its belongings. We may have to bear with our own temptations, and with the infirmities of others, and we may have to do much that seems too mean for us, or too hard for us; but the eager and zealous utterance of the heart on all occasions is, 'The will of the Lord be done; that is my desire, that is my trust, that power is my strength.' Thus must we recognize that the divine will has called us, and also those round about us.

The variety of individual character and work draws forth the treasures of a common grace.

There is necessarily a variety of persons, and of kinds of person, a variety of tastes, tempers, dispositions in a community. Hence there is need of mutual forbearance, co-operation, unwearying

[1] See Note D at the end of the chapter.

energy, triumphant love, to enable us to live and work together. In this spirit we shall not want to do one another's work; and we shall not think much of the work entrusted to us. Every work is in one sense of equal importance, because it is the call of God to work on behalf of the community. By partaking thus in a common work, we are partakers of one another's grace. There is a real spiritual communication of divine grace in the community, so that whatever we do in it draws forth all the treasures of this common treasury of grace. This is the stay of the soul amidst all the multitudinous cares it may have. Are we distracted by many occupations, and much merely secular work? We must realize the peace of the reposeful contemplative life of the Society, sustaining us through them. Thus shall we be sustained by the grace of the Society.

Then, too, in times of contemplation and repose, in all our meditations and private devotions, we must realize that we are gaining and storing up strength and grace for the Society; and this without losing ourselves or our own gain, but rather the opposite. 'The more he gave, the more he had to give.' It is not as a flood caused by the pouring forth of a river, which grows shallow as it irrigates that which is around, but it is rather as the widow's oil in the vessel, filling other vessels, and giving forth until all are filled (cf. 2 *Kings* iv. 1 ff.). In the unity of a common grace we become partakers of one another's grace. Thus we realize what a supernatural entity our Society is. Our organization is called together by the voice [All contribute to and all share in the common grace of the Society.]

of God, and this will strengthen us in all things.

<small>The need of mutual forbearance in reverence to the divine call.</small>

There will be at times much to bear in a community, but this will help us. We must bear with one another, not by courtesy only, or as in a family, but out of the necessity of divine charity, and of reverence to the divine power which has called us together and is dwelling in each and all of us. It is a very necessary part of our discipline and life that we should bear with difficulties in those round about us, and it enables us to test the workings of divine grace within ourselves. It will help us if we recognize Christ in one another, and so reverence Christ in one another. For the voice of God is the revelation of the Word of God within the soul, and we must reverence this presence even through the infirmities of the outer vessel. Every soul that has received such a call must be reverenced, as possessing a special presence. Whether it is true or untrue to its vocation matters not; the presence is there, if there has been the vocation.

<small>Simple conformity to the will of God.</small>

So, then, let us not be anxious that the Society should do any special work, but only that Christ may be manifested in the midst of a fallen world. Let us not think what the world will expect, nor of the fashion of the religion of the day, but let us think of the eternal divine love of Jesus Christ; of what that love expects, and of the manifestation of that eternal love in the midst of a fallen Christendom. Think only—the Word of God has come to me, and to the Society. We know not whether our work is to be mainly active or contemplative, whether winning souls or suffering, whether we shall win many or few, or in what part of the world we may be; but we look at our Society, and we look back at its origin, and we know that that is nothing if not the will of God.

So let us strive to realize the great principles of community life, and its supernatural aspects; that it is a vocation of God, and, therefore, the revelation of Jesus Christ. Our whole life is derived from the voice of God, and we live by the vocation of God. To this we must be true. We must test it, and then go forth in collective unity in this power. God, who has called us, will work with us, until His grace is perfectly manifested in us. Life in community a revelation of Jesus Christ.

Note C

'*The existence of smaller communities than the whole Church certainly implies something wanting, some imperfection in the state of Christendom.*'

Individual asceticism, or the strict following of our Lord in the spirit of poverty, in the practice of prayer and fasting, and in the service of the sick and poor, had always existed in the Church, but it was not until the fourth century that the coenobitic life, or life in Religious communities, began in the deserts of Egypt, and thence spread rapidly to Palestine, and so to Rome and Europe. The earliest dwellers in the Nitrian desert of Egypt were hermits, who in the third century fled there from the Decian persecution for the practice of their religion in safety. These gradually increased in number, and their great leaders were St. Paulus and St. Anthony, a native of Upper

Egypt, who as a lad of eighteen heard the call to renunciation and followed it. Then later, when peace came to the Church with the conversion of Constantine, those who had now lived long in solitude were unwilling to leave the life they had learned to love, and began to be organized into communities, as disciples around great teachers, the earliest of the great founders being Macarius and Pachomius. The fame of these Saints drew many to the Thebaid, who desired to give themselves to penitence and contemplation; but as communities began to be established in the great centres of Christian life in the Roman Empire, the sight of these families of devotion and mutual charity attracted increasingly those who felt that, in the new popularity of the Christian religion under Imperial favour, the world had begun to leaven the Church, and the true standard of Christian life had begun to be lowered. It is to this that Father Benson especially refers.

Note D
'Natural unfitness' for the work of God.

Father Benson very frequently in his retreat addresses on the Incarnation dwells upon the weakness of the human nature assumed by the Word of God in the womb of the Blessed Virgin in its simplest elementary form, to be developed by its union with Himself to the most perfect manifestation of power, accomplishing the divine purposes and revealing the divine glory in the power of the Spirit. In itself, and by itself, human nature cannot do the works of God. It was created for fellowship with God, by whom it is ever sustained in existence, and by means of that fellowship to do His will. It was by the breath of the Spirit that man was to live. We are to use the powers which God has given, and which God sustains, in continuous fellowship with Him, not acting from ourselves and then asking His blessing, but acting from our fellowship with Him in the power of the Spirit, sure that His blessing will go forth on all that we do. He will be acting in us—'The work is wholly His. No skill of man can fashion any work, so that God shall come, and approve of it, and finish it. He begins and He finishes the work; and so He begins every work in the greatest possible form of weakness. Therefore in all divine works, instead of being discouraged because things seem to be weak, we are to recognize this weakness as an almost necessary form of divine co-operation. God delights to begin a work when man's weakness is specially manifest, in order that it may be perfectly manifest that all the work is His. God delights to show His favour just when man can do nothing else than feel his incapacity' (*S.S.J.E. Retreat*, 1876).

CHAPTER VI

OF THE THREE VOWS

'THE disciple whom Jesus loved, whose name we bear, and whose mind we must especially seek to cherish as being filled with the inspiration of divine knowledge, hath written unto us, that we love not the world, neither the things that are in the world. If any man love the world, the love of the Father is not in him; for all that is in the world, the lust of the flesh, and the lust of the eyes, and the pride of life, is not of the Father, but is of the world; and the world passeth away, and the lust thereof; but he that doeth the will of God abideth for ever. We must therefore seek to be conformed to the will of God by poverty, chastity, and obedience.

'All who enter the Society must seek to carry out, not only the letter of their vows, but the fullness of the spirit thereof, that they may attain to the end to which God is calling them by these counsels of perfection.

'The heart must be detached from the world in every possible form, if it is really to be filled with God. It is an eternal glory that is set before us, even eternal life in union with the Son of God. We must, therefore, purify ourselves, even as He is pure; coming to buy of Him gold tried in the fire, and the white raiment of chastity, and the eyesalve of humble obedience, that we may see the things hidden from the fleshly mind.'

OF THE THREE VOWS

In considering our three vows, we must remember that their whole value is that they bind us to Christ. Natural moralists have their laws by which they would train their disciples, but Jesus does not merely leave a law behind Him; He is Himself the fulfilment of the law, and He binds us to Himself while we accomplish the law. And so this threefold law of perfection is a law of union with Christ. If we want to know how to fulfil the law, we must see in what way Christ reveals Himself to us as fulfilling it. Whatever be our point of difficulty, let us come to Christ, and see what Christ would do, and we may be quite certain that He will reveal to us whatever is good and important for us to know. In every matter in which our three vows are concerned, we must remember that the object of these vows is to make us like to Christ. What, then, would Christ have done? How would He have accomplished this vow? How shall I accomplish my vow, so as to be like Christ? If I keep my vow ever so truly in the letter, and am not in some way like Him, then it will have profited me nothing. The purpose of my vow is to bind me to Christ in the fellowship of a holy life, in the unity of a changeless spirit of holy action. *[The vows of Religion a law of union with Christ.]*

Many are the rules of moral discipline which may be laid down for the world, and many of them good, but such rules do not always bind us to Christ. They may put us in the way of becoming bound to Christ; they may be counsels of penitence, or of discipline, but counsels of perfection only are such as really bind us to Christ, and *[The counsels of perfection develop the likeness of Christ within us.]*

unite us in the likeness of Christ. We may perform certain actions as vengeance for our sins, because we are unlike to Christ, as actions of discipline of our outer nature to check the sinful tendencies which keep us unlike Christ; but these are counsels belonging to imperfection. Counsels of perfection are those which develop within us the real likeness of Christ. Jesus Christ was poor; see that poverty does really develop within you the life of Christ. Jesus Christ was chaste; see that chastity develops the life of Christ within you. Jesus Christ lived in obedience; see that obedience does really develop the likeness of Christ within you. Unless we are acting in these three ways, we are losing somewhat of the likeness of Christ. However well we may spend our wealth, we are forfeiting somewhat of the likeness of Christ. However pure may be our domestic affections, we are forfeiting somewhat of the likeness of Christ. However wise our exercise of authority, we are forfeiting somewhat of the likeness of Christ. Christ had the riches of God, Christ hath bound all unto Himself in the love of God, Christ ruled all with the wisdom of God; but in His human life He lived according to these counsels of perfection which our vows perpetuate.

They perpetuate the principles of His incarnate life. So we must be constantly mindful to keep the thought of the three vows distinct from all counsels of moral improvement, however good they may be; otherwise we shall fail to recognize the supernatural virtue and power of our three vows. If we look upon them merely as external modes of moral discipline, we might very likely find them less suited than other modes to our own individual case. But if we recognize the likeness of Christ, then we see in them that revelation of divine grace which not only fits our own particular case, but which fits us because it is the life of the Incarnate Word, the Son of Man, the head of the Body, whose members we are, whose life we have received, and whose actions and mode of life we are called to perpetuate. In the fellowship of His earthly life, we are to live upon the earth in order that we may be trained, not for such a heaven as would suit our own particular taste, but to rejoice in that heaven in which the Son of Man ever lives. So be always watchful to distinguish the three counsels of perfection from all mere rules of earthly moralists. Be careful to remember that other rules are empty, until filled with Christ. He is the fulfilling of the law, and the law is empty and weak through the flesh; but those forms of life which grow out of His humanity are forms of substantial power, which communicate divine life to those who are really incorporated into them. We must, then, dwell upon this thought of our substantial union with Christ, our incorporation into Christ, our subjection to the law of the Body of Christ, which these three vows effect.

And then we should be very careful to keep these vows really in the spirit which belongs to Christ, for it were in vain for us to trifle with Christ. It were in vain for us to imagine that Christ would be pleased with our taking a vow that we

The vows can only be kept in the light of the example of Jesus.

did not keep: 'Better that thou shouldest not vow, than that thou shouldest vow and not pay' (*Eccles.* v. 5). It is not the mere acceptance of an outward form of life which makes us like to Christ; it is the endurance of the privations which belong to that form of life. We should be constantly looking to Christ as exemplifying what we ought to be setting before ourselves, the pattern of our true selves. How would Christ have lived in our circumstances? All persons ought to set before themselves this ideal. There is no Christian life which is not a call to the likeness of Christ, which is not really a perpetuation of Christ's law of action, in which we may not thus look to the example of Jesus Christ. But the higher the form of life, the closer in its outward details to the earthly life of Christ, so much the more must we look to see what Christ would have done. We must be careful to take Him as our real pattern, to take His life as the exponent of the law which He taught—'all that Jesus began both to do and to teach' (*Acts* i. 1). We cannot accept His teaching unless we see Him doing. With other teachers we must take their teaching rather than their works, but with Jesus Christ we cannot understand the teaching unless we contemplate the works. 'The works which I do, they bear witness of me' (*St. John* v. 36), and the works of Christ explain His words.

We must fulfil them by the light of His presence. We must, then, accustom ourselves to look to the likeness of Jesus Christ as really illuminating us, that we may know what our vows require. He is the light of the heavenly Jerusalem. He is that central diamond, shedding forth its lustre in crystal brightness on all sides at once, the central foundation, and the central illumination of the city of God. If we are not looking to Him, we cannot see our way about the streets of the city. It is His light, the light of His presence, which sheds its brightness all around. So we must be watchful to see this light, the presence of Jesus Christ, making plain what it is that He would have us to do.

But this light is not a mere external light, as the Pillar of fire, illuminating the surface of things round about us (cf. *Exod.* xiii. 21); it is internal, illuminating our hearts. It is not an outward light like an outward revelation, removing the darkness of things round about us; rather, it is an inward light filling our souls, and enabling us, as it were, to see in the dark. The darkness remains externally round about us, the darkness of the world, but the soul which is living in the light of the heavenly Jerusalem sees by reason of the light of the inner presence of Jesus Christ. 'The light of the body is the eye' (*St. Matt.* vi. 22), and the eye, the supernatural eye, has its own light within itself; it sees by reason of its own supernatural power. We must thus look to Christ, to Christ really dwelling within ourselves, the central light of the heavenly Jerusalem, if we would really live according to this law of the city of God.

We must, then, seek to have these counsels of perfection exhibited, and brought home to our conscience, by the likeness of Jesus Christ; and

[margin: The presence of Christ is an inward light, illuminating our hearts.]

[margin: As we see Him so we follow Him.]

if we do so, we shall certainly delight in this law. For we cannot know what Christ does without living it; we cannot see and admire it, and stand aloof from it. To see Him is to be drawn to Him, into the fellowship of His life, so as to be united to Him. We cannot see what Christ would do, and be content to do anything different. A real vocation is just the revelation of what Christ does. There is our vocation! If we are not drawn to live in the same life that He lived, there must be some obscurity in the revelation. We could not tolerate ourselves in being different from Jesus Christ, if we really saw Him in His truth.

If our gaze on Jesus Christ is kept clear, we can keep our vows.

So then our vocation is just a revelation of Jesus Christ within us, and we must be true to this vocation. We must keep our gaze upon Christ clear, and prevent any of the fog of earth coming between us and Him. We must accustom ourselves to gaze upon Him, to be filled with the light of His presence. We must accustom ourselves really to feel everything a burden which holds us back from Him, and everything a joy in which we are enabled to become like to Him. So must we look to our Lord Jesus, as really teaching us to practise, and also to love, these counsels. What if they are sometimes hard to the outer nature; is that any reason for shrinking? O my Jesus, didst Thou not come into the world, in order that Thou mightest draw me away from all the desire of the fleshly mind, in order that Thou mightest separate me from all that the natural heart desires? O my Jesus, have Thou mercy upon me; guide me to behold Thyself, that I may indeed praise Thee, casting aside every burden, rejoicing in all I can suffer, for only thereby may this nature of sin be mortified, and done to death.[1]

Our Lord Jesus Christ does then indeed set before us His example to draw us unto Himself, and by the revelation of His supernatural sweetness to strengthen us to bear whatever may be irksome to the outer nature. We are not to imagine that we can rise up to the one, except by bearing the other. We are not to think that we can be so spiritually minded, that we can rise up to the perfection and knowledge of Jesus Christ in any other way than by stern discipline, the wearing down of the outer nature, the natural mind, the natural heart. All this whole earthly system of nature requires to be crushed before the soul can really rise. We are not to imagine that we can keep it so regulated that we shall be always rejoicing in the Lord. No, we have a very hard struggle, and a very long-continued struggle, to undergo, and there must be the mortification of the outer nature. Poverty must at many times be felt as a real difficulty; chastity has its own terrible temptations; obedience must crush the inmost mind and judgement: otherwise we cannot really get free of all our own selves, and live according to the vocation of Jesus Christ. Jesus Christ calls different persons to different degrees of mortification, that they may come nearer to Him, but us He calls to an entire mortification, that we may belong to the world no more than

By our vows the outer nature must be wholly mortified.

[1] See Note E at the end of the chapter.

He did. 'As He is, so are we in this world' (1 *St. John* iv. 17).¹

Jesus makes us triumphant by giving strength for the conflict.

We are very apt to have an idea that as Christ has died and risen and ascended, we ought to find ourselves triumphant over the world by the subjection of all our enemies. But we are to find His power, not by triumph, but by strength for the conflict. He strengthens us that we may fight. And we are to be thankful that we have to fight, and that God in calling us to this struggle does give us the necessary grace. The power of Jesus Christ is not manifested by Jesus sheltering us, but rather His power is manifested by His leaving us, as it were, in the serried throng of armed antagonists. They are round about us on every side, but it is in this conflict that we are to show the strength of Jesus Christ. He says, 'The Philistines be upon thee,' but He does not leave us, as she of old left Samson in weakness in the midst of his enemies (cf. *Judges* xvi. 20). Rather He says, 'The Philistines be upon thee, but I am within thee; I will strengthen thee; the more thine enemies, the more thou shalt find my strength.'

The conflict is in proportion to our nearness to Jesus Christ.

So it must be, that we are indeed to bear many trials, many difficulties, many sore and terrible temptations, more than other men in proportion as Jesus Christ calls us near unto Himself. How was it that the Saints attained to that sweetness, that tranquillity, that patience, that self-forgetfulness which constituted their being? Was it that they were always sheltered, growing up as tender

¹ See Note F at the end of the chapter.

plants? Nay, it was because they were exposed to manifold difficulties, so that the whole outer nature was rubbed off in the conflict, was burned through with that fire of God which penetrated their being as it burned out the fire of the world. Yes, our nature requires thus indeed to endure a great struggle in order that it may be sanctified. Our three vows are surely to bring this struggle along with them. Our Lord Jesus had to suffer much in carrying them out, and so must we also. But, never mind! we are to go onward in the strength of Jesus. Our vows are given to us in order that we may become like Jesus.

In the likeness of Jesus we shall find the glory of the spiritual life. In the likeness of Jesus we shall find all difficulties solved. When we are in doubt, whether this or that is consistent with our vows, let us not ask, 'Is it consistent with the letter of my vows?' We are able to make almost anything consistent with the letter of our vows. But let us ask, 'Is it consistent with the likeness of Jesus Christ?' Then Jesus makes His light to shine, and we can see at once what is consistent with Him, what He would have done, what He would have avoided, how He would have lived in poverty, what that chastity of soul was in which He ever lived in the love of the Father, how He would have been obedient to those over Him. Thus must we learn to surrender our whole nature to the likeness of Jesus Christ, that we may indeed find in our three vows that perfection which comes from Him alone.

The likeness of Jesus Christ is the law of our perfection.

Note E

'This nature of sin.'

In using the words 'nature of sin' Father Benson seems to have had in his mind St. Paul's words, 'Knowing this, that our old man is crucified with Christ, that the body of sin might be destroyed, that henceforth we should not serve sin' (*Rom.* vi. 6); a phrase similar to that in the cry: 'O wretched man that I am! who shall deliver me from the body of this death!' (*Rom.* vii. 24). Sanday and Headlam in their commentary on the first of these passages paraphrase thus: 'That the bodily sensual part of us, prolific home and haunt of sin, might be so paralysed and disabled as henceforth to set us free from the service of sin' (*Commentary on Ep. to the Romans*, pp. 154, 155).

In the following paragraph, where Father Benson speaks of the 'outer nature,' the 'natural mind,' the 'natural heart,' the 'whole earthly system of nature,' he is using these expressions in the same sense as St. Paul when he speaks of the 'flesh wherein dwelleth no good thing' (*Rom.* vii. 18), the 'carnal mind that is enmity against God' (*Rom.* viii. 7), the 'deeds of the body' which must be mortified if we are to live in Christ (*Rom.* viii. 13).

In his *Commentary on the Epistle to the Romans*, on this last passage, Father Benson writes: 'The practices which we have to mortify are such as belong to the fleshly nature. We are not idly to acquiesce in any incapacity, nor to neglect the faculties of action which God has given to us in our bodily nature. No, the bodily faculties must be exercised on behalf of the higher purposes of the Spirit. The practices which originate in the body for its own gratification (and the word includes the whole bodily or fleshly nature) must live only for the Spirit, and all its powers must

be cultivated so as to practise what the Spirit desires.
... It must be dead to its own impulses, else it will
be our destruction' (*Commentary*, in loc., pp. 312,
313).

NOTE F

'Obedience must crush the inmost mind and judgement.'

The vigour of the Father's phrase might easily lead
to misunderstanding, as though he meant that the
inmost mind and judgement of one who lives in holy
obedience must necessarily become paralysed and
inoperative. If mind and judgement were in that
sense crushed, there would be no subject matter left
for the continual joyous offering of the surrendered
life. What Father Benson means is that the real test
of obedience will come when there is a real disagree-
ment about some course of action to be followed, or
some change to be adopted. When a decision has
been made by constitutional authority 'there must
then be the surrender of the judgement in all matters
accidental' (*S.S.J.E. Retreat*, 1873). 'It is in the
surrender of the judgement that the chief fruit of
obedience is found. It is not obedience if we only
do what we agree with. It is obedience when what
is required may be to our judgement distasteful or
undesirable.' But such obedience 'is limited by
obedience to Almighty God. We cannot put any
one in the place of God. We must be careful to
acknowledge divine authority in all its fullness'
(*S.S.J.E. Retreat*, 1874).

The obedience of the Religious has to do with all
matters in which apart from his vows he would have
been free to follow his own will, and act by his own
judgement. It is an obedience that flows from his
vocation of God. He renounces now the right to

make his own judgement the arbiter of his own determination. Called of God to the Society he will now find the spring of all his actions in the will of the Superior, coming to him as the will of God, and the practice of a ready obedience however costly, and in proportions to its cost, will be the best security for God's blessing, and guidance. 'The more readily we obey the more we shall find the wisdom of God manifested in the Society' (*S.S.J.E. Retreat*, 1873).

Speaking of obedience, from the point of view of poverty, St. Francis of Assisi taught: 'A man has not abandoned all for God as long as he keeps in his hand the purse of his own opinion' (Le Monnier, *History of St. Francis of Assisi*, p. 457). Father Benson, speaking of the blessing flowing from obedience, which renounces its own previously conceived ideas, spoke similarly: 'In proportion as the soul is given over to God, so is God given over to the soul. She who had put aside the thought of the Mother's joy, received the unspeakable joy of the divine maternity' (*S.S.J.E. Retreat*, 1872).

CHAPTER VII

OF LIVING UNDER RULE

A LIFE in community without Rule would be a mere collegiate life; it would not be the Religious life. To realize this life, it is necessary that we should live strictly by Rule. *The Religious life a life under Rule.*

The great foundations of Rule, which are common to all societies, are the three vows of poverty, chastity, and obedience. Poverty breaks the soul from the world; chastity lifts up the soul to God; obedience binds the soul under the common law of the community. *Every Rule is based on the three vows.*

The Rule of any community will necessarily vary according to the circumstances for which it is set apart. In the contemplative life the Rule will be carried out with minuteness for the actions of each day. In a mixed life, such as ours, the details of the Rule cannot be marked out in the same way, or they would be encumbrances to us rather than helps: but then the principles must be cherished all the more, to secure for the individual the grace of fellowship. *The Rule is adapted to the purposes of the Society.*

It is true that the life of obedience is a life of restriction, but it is also a life of power. We must, then, take very great care to abide within the limits marked out for us by the vows of poverty, chastity, and obedience. Any special rule which *The Rule restricts our life.*

may be given to any individual is intended to develop these principles within him, and not to rule his life apart from the community.

The restriction of the Rule a source of blessing.

It is necessary that we should feel the life to be a life of restriction. Poverty may seem sometimes to cut us off from doing much good, but then we may do greater good in other ways, and we must realize that we shall obtain the grace of the Society, which has made the vow. It will constantly seem to us that by wayward, fitful impulses we might effect much, but we must look upon these things as temptations, as the effort of the evil one, attempting to draw us away from the grace of community. We must realize the Rule as God's will for us, and the performance of it as the way in which we are to gain His blessing.[1]

The less detailed the Rule the more carefully the principles of the Rule must be observed.

The distractions of the present day, much more manifold and embarrassing than in the earlier ages of the Religious life, prevent any great detail of Rule applicable to all under all circumstances; but we must keep the great principles of the life very strictly in view, and be attentive to the observance of the rules we have, especially in the early days of the Society before the detailed Rule has had time to develop.

The Rule is intended to develop the life of the Society in the individual.

The observance of the Rule will tend to check individualizing, which indeed would be the death of the Society. There should be in all a great family likeness. The individual thus becomes effective for greater purposes. Elasticity may display itself in a variety of works and actions, but if our elasticity succeeds in binding

[1] See Note G at the end of the chapter.

us down within the Society's Rule it becomes real power, and shows itself in the perfection of the action done. We must see, then, that we act, at all times, according to what the three vows involve.

This life under Rule gives us a great and continual opportunity of triumphing over self, and this, not only by the restraining of what is evil, but also by the disciplining of what is good. As the gardener removes from his trees fruit which might have come to perfection, in order that the rest which is left may become more perfect, so the mind that is disciplined will be able to give itself up to the perfection of the acts to which it is restrained. Natural society eschews wildness and independence in its higher forms, and in refined society the individual who sacrifices himself for it is helped on by it. So we shall find that the high aspirations of the soul, together with its philanthropic emotions, run continually to waste unless they are held down by the higher impulse of divine love, that is, by obedience. When they are thus held down, they act inwardly instead of outwardly, and at last come forth in the fullness of power, in whatever act the well-disciplined soul may be appointed to perform. *The discipline and fruitfulness of life under Rule.*

Realize, then, that your life under Rule is a life of power; that restraint is a source of power; and that it can only be so when you feel that it is a restraint, and not otherwise. So in reference to the rules of the House, though very simple, and sometimes seeming to clash with things that seem *The obligation of faithful observance of the Rule.*

more important, we must be very careful. No merely immediate impulses, nothing but a plain duty of actual necessity, not of choice, should make us even argue with ourselves about violating these rules. When some plain matter of actual duty comes in the way, for which we must set the Rule aside, this will be no violation of it, for there is the intervention of a higher rule. We must always bear in mind that the rules of the Society are not given to us as a substitute for that higher rule. We must recognize also the mutual dependence and subordination of rules. The Rule of the House if carefully observed will give peace and light to the conscience.

The careful observance of the Rule binds all in one spirit.

The less detailed and the fewer our rules are, the more watchful must we be that we are observing their spirit. By this careful watchfulness we shall be united in spirit however much we may be separated. Whatever our work may be, and in whatever place, we must realize that all is given to us to be done by the Society. We must, therefore, abstain from any spontaneous action, unless imperative necessity require it, and we should not act without the permission of the member of the Society who is Superior in that place where we may happen to be. It is a great stay in separation to feel that we are under these mutual obligations, and that our mutual sympathies well forth from the three vows. We are thus taken away from individuality with all its sparkling weakness.

The unity of our life in the Society, abiding before God.

So whatever different works we may be called to give ourselves up to, let us ever remember that they will pass away; but the bond that unites

OF LIVING UNDER RULE 107

us as members of a Religious society will pass through time out into eternity. We shall have to appear before God as having been united by that bond, as Religious. May He grant that our union may not cease when this life is over.

Note G

'*We shall obtain the grace of the Society, which has made the vow.*'

Father Benson, if his words are correctly reported, seems to mean that it is the existence of the Society, as founded upon the vows of Religion, which becomes the occasion of those vows being taken by those who are called of God to its membership. It 'makes the vow' in the sense that it is the occasion of it. It sets the vow before us as the condition of membership, and the keeping of that vow will be the assurance to us of our being upheld by the grace of the Society.

It seems less probable that he meant that it was the grace given to the Society which has made the vow. In this case, however, his meaning would appear to be that as it was the grace of God which called the Society into existence, so it is the grace of God which has made the vow of obedience in it possible and right. The same grace that created the Society creates also the state of life, constituted by the vows.

The difficulty, however, is only one of the expression used. The truth that he is concerned to enforce is that faithfulness to our vows is the pledge to us of the grace that belongs to us in the Society in which those vows were taken. It would have been entirely consonant with his meaning if the words had run simply, 'in which the vow has been made,' or even 'which is based upon the vow.'

CHAPTER VIII

OF OBEDIENCE

Obedience a counsel of perfection because it secures humility.

'AS pride is the principal root of all sin, so is humility the foundation of all virtues ; and this foundation is laid in the powerful concrete of holy obedience.'

We must be watchful to cherish always this spirit of humility. Remember that obedience is a counsel of perfection, not because it secures wisdom, but because it secures humility. Wisdom grows out of humility. There might be a great organization and wise government in which there were no humility, and such wisdom would profit nothing. Obedience is of value in the mere societies of the world, because it tends to unity of purpose, concentration of aim, wisdom of deliberation, and the like; but it is not for this purpose that we seek obedience in our vows. It is in order that we may learn to be humble; so that in fact sometimes the very outward defects of authority may tend to the greater virtue of obedience, and when we have to surrender our judgement to that which seems to us to be less fitting, we may be exercising a spiritual virtue which shall be to us of the greatest profit. We must be careful, therefore, to cherish humility in all the parts of obedience, not merely in obedience to this or that authority, but in obedience to whosoever may at any time be set over us, even to a subordinate, even to one who may be in the Society inferior to ourselves.

We are to learn humility in the way of holy obedience, the entire setting aside of self, the losing of self in the Society so that the Society lives in our persons. As the Society is a special means by which we seek to develop the grace of Christ, so Christ dwells in the Society, and the Society in us. The Society, therefore, must be to us a real means of the indwelling of Christ. We must lose ourselves in the Society and so in Christ, so that we may be able to say, 'I live; yet not I, but Christ liveth in me' (*Gal.* ii. 20). While we are living as independent Christians in the Church at large, we have constantly to exercise our own will. That will seems to come between us and Christ; but it is the surrender of our will in holy obedience that enables us to welcome the will of Christ. We must take care, then, not only to be merely obedient in the outward letter, but to be cherishing this real spirit of obedience, and seeking Christ therein. Obedience is one means by which we follow the example of Christ. We cannot follow the example of Christ unless we are acting in the power of Christ. Christ must be as truly obeying in us as in another sense He is ruling in those that rule, and as truly working in us now as He was in His own Person during the years of His earthly career. We must thus seek indeed to lose ourselves in Christ by the exercise of holy obedience.

We are to lose ourselves in the Society, that Christ the life of the Society may dwell in us.

'*Obedience must be no mere servile acquiescence in that which is enjoined, but the hearty self-surrender of trustful love accepting the voice of God in those who are set in authority over us. It must be prompt, hearty, and complete.*'

<small>Obedience is the surrender of self.</small>

Obedience must be a hearty self-surrender, and giving up of self; so that, in fact, there will be the greater joy of obedience when there is the consciousness of having given up self. We realize obedience as a triumph over our own self, when we set self aside. Thus after an act of this kind, in which self has been set aside, there comes the tranquil life of holy obedience, and our life goes on like a boat gliding on the surface of a stream when it has received an impulse; it is borne on without any jar or shock, tranquilly yielding itself to that power by which it has been moved. So the life after a surrender, or struggle, of obedience should realize the joy of that divine peace which God extends like a mighty river (cf. *Isa.* lxvi. 12), flowing on in its calmness to the faithful, humble soul.

<small>The surrender of self, an act of trustful love.</small>

There must be, then, this self-surrender in obedience, without thought of self. If our own will, or our own mind, or our own fancy, or liking, or judgement rise up, we are just to put it aside, accepting the will of God. There must be this hearty self-surrender, knowing how truly God does welcome us while we give up to Him, and so it is done in trustful love. It is not done as a matter of course. It is a matter of divine love. Whatever command we receive, we receive it with the intensity of divine love, as expressing the divine will towards us. It is done with trustful love, for we are sure that God has given it to us; it is His vocation, and we are sure He will guide us in it. He can overrule even the mistakes of those in authority, even the sins and faults of men. He can, He will, overrule them for our personal good. So it is for us to live in personal trustful love, loving God as we know that He loves us, trusting Him as we know He rules us.

God speaks to us. As the voice of God came amidst the trees of the garden (cf. *Gen.* iii. 8), so the voice of God speaks to us, and we are to recognize that voice; and every act that we do, really recognizing that voice, is an act that is sure to obtain His blessing. So obedience is not to be the mere dull, servile, routine observance of what is commanded, but it is to be a real watchfulness for the divine voice. We do a thing altogether differently when we do it as a matter of course, and when as a matter of divine love. Great is the difference between doing a thing as a matter of course and as a matter of human love, but greater than doing it as a matter of human love is the doing it as a matter of divine love. Watch, then, for God's voice, whether it be to call us to this work, or to set us aside from that. To know that God speaks to us is full of joy. 'The Master is come, and calleth for thee' (*St. John* xi. 28). And whatever it be that we are called to, the bell calling us to chapel, or to meals, or some call to a lecture, or to work in the garden, or to whatsoever it be, it is the voice of God. We must strive upon each occasion to hear the voice of

In obedience we must be watching for the voice of God in love.

God speaking to us. 'I am to go and do this act, because it belongs to that eternal life in which I am living in God.' The people of the world act upon necessity, and they act upon routine; but the faithful, the elect, hear the voice of God, and they act in love. Whatever it be they have to do, they go forth to do it in the power of this divine voice, for they hear the voice of God.

As we act in obedience to God we glorify Him outwardly, and inwardly in our own souls.

Constantly to be listening to the voice of God is a great stay to the soul; constantly to be listening for this voice of God, to feel that God has His own special purpose for our own selves, that though it be one of the commonest acts of the house we have to do, nevertheless it is God's purpose for us; to measure the act, not by its necessity, or its wisdom, or its dignity, or by the praise it will win, but to know it simply as the appointment of divine love, as something we can do for God. The life really sacrificed to God recognizes every breath as belonging to God; and so every act must be done, not simply for the glory of God externally, or for the advancement of His glory in the world, but really and truly for the glory of God in our hearts, for the advancement of His glory in our own lives; really and truly for the glory of God in our own selves, that interior glory of God by which He fashions us for the participation of His own interior glory throughout eternity. He trains us by His external glory and by the discipline of the outer life, that our lives may be to His external glory while we exhibit His sanctity.

OF OBEDIENCE 113

But love is indeed a secret bond between the soul and God, 'a garden enclosed, a fountain sealed' (*Song of Songs* iv. 12), and God delights in the soul which is thus secretly given up to Himself, which really lives in this interior delight of His divine presence, which really welcomes the manifestation of His love, and which, therefore, is quite content to do anything, whether it be great or small, whether it succeed or fail, content to do anything in the simple power of love, and so to His glory. God was as glorious in all those ages of eternity before the world was created as He will be when He has brought all things to their consummation; and all that interior glory of the divine love He communicates to us to be the interior glory of the loving soul. If He calls us to co-operate with Him in outer works, manifesting that interior glory, yet it is because He has taught us how great that glory is. The hermit soul that is simply shut by, living in some insignificant actions but living in the fullness of the love of God, lives in the consciousness of glory, far greater than any outward manifestation which belongs to the outer life. So it is for us in all the routine of our daily observances to realize, to live in, to rejoice in this glory of God, which He pours forth into our souls, and which He calls us to contemplate; which He calls us to contemplate, that He may indeed make Himself manifest in us.

To act in the power of the divine love is to participate in the divine glory.

'*If the life is given as a sacrifice to God, it is better that it be consumed in the fire of holy obedience than that it should have ever so much brilliancy in the glitter of worldly applause.*

'*The worldly heart delights in that which itself has chosen. The disciple who would abide in the love of Jesus delights in doing not his own will, but the will of Him that sends him. We must be content on all occasions to act or to abstain from acting, to follow or to tarry, as may be the will of Him to whom we are given, made known to us by those whom He has set over us.*'

<small>By obedience we seek to act in the love of Jesus.</small>

We must delight thus to rest in the bosom of Jesus, knowing that herein is the greatness of that love in which He unites us to Himself, that we do His will and not our own. While we do our own will, we cannot rest in the love of Jesus. We must find our rest in the removal of every natural impulse. We must abide in the love of Jesus, by having that love as the motive power of our life.

<small>By obedience we lay aside every personal choice.</small>

We may have to tarry until Christ come, or we may have to follow in some way of suffering, but we must be just as ready for the one as for the other. We are not to think that we shall lose any divine glory, because God holds back from us some form of action, or suffering, on which we have set our heart. We are not to set any medium before us as the particular medium to some divine glory, but we must lose ourselves in the manifestation of the love of Jesus. If our whole self is bathed in that love, without any veil between us and it, then indeed we shall find the fullness of divine glory. So must we just leave ourselves in His hands, assured that He will guide us in that way which He knows to be best.

OF OBEDIENCE

'*Humble obedience is secure against any possible humiliation, for the great glory of the obedient is to recognize no existence except what is derived from the superior authority. Our object is that we may be purged from self-will, and what would be to the worldling a humiliation is accepted by us as the means of destroying that self-will, which is the great hindrance to Christian perfection.*'

Yes, there is great glory in obedience, for the more we humble ourselves in outer acts of obedience, the more does the soul rejoice in the manifestation, or contemplation, of the power of God. As when toilsomely we climb some height and see the distant vision, so when outwardly we are subjected to some humiliation we are really climbing the height of holy light, and with every humiliation we gain a wider prospect of the heavenly land. It is not merely that we darkly hope for it, but we really attain to see. And so we must find a real glory in every humiliation to which we may be exposed in the way of holy obedience. If it be the mere scorn of some worldly heart which does not understand our motives, every word of scorn which we hear should at once wake within us, not a soreness, not a sense of being wounded, but rather an intensity of delight; for Jesus is longing to manifest Himself to the soul, and the outer reproach will make us at once take refuge with Him, so as to taste the sweetness of His love.

By acceptance of humiliations in the way of obedience we gain fresh visions of God.

We are conscious how much there is of self remaining while we are in the world. This natural self remains until the great purging of the

By humiliations we are purged from self-will.

Last Day. Oh, what will it be, being thus thoroughly purged from self, to exist within the very being of the glorified Saviour, yet with an individuality of life! A personal consciousness remaining, yet with nothing that separates; the reality of self without its feebleness, the glory of God filling our whole nature. So by every act of humiliation that we have to bear in the world, by every mortification of the will, we are just to learn that our own will is being gradually purged off, and we ourselves are being stablished in the being of Christ. We have to welcome that being of Christ; we must welcome it into our own selves.

'If obedience is to be hearty, it must be the instinctive expression of love co-operating with the will of the Superior. It is not enough to go into the sepulchre of obedience, unless we see and believe the mysteries whose glory sanctifies that shrine of burial. Obedience must therefore open the heart to live in unity of purpose with the superior authority.

'Such hearty obedience causes that the special gifts of each shall be combined in forwarding the common work of the Society. The spirit of obedience is the holy anointing whereby all are at once illuminated, united, edified.'

The life of obedience a burial with Christ. We are, then, to realize how obedience does indeed bury us. It implies that we are indeed dead to the world, that we are taken out of the world; and as we go into this grave of Christ we are to see and believe the mysteries of the death of Christ. We cannot be really buried along with

Him until we have seen where He lay, and in that sight have come to believe all that He taught. So our life in obedience must be a continual watching of the buried Saviour, watching where He was in order that we may be buried there, watching in the knowledge that His burial is indeed but the other side of His Resurrection, watching there, and knowing that for us to be buried along with Him is to rise with Him also.

It is the holy anointing of the spirit of obedience that binds us in this oneness of new life, that so we may all act together as of one heart and one mind. 'Behold how good and joyful a thing it is, brethren, to dwell together in unity' (*Ps.* cxxxiii. 1).

By obedience we live in unity of life.

'*The actions of life must thus be nourished in the deep soil of holy obedience, and not spring out of the shallowness of individual conception.*

'*If things which we think to be needful are in any way set aside by authority, even though it may seem to be only through forgetfulness, yet must we realize it to be a great gain to ourselves that we have thus an opportunity of surrendering something valuable. The sacrifice is lost to sight, when the fire consumes it, and what we offer to God must be lost to our own sight, ere we can receive it back from God, in the glorious resurrection-power of His divine acceptance.*'

So the blindness of obedience must pass on to the vision of God. We shall see God more and more, in proportion to the blindness with which we obey. If we yield up what we do simply to Him, we shall find that it is indeed consumed, but

The more perfectly we obey the more the sweet savour of the sacrifice of Christ rises up in us.

it does not perish. The sacrifice is burned; the particles pass away from view, but not one of them is lost. They rise up, filling the air with that which is so acceptable to God as a sweet-smelling savour. So it is with our acts of obedience, in which we are consumed; our life rises up as an offering of sweet savour unto God. True indeed it may be that our life has no sweetness that God should accept, but indeed it does rise up with all the sweetness of the life of Christ. The sacrifices of the old law had no natural sweetness, but a typical sweetness as they symbolized the offering of Christ. The sacrifice of the new law has indeed no natural sweetness; there may be much in our life of which people could say, 'Of what use is it?' and, 'Why should God delight in it?' But we must take care that our life has a sacramental sweetness of the life of Christ: not merely a natural sweetness, nor a typical sweetness, but a life consumed in the power of the Holy Ghost, and sweet to the eternal Father, with all the merits of the grace of His well-beloved Son.

CHAPTER IX

OF CHASTITY

'THE disciple whom Jesus loved, which also leaned on His breast at the Supper, to whom also in dying He commended His Virgin Mother, must always be regarded by us as exhibiting for our example that purity dear to Jesus which alone can fit us to rest in Him by holy contemplation, or to labour for the well-being of the Church.'

Without this purity we cannot be taken into the love of Jesus. Without this purity Jesus cannot reveal to us His purposes. Without this purity Jesus cannot raise us up to contemplate His mysteries. Without this purity Jesus cannot call us near to share His work. We must be prepared, then, to suffer much in the maintenance of purity, if we would cling close to Jesus. Great is this gift. Jesus values it, and Satan knows its value; and it is for us to know its value also. Jesus values it, and He will help us to abide in His purity. Satan knows its value, and he will strive in every possible way, in ways beyond our thought, to take us away from it, to rob us of it. But we must know its value, and in the sympathy of the love of Jesus we must seek to abide in that chastity which Jesus loves.

The necessity and value of purity.

Purity flowing from fellowship with Jesus.

Be sure of it, there is no possibility of abiding in this, except by closeness of fellowship with Jesus. The natural heart may think it is pure, while, nevertheless, it is being encrusted with an earthliness which entirely shuts heaven out. We must have that purity which Jesus loves, or it is no real purity. That purity we can only have in fellowship with Him; it is a living purity, and He is the Lord of life. He makes us pure by pouring into us the energies of that supernatural life of purity in which He dwells. This purity is a living power. It is a divine gift. It makes the fullness of the glory of God to shine through the nature, purging all the avenues of sense, and expanding the faculties that they may apprehend the things of God.

St. John the pattern of purity, ever rejoicing in, and still looking for, the revelation of Jesus.

We must, then, be always careful to look to our dear Patron as the pattern of that purity, abiding close along with Jesus, resting in the bosom of Jesus, rejoicing in the revelation of Jesus, evermore living on in the world as He lived, simply waiting until Jesus comes (cf. *St. John* xxi. 22). We must be always waiting until Jesus comes, looking for Him to appear. Let every knock at the door be to us as a reminder that it may be Jesus who is coming. Let every change always make us watchful for the appearance of Jesus. Our hearts must be continually waiting for the manifestation of Jesus, as they rest upon the bosom and upon the grace of Jesus, resting in that which He has given, waiting for that which is yet to be revealed. So must we indeed find a twofold advent as two hands, one sustaining and the other directing us. We must feel our life to be thus enclosed within the very being of Jesus, otherwise it is impossible that we should keep ourselves pure in the midst of this evil world. The beloved disciple was waiting until Jesus should come, not knowing how soon, but longing for His appearing, rejoicing as from time to time revelations were given, and yet each revelation only made him long the more for Him. 'Surely I come quickly. Even so, come, Lord Jesus' (*Rev.* xxii. 20).

If, then, we would be living in the purity which our dear Patron teaches, we must be living in this earnest longing, this constant expectation of the coming of Jesus. So shall we indeed rest in Him by holy contemplation; and whatever the toils and labours and embarrassments we may have in the world, we shall be restful in the midst of all, not disquieted, if we know that Jesus is coming and other things are passing away. We know that Jesus is coming, but we know not how soon. So must we rest in Him by holy contemplation, and realize that His eye is really upon us. If He seems to be far off from us, yet we are not far off from Him. He sees us, and we are close under His care. We must, therefore, rest in the knowledge that He is looking on us. Yea, do we not rest on His bosom? He gazes into our hearts; He knows all the thoughts that are there. He watches us when perhaps Satan assaults us with manifold evil thoughts; He watches whether we do indeed manfully resist. He encourages us to be strong, to put all thoughts of evil away, to keep

The contemplation of Jesus the strength of purity.

ourselves continually gazing upon Him; and if we will only live in His love, then no power of the enemy can tear us away.

<small>The contemplation of Jesus the condition of our work for God.</small>

We must rest in Him by holy contemplation, and in Him we must labour in all purity for the well-being of His Church. We may toil much for the Church of God, but if we mingle the impurity of our nature with what we do, we destroy our every work; we canker the gold with which the temple of God should be built up, with the quicksilver of our earthly nature; we weaken and destroy the whole fabric we desire to build. Let us realize the great necessity of purity of heart for seeing God, and for doing the work of God; for we cannot do the work of God unless we see God. 'The Son can do nothing, but what He seeth the Father do' (*St. John* v. 19); and we can only do the work of God really and truly in proportion as our eyes are open to see what God is doing. All that impurity which mars our own vision mars our work also. So, then, we must be careful really to abide in this purity of heart along with Jesus, following the example of our dear Patron.

'*The affections must be purified from all earthly desire by continually reposing on the holy heart of Jesus. So must all the brethren dwell upon the remembrance of that which Jesus loves, and in the sympathy of His adorable purposes, that thus all the impulses of earthly desire may be hushed within us, and the eye of the soul perfected in the vision of the heavenly peace.*'

OF CHASTITY

We are not to form our own idea of purity, but we are to lose all thoughts of our own in the sympathy of Jesus. We are not to lie upon that bosom, as if we needed to lie there for rest, but it were void of sympathy for us. No, as we repose upon the bosom of Jesus, we must know the fullness of the love of the heart which beats under that bosom; then in each of those beatings we must recognize the fullness of that love wherewith Jesus loveth us. It is the knowledge of that love which purifies the soul. It was not in any self-gratulation that St. John delighted to speak of himself as the disciple 'whom Jesus loved' (*St. John* xiii. 23), but it was because the contemplation of that love was the only thing that could make him worthy of that love. The more he recognized that love, the more did he rise up to the sympathy of that love. 'We love Him, because He first loved us' (1 *St. John* iv. 19). It was not in any spirit of pride because he knew that Jesus loved him, but in the spirit of gratitude that he thus delights to speak. For by that love Jesus made him what he was, purified him from all imperfection, opened his eyes to the contemplation of divine mysteries, and strengthened his love for the fullness of divine work.

The knowledge of the love of Jesus for us purifies our hearts.

We must, therefore, always rest upon Jesus, in the knowledge of the intense love wherewith Jesus welcomes us. The knowledge of how He loves us is that which will keep us true to His love. If we know how He loves us we cannot sin against that love; we cannot let ourselves be drawn away by any other affections whatsoever. To know

The knowledge of the love of Jesus keeps us true to Him.

how Jesus loves us is to be drawn by an irresistible power. We may as well attempt to move a mountain resting upon its base, as to move a heart rested and rooted in that blessed gravitation of the love of Jesus. We do well constantly to dwell upon the thought of that love wherewith Jesus loves us. And let us not think how we can be worthy of it, but that we have received it, and that we may rise up to its requirements.

The love of Jesus a transforming power. And this love—as we behold it, we see its transforming power. It is an active love. Often when we love some one, however intensely, upon earth, there may be the mutual gaze of loving eyes, but that gaze leads on to no further action; it simply stays in inaction, in the knowledge of love. But it is not so with the love of Jesus. We cannot know how Jesus loves us, excepting by knowing all that Jesus is; we cannot know what Jesus is, except by knowing what He does. So while we behold Jesus looking upon us with that eye of intense love, we have His purposes and His actions revealed to us, and as they are revealed to us, we find ourselves drawn to take part in the same; we become transformed thereby—conformed to Him.

The love of Jesus calls us into sympathy with His holy purposes. So must we indeed, gazing and resting upon Jesus, learn to sympathize with all the purposes of Jesus, learn to rejoice in all His wisdom, learn to desire all He teaches us to desire, learn to accept all He bids us to accept, learn to do all He trusts to our accomplishment. We must really enter into the sympathy of the love of Jesus, while we rest upon Him, worshipping His holy purposes; for He is the very life of God, and all the purposes of God shine out therein. He does not diminish His purposes, in order that He may enable us to sympathize with them, but He calls us to be enlarged along with Himself, in order that we may rise up to the measure of His purposes. And so earthly impulses are hushed. The world has power over us, our passions are strong, while Jesus is out of sight; but the moment Jesus is seen, at that moment do all vile passions hie themselves to their dens, and the joy and thrill of the divine life fills the soul.

'All must cultivate a habit of secret converse with Jesus; for it is not enough to be brought near to Him at His table, unless the soul open out to His willing ear all griefs, doubts, fears, temptations, sins, and hear His voice, and find His will making itself manifest in all the tokens of His controlling providence.'

Thus we must accustom ourselves to speak with Jesus, assured that He delights to have us to speak with Him. He delights to have us unfold to Him all our griefs. Whatever be the assaults of Satan from which we are suffering, we are not to think that they are of such a kind that we dare not speak of them to Jesus. The worse may be the assaults of Satan, the more necessary it is to come to tell Jesus of all, in order that He may be our heart's real and true deliverer. Do we cry out to Him? As the sheep that is caught in the thicket, so must we cry out to our good Shepherd, and He will surely come to set us free. Oh, yes ! though we be bleeding and wounded, we need not fear to come to Him. We cannot find life until we do.

Openness of heart with Jesus.

We must come to open out all to Him, for He is the Word of the Father, and as His very existence is to make the Father known, so He wills also to take into Himself the very knowledge of our needs. He cannot gaze upon us in dumbness, neither can He gaze upon the dumb. His whole being is an existence of utterance, and if we are to know the truth of His love, we must utter ourselves to Him as He utters Himself to us. So let us seek always indeed to make known our wounds to Him, and to rejoice that He does thus call us. He calls, and we need not attempt to keep anything back from Him.

<small>The confidence of trustful love.</small>
But do we attempt to keep anything from Him? How foolish! He knows what we are disputing by the way, though we may sometimes fear to tell Him (cf. *St. Mark* ix. 33, 34). If we have really come to Him to repose in His bosom at His banquet, there must now no longer be any hiding up to Him. We can tell all to Him, and of Him ask all. If in difficulties and troubles we are not to gaze round in bewilderment, let us remain where we were in the bosom of Jesus, and looking up in His face let us ask Him. Whatever it be, Jesus will speak to the soul that really has confidence in Him. If our anxieties are more than our confidence, then Jesus cannot speak; but if we lay our anxieties aside, and just repose in Him and ask Him to bear them, then He will speak. We must not even too much distress ourselves, whether we are abiding in the love of Jesus. Oftentimes fear of our weakness may prevent our laying hold on the strengthening grace of Jesus

Christ; rather it is for us to lay hold on that strength, not thinking of our own perseverance. Then we shall persevere, for we shall be at rest.

'*If we would have our affections purified for Jesus, they must be carefully guarded from the sight of impure objects, whether animate or inanimate. All must, therefore, carefully exercise a guard upon their eyes, never to look unnecessarily upon things dangerous to purity, but rather to turn away at once and recall the image of Jesus instituting the Holy Eucharist, suffering upon the Cross, or glorified in Heaven.*'

The guardianship of the eye is a most important feature of the Religious life. There may indeed be various degrees of it, various degrees in which the world is shut out in order that Jesus, the light of heaven, may be more and more revealed to the soul. That enclosure were nothing worth which did not bring along with it this fuller revelation. We may be certain that we cannot have the revelation of heaven unless we do carefully shut out the world. We must, therefore, be very watchful to keep from the sight of things unseemly and vain, and in our own degree, as God calls us, each one of us, to keep from the sight of the mere ordinary objects of nature. God calls different souls to different degrees of the enclosed life. We have to deal with the world, and therefore we cannot have this enclosed life in its strictness, but we must be ever watchful to keep a guard upon our eyes. In fact, the more we are in the world, the more important it is to keep our eyes thoroughly guarded.

[margin: The watchful guardianship of the eyes, the more necessary the less strict the degree of our enclosure.]

We are in the world as buried with Christ.

It is not only the worst objects of the world which awaken unholy desire in the soul; the sight of the outer world is very apt to awaken the worldliness of the heart, and we do not see the evil of that worldliness. But as we gaze upon the objects of the world, we must always be careful to gaze as if we were looking through the door of a sepulchre. We must feel that there is a stone, rolled upon the door of the sepulchre. Though it be a transparent stone, so that we see the world through it, yet we feel that we are separated from the world, and from all that we see, abiding within the enclosure of the buried life. We must seek to be constantly lying hid, separated altogether, shut up. Whatever we may have to do, there must always be this real separation between us and that on which we gaze. We must gaze upon it, as we can fancy a spirit would gaze upon the things of the world, visiting them from another world, while itself had no share in all the things in the midst of which it might be.

The love of Jesus the true enclosure of the heart.

What is that which can thus enclose the heart? Nothing else but the love of Jesus. There is no power through which we can see the world, and yet remain separate from it, but the power of the love of Jesus. The love of Jesus is indeed a strong tower in which we may be enclosed, and through which we may look safely upon other things (cf. *Prov.* xviii. 10). The love of Jesus purges off the evil of all on which we gaze. The love of Jesus keeps us within its sanctifying power. Let us be careful to abide in this love, and see nothing except as it is seen in the heart of Jesus. Yes, as we bury our faces in the bosom of Jesus, we must see the world reflected in the heart of Jesus. As we see how Jesus loves the world, so must we learn to love it and work for it. And as we see how Jesus hates what the world loves, so must we learn, while working for the world, not to love what the world loves; not to love as the world loves; but to keep ourselves detached, beholding all things in the heart of Jesus, and labouring simply in the fellowship of His love.

'The frequent remembrance during the day of the morning meditation, and a careful attention to its resolution, will be a great means of thus abiding in contemplative purity of heart along with Jesus.'

We are not to let the thoughts which Jesus brings into our hearts just pass away. We are constantly to gaze upon them within our own hearts throughout the day, so that they may become to us a real law of life. We must not leave them, as an ostrich does her eggs, but must dwell upon them, until these thoughts and resolutions, which our meditations may have brought to us, become perfected in holy actions, and become a real part of our life. The forgetfulness of what Jesus has said to us is apt to make us very remiss in accomplishing His work. We intend perhaps to act; then we forget; then perhaps we suddenly remember, and try. But as we have forgotten, we have lost the impulse, the spiritual power; we begin to will to act, but by our sin we have forgone all the power of the will of Jesus by which we might have been sustained. So we

Our union with Jesus sustained by the recollection of the fruit of our meditations.

find ourselves unable to take up again what we have forgotten; we find ourselves baffled in doing what we propose.

<small>The value of the repetition of our meditations.</small>

In the remembrance of our daily meditation and of our resolution, we must be constantly recalling it with many an ejaculatory prayer; so that it may mingle its holy light with all we do in the day, that all the other thoughts of the day may gather some of their colour and glow from it, that all our actions may be invigorated by it. The continual repetition of our meditations will be one great means of our really thus deriving the full value from them. We are not to want to meditate upon something new, in order that we may acquire some fresh thought, but rather to rejoice to feed upon that which we have already contemplated. Some have found it well to go on with the same meditation for a great length of time, until they have come to appreciate the full truth. We must be constantly recurring to our meditations, taking them up from day to day, looking back to that which God has said to us in time past, considering the way along which God has led us, coming back, and retracing, and living in the past. Thus living in the past we are living in God; God will thus guide us onward for the future. It is by thus abiding in these thoughts which He has vouchsafed to us by the power of His Holy Spirit, that we shall really be enabled to abide in the purity of His love.

CHAPTER X

OF POVERTY

'*NO one who enters the community shall retain any property for his personal use. The wealth of this world is a burden in its acquisition, its retention, and its expenditure. Joyful is the soul which feels itself to be free from the embarrassments which worldly wealth brings. Silver and gold have I none! If we have parted with it for Christ, we may be sure that we have that which is much better, the riches of divine grace, ever abounding so as to make all our actions mighty through God by His blessing upon the outward weakness of our position in the world.*'

We must remember that our Religious life is to be a life of entire detachment. And we are to be detached not only from great things, but from small. We are to be detached from all earthly things, in order that we may live in the love of God, that we may have God for our only true possession. As we put away earthly things, we must realize that we do indeed take hold upon God, that God gives Himself to be our portion (cf. *Ps.* lxxiii. 25). Oh, the greatness of the riches of God to those who really do appreciate Him! Think what it is to know that we have all the power of God in our hands! To know that we have all the goodness of God pouring itself

<small>The Religious life a life of detachment, laying hold upon God;</small>

forth upon our hearts! To know that we have all the wisdom of God quickening our life! Any earthly thing to which we cling just prevents this entire surrender of ourselves to possess God, and to be possessed of Him. We must come to God to abide in God, with a consciousness that He knows all our needs and that He will supply them. 'Your heavenly Father knoweth what things ye have need of, before ye ask Him' (*St. Matt.* vi. 8).

reaching out after heavenly things;
The teaching of our Gospel in this week (*Fifteenth Sunday after Trinity*) brings home to us the blessedness of an entire dependence upon God, and teaches us to seek first 'the kingdom of God and His righteousness' (*St. Matt.* vi. 33), and all other things shall be given unto us. We must take care that while by the law of poverty we put away earthly things, we are really reaching out after heavenly things. It is not just to fall, as it were, into the water with our arms closed, but to spread them out as one that swims, and then we shall find how they bear us up. So we spread out our arms before God in the energy of holy prayer, and find the sustaining power of the glory of God, that ocean of divine life, in which we come to find a new life.

and concentrating the mind on the love of God.
So then there is the entire putting away of all things, even the smallest, to which we have any claim, the withdrawal of all affections towards any mere earthly objects, the concentration of the mind upon the love of God, as the one object of interest, that we may behold the love of God in all things, and in all things seek to obtain more of the love of God.

'We must put away, not only the reality of wealth, but even its desires; and we must not desire it for the Society any more than for ourselves personally.

'We should often consider with much humility that there are many parish priests and others, who are suffering from grinding poverty while living in their natural spheres of duty, while we, who are living under the vow of poverty, have our wants continually supplied.

'We must be thankful when we do suffer some inconvenience, whether in our personal life or in our special department of the work, because of not having the necessary means to supply some deficiency.

'All must gladly forgo anything, at whatever difficulty, if the Superior does not see fit to provide it.

'Never think that God is the less glorified because you may not have the means of doing something, as you think, well; but remember that He is glorified by cheerful poverty, whereas He would be dishonoured by wealthy self-satisfaction, even though you could do things outwardly with the utmost correctness.

'If the Society is wealthy in any place, remember that the wealth is a great burden and needs to be lifted up to God by the energy of many prayers. You should pray especially for the Superiors, with whom the outlay rests, that they may use all to God's glory.

'If the Society in any place is poor, look to God to do great things by it. God has chosen the poor, the weak things of the world to confound the mighty. Think of the blessed poverty of Bethlehem, Nazareth, Calvary.'

We must remember that God calls us out of the world really to do His work, and will enable us

The wealth of this world often a great hindrance. to do His work according to His will and in His measure. The worldly means which God puts at our disposal often bring with them great embarrassments; we must take great care that there is no spiritual forfeiture. We must take great care in the dedication of our worldly goods to God, that we do not imagine for a moment that the work of God is strengthened by such dedication. We ought constantly to bear in mind that the work of God has been hindered by wealth. Whenever we bring in worldly wealth to God, we ought to tremble lest we be hindering instead of helping. How many societies have served God faithfully, while they had nothing; then as property has come round about them, they have gradually lost their fervour, and have settled down to live as the people of the world. How many a man has begun life in the poverty of some curacy, living years of devotion with much struggle and difficulty, and as he has gone on in life, his spiritual fervour has gradually been done away, as he naturally rose up to positions of greater comfort. We should bear in mind how many a work of God has thriven in poverty, the spiritual power of God showing itself forth in it, and then afterwards has become crippled, imprisoned as it were with wealth.

All gifts of money must be purified by the divine love in which they are given. So we must be very careful not to think that gifts of money are of necessity helps to the work of God. If they are to be helps to the work of Christ, we must take care that they are thoroughly purified in the fire of divine love. The furnace of divine love must have melted the pure ore from all the dross which was with it. Every earthly gift, if it is to be really helpful, must be given with the spirit of entire detachment—'All my goods are nothing unto Thee' (*Ps.* xvi. 2). We must understand that if we could found or perfect ever so many institutions, yet all will gradually consolidate itself into mere earthliness, unless it be glowing with this fire of divine love which burns away all that is wood (cf. 1 *Cor.* iii. 13). We must each of us be watchful that we do live in the Society with this thorough spirit of poverty; with a real shrinking from this world's wealth, using it as a dangerous thing, handling it as if we knew it to be infected with a poison, knowing indeed that it does thus infect our hearts, and that it is nothing but the fire of divine love that can burn that infection out, and keep us safe.[1]

We need to keep ourselves constantly in this remembrance of poverty, cherishing this spirit of poverty. We have to compare our own life with the hard poverty of the world. How many there are in the world who are poor, struggling with manifold difficulties! How many there are in the priesthood who are struggling with manifold difficulties from which by the providence of God we are exempted, so that if we reduce our life to the lowest degree, yet we are free from those manifold anxieties which eat out the soul of so many. Let us seek, then, to cherish a spirit of poverty, resting simply in God, and looking up to Him, so that we may find the fullness of His riches (cf. *Phil.* iv. 19). For we are to look as

The spirit of poverty to be cherished that we may lay hold on the riches of God.

[1] See Note H at the end of the chapter.

earnestly for the riches of God as we look suspiciously upon the riches of the world.

<small>The crippling of outward poverty should quicken our sense of God's power.</small>

Yes, we are to look for the riches of God. We are to look for God, to make the power of the divine wealth more and more manifest within us. We must be seeking these riches of God continually, and we may be assured that He will give them to us, just in proportion as we do hold ourselves detached from the use of any particular objects, and ready to go without anything, however important it may seem or may be. Things will seem to us of importance for outward appearance, or, it may be, of importance for carrying on effectually that particular work which we have in hand, or for our own personal comfort. But all this is just simply to be lost sight of. We are to be thankful if we are hindered, crippled by poverty. It is that crippling by poverty which will enable us to lay hold upon the riches of God. I do not say that because we are crippled, therefore we shall have the riches of God. It depends upon ourselves whether we are laying hold upon them. Many are suffering in poverty who do not lay hold upon the riches of God. But there is no one who really feels himself and his work hindered by poverty who cannot find therein the greatest possible life and power, if he will make it the occasion of reaching out to lay hold upon God. Our apprehension of the divine power must be quickened by the consciousness of the outward need. We are to look up to Him, knowing that He knows our need. We are to look up to Him, quite convinced that He will supply us in that way and time which will be most beneficial to us. We must live in entire dependence upon God.

If, at any future time, any of us may be in some distant mission work where the very necessities of life may be precarious, we are still to look up with confidence to God. We shall not look up then, if we do not look up amid the easier life. We must learn to apply to God in all the little difficulties of life, and so shall learn to apply to Him in the greater difficulties by and by. It is like a child being taught to swim in shallow water, or it is like having the muscles strengthened for action by the bearing of weights accommodated to our little strength until we can bear more. So we must realize that God would train us to look up to Himself. We must see that we are looking up to Him with a constant habit, not looking up to Him to supply our every need in any way we should fancy, but in whatever way seems good to Him.

We must learn the habit of looking up to God.

It may sometimes happen that persons opposed to us have power, and we are kept in check while they get some position of influence. We are to remember not to feel ourselves really hindered by that. It is for us to look up to God, and draw out of the fullness of the power of God. If we can but look up to God, and draw out the fullness of the power of God, then it shall be as a fire which shall burn off the outward wealth of those who may be hindering God's works. There is no power that can really withstand the fire of God, if we will only see that our hearts are so empty that the fire of God may take possession of them. If

As we look up to God, we must keep our hearts true, that His power may be with us.

there is anything in our hearts inconsistent with our vow of poverty, then the fire of God causes a conflagration within them, instead of passing through our hearts to destroy that which is outside. We must take care that there is no affection to earthly things in our hearts, which the fire of God's presence may change into a real principle of destruction. If the fire of God's presence finds our hearts empty of all earthly things, then that fire will indeed pass through and will burn up all that is opposed, and will kindle the world with the fullness of divine love.

'*The Superior shall from time to time change the articles in the various cells in order to preserve a spirit of detachment.*'

Our hearts must cherish a spirit of detachment.

It will probably be a good thing for us that our cells should at times be changed; a habit of passing into a new cell tends towards a spirit of detachment. With some communities it is usual to change the cells just before Christmas, in honour of our Lord's Incarnation, that as He came to live a detached life upon earth, so we may begin with a fresh detachment year by year. We need to keep this spirit of detachment constantly in our minds and hearts.

'*If any one be rich and contribute largely to the funds of the Society, he must not think that on that account he is to receive any favours above those who contribute less. He must rather fear lest his spiritual defects be more injurious to the Society than his pecuniary assistance is helpful.*

'*All, whether contributing in money to the funds of the Society or not, must remember that it is their duty to help the Society forward by the exercise of all spiritual energies which they possess. No contributions can bring any blessing to the Society, or to the individual, unless they are given in a real spirit of poverty. Poverty is not redeemed from its penal character, unless those who may be poor in the world give their energies to the glory of God by labouring in the Society with at least as much diligence as would be necessary for them if they had to earn their daily bread.*'

The law of poverty is not intended to be a hindrance in such ways of intellectual improvement as may be consistent with our calling. We have to cultivate those gifts which God has given to us to the best of our power. Hard labour is one of the laws of poverty. We have not got to labour hard to maintain our life, but as poor persons we must labour hard, only in a different way, for the glory of God; not in order to maintain the life of this world, but to maintain the glory of the eternal life. So our own intellectual improvement is one of the ways in which we have to labour hard. Our work must be no desultory work, but as if we had to get our living by it. How differently those persons work who have really got to get their living from those who do certain things merely as a matter of pleasure. How different is the work of a professional artist from that of an amateur, even of the highest kind! And why? Because there is the pressure of a necessity to bring his work to the sharpness of perfection, which the external measure of its value

The law of poverty demands that we should cultivate whatever gifts God has given us.

demands. So we must take care that our work is really worthy of God in all these ways, and that we are really cultivating our spiritual life, our intellectual faculties, our moral nature; doing our work, our study, our teaching, our visiting, our sermon-writing—doing all so as really to work out the glory of God.

We must work, as for our daily bread.

We must take care also that all our manual work in the house or garden, as the cleaning of our cell, or the cultivation of the garden, or any work such as the cleaning of the sanctuary—that all of this is really done as if we were doing it for our life, knowing that our life is dependent on our doing it in a manner worthy of the glory of God. If we do not do it thus, we are not earning our spiritual bread. We must see that we are thus careful to carry out the law of poverty as those working for their livelihood; and our livelihood is not of time, but of eternity, and is gauged by the measure, not of a mere human judgement, but of divine approval. So we may be permitted things for the carrying out of this in so far as the requirements of the Society allow it.

We must learn to do without what seems necessary if we cannot have it.

At the same time we are to be ready also to forgo things which the necessities of the Society prevent us from having. So that we are not to think it hard if at times we cannot have our full time for intellectual cultivation, or for doing any work in which we are interested. We must be just as ready to forgo these things when the necessities of the Society require it, as to be diligent in the using of them when we have them. It is part of the spirit of poverty to be content to be unable to do certain things. How many there are who are unable to cultivate their intellectual powers, because they have not the means; who are unable to begin certain works in their parishes, because they have not the means. We are not to think that because we are in a Society therefore we ought to have the world putting everything at our disposal. We are to be quite ready, and willing, to go without anything, whether it be for our own cultivation, or for the carrying out of our works. We must just take what God gives, and use it to God's glory, and desire nothing more. If there is anything really wanting, the want should at once be made known. It may be that whoever is in authority may not think fit to supply the want; that rests with him. But if there is any real want, anything important to any part of the work, the want should be made known.

'*None of the brethren may receive the smallest thing by way of presents from externs, nor may they receive payment for anything done, unless the Father Superior gives consent.*

'*Whenever any presents are given to those who are engaged on work, they must, if accepted at all, be accepted in the name of the Society, and handed over to the Father Superior immediately upon return.*'

We must be careful that in all our work, our mission work and the like, we are really doing it in a spirit of poverty, so that people understand we are not looking for any external payment. At times courtesy and good nature may require that we should receive presents. They may be of little

Gifts may be received for the Society, but not for personal use.

pecuniary value, but may be something which persons may wish to give. We must be careful that we understand that we do receive such gifts, not for our own selves, but for the Society; and especially we must be careful that we cannot receive anything to be personally worn or used. See that what is given is thankfully received, on behalf of the Society.

'*Often think of the poverty of death. Naked shall I go whence I came. The deadness of the Religious life must anticipate the poverty of the grave, that it may know the wealthy joys of Paradise.*'

<small>The law of poverty demands the careful use of all we possess or handle.</small>

So we must seek to live in a real spirit of holy poverty, looking for the riches of God, dependent upon the will of God, rejoicing in the goodness of God, exercising the power of God, devoting all we are to the glory of God, taking care of everything round about us because it belongs to God, looking upon everything as a trust. So we shall be careful of the use of everything in the house; careful not to leave the gas burning unnecessarily; in all use of the books, careful not to leave them lying about on the tables, so as to spoil them, careful to keep them clean, so that they may not be destroyed or stained; above all, careful of all things connected with the sanctuary, that the brass work may be thoroughly bright, and not destroyed by negligence; careful in all matters of food that none is wasted; in all these ways careful of everything, as belonging really to God.

If we realize that we have nothing, and that everything around us belongs to God, then we shall find everything possessing a sort of sacramental value. The life of the Religious ought to communicate a sort of sacramental power to all he touches. In whatever he touches, the virtue of God ought to meet him, because all things exist by the power of God. There is nothing which exists without the power of God within it to sustain it, and the eye of the Religious should see that power of God sustaining everything, so that, as we touch it, that power of God should correspond to us. Like the shock coming out, when you put your knuckles to an electric machine that is charged, so there should be a response of divine power. The Religious will look upon nothing as worthless, since all is sustained by God. He will look upon everything as demanding his own special care, because all is sustained by God.

<small>All things are God's, and in our use of them we should find a sacramental value.</small>

If things seem to us of little value, we ought to remember how much value many people set upon them. We are not to neglect things because they may seem to us of little value; we should think of the value they might be to many. And so we must learn to use all the things of this world as a real means of clinging to God; and then we shall indeed find the blessing of God coming out to us. It is not a mere intellectual apprehension. Where God is, there the love of God is. If we recognize the power of God in everything, we shall find the power of the love of God in everything. God will make everything to be a channel of His love to us, if we are only looking to Him in the use of it.

<small>All things of however little value can become channels of God's love.</small>

Note H

'Knowing that it does thus infect our hearts.'

In the manuscript text the words are, 'Knowing indeed that it is infected.' The sense of the passage, however, seems to require that it is the infection of our hearts that needs to be burnt out, and an alteration has been made as above in the present text. Father Benson was speaking especially to those who were living under the vow of poverty, but his words have also a wider application. Deeply immersed in the language and spirit of St. John, he teaches that there is a malign influence in the wealth of this world which belongs to it, not in itself, but as an instrument in the hand of Satan, the prince of this world, appealing with a fatal attractiveness to the desire of possession in our fallen nature. 'Love not the world, neither the things that are in the world. If any man love the world, the love of the Father is not in him. For all that is in the world, the lust of the flesh, and the lust of the eyes, and the pride of life, is not of the Father, but is of the world' (1 *St. John* ii. 15, 16). For 'we know that we are of God, and the whole world lieth in the evil one' (1 *St. John* v. 19. The same teaching is found in the Gospels. 'Take heed and beware of covetousness: for a man's life consisteth not in the abundance of the things which he possesseth' (*St. Luke* xii. 15). It is the divine love possessing the heart which purifies the possession of wealth, which otherwise would taint and kill the heart that thought to find its life therein. Similarly our Lord uses the expressions 'mammon of unrighteousness,' and 'the unrighteous mammon,' in contrast to 'the true riches,' in reference to those who have made mammon master (*St. Luke* xvi. 9, 11).

CHAPTER XI

OF CONFESSION

THE confessions of Religious, my dear brethren, ought indeed to be full of tender love. When we think what our life ought to be, given up to Christ, we ought to mourn over our sins with very special sorrow.

The deep penitence of the Religious.

Our sins acquire a double character—the sins of a Christian intensified by the character of the priesthood, and then by the character of the Religious. Things which are trifles in the laity are enormities in priests, and if we have given ourselves to Christ by a special Religious dedication, how immeasurably does the weight, and burden, and bitterness, and grief of our sin become heightened. The life of the Christian was given to us as a necessity, and we were called to the life of priests for the necessities of the Church; but we are called to the life of Religious for our own sanctification, and our sins are not merely sins against the law of God, but against the very special end of our Profession. As priests we are to help others out of their sins, to help them to triumph over evil habits and attain to good. As Religious, whether laymen or priests, we are called to rise out of our own sins, to rise into habits of self-sanctification. This is our call, and this is the calling we have accepted and voluntarily taken

The special character of the sins of a Religious priest.

upon ourselves; to rise thus to live in the full light of the presence of Jesus, to rise to have nothing hidden, to live in openness of heart to Him, and in an openness of heart to one another also, which the world does not know of, to tear away the veil which hides our hearts, to have our inmost life standing out in the presence of God. This is the life to which we have been called, and this is the life which we have accepted.

<small>We are bound by the spirit of our vows.</small>
When we come to our confessions, we come to see how far we have come short of it. Let us be very careful not to think of the more technical matters of our Rule as if they were mere technicalities. Let us think of all the technical matters of our Rule as real links which bind us to Christ, which should be full of sanctifying grace. The observance of the spirit of our three vows—what a terrible thing it is to fall away from that spirit! We may not violate the letter, yet what a terrible thing it is to have the letter standing out to our hearts, simply as a witness to the depravity of a heart which remains unchanged! How must we mourn over every movement in our hearts, every affection, by which we turn back to the world, every affection by which the world begins to crop up again within our hearts! How very watchful we ought to be, as we make our Confessions, that we really do it with that intensity of contrition which befits our Religious character.

<small>Yet we must be equally careful of the fulfilment of our external Rule.</small>
And then the outward matters of our Rule, our silence, our punctuality, and the like. We must remember that our law of life is indeed instinct with a supernatural character; and that in order

to gain that supernatural character in its fullness, we must be living up to all of it in its preciseness. If there is some dislocation in the natural body, even of some smaller part, how great is the pain and the disorder! And we must realize that our preciseness in correspondence with the laws of God, as manifested in our Rule, is of the same importance. Our preciseness of conduct is just that which will enable us to realize the joy of the divine life, and every failure in it must be attended with proportionate pain and loss, spiritual loss to our own selves. We are, then, to be very careful in all our confessions to see that we do recognize all our failures, as so much forfeiting of that union with Jesus, for which we are set apart.

And then there must be a consciousness of sin, as against that special love wherewith Jesus has called us near to Himself. We are not to think that Jesus loves the Religious just as He loves the rest of the world. He would not have called us out of the world if He had not called us to a special love. Every call of God is a creative call. God is the Creator, and He cannot speak to the creature just to leave him as he was. Whenever God calls, something is done in the creature to whom He speaks. So when God called us into the Religious life, it was a creation. And every creation is an object of special love to the creator. God did not call us into the Religious life as a Commander-in-Chief might call certain soldiers to certain works. It makes no difference in his feeling about the soldier where he puts him. But *The Religious the object of the special creative love of Jesus;*

Jesus called us into this special life; it is our Creator's call, and it is a creative call, and, therefore, it is a call to a special love. We must think of our Religious life as binding us to this special love of God, who has called us unto Himself. So we must think of all our failures and sins as being greatly heightened by the terribleness of outraging such immense love. Oh, the love of Jesus which calls! Oh, the misery of having lived so little for that love of Jesus! O my Jesus, I have thought that I was taking this life upon myself, and if I have fallen, I have seemed to fall from my hope. But I have not taken it upon myself; Thou hast called me. Strengthen me, perfect me. I have disappointed Thee. Yea, too, I have changed Thy love, Thine eager love, wherewith Thou hast rejoiced over me. I have changed it into the bitterness of disappointment and sorrow. What couldst Thou have done more for me than Thou hast done, ever since Thou calledst me into this life? How little I have thought of what Thou hast done! What a pain it was to Thee, that I was not thinking about it! Help me to measure my sins by the greatness of Thy love.

a love which intensifies the grievousness of our sins.

We must see that we do come to our confessions with a deep and special contrition; not merely as the world goes, but as those chosen out of the world to live in the light of God, to live in an open-heartedness before God greater than that of others, to live in a strength of sanctification received from God greater than that of others. We must mourn our sins proportionately to all these circumstances which aggravate them. Let us see,

The tender contrition of the Religious as the bride of Christ.

then, that we do indeed come to our confessions with a deep contrition, a deep sorrow of heart. Let us come with that tender love with which the bride draws near to her husband. Oh, that tender love! our souls ought to have it for Christ. Do we recognize Him as the husband of our souls? Do we recognize our life as being thus really betrothed, dedicated to Him, accepted of Him, identified with Him? We must think of the closeness of this relationship as causing such a terrible aggravation of all our sins, and we must confess them with such an intimacy of affection as the world cannot know.

The sorrow which is in fear is a sort of colourless sorrow, but the sorrow of love is a sorrow whose colour is manifested in the full brightness of the sunshine of God's presence. The sorrow of fear is a twilight shadow, but the sorrow of love is like a dark shadow of noon. The sorrow of fear is a sorrow that seeks to be as little definite as possible, but the sorrow of holy love has its outline clearly marked. Oh, we know indeed what we are sorrowing for! Like a shadow which clearly marks out the form of the object from which it is derived; not a dim, elongated, shapeless shadow. We must indeed see that our sorrow rises up to the full proportion of our sin, as being called to live in the perfect sunshine of the divine love, the love of Jesus.

_{The sorrow of love.}

Our confessions, then, should rise up to this fullness of holy love. We must look in our confessions to attain that perfect purity which Jesus

_{By our confessions we are to lay hold of the strength which our life gives us.}

gives. We must long to rise out of those habits of sin which still hamper us and hold us down. Our Religious life gives occasion to many sins, but it should also give strength to resist. Are we living in the real strength of our Religious life, so as to resist sin? We find ourselves exposed to manifold temptations of which the world knows nothing; we find that the world's temptations are stronger here; but do we realize the strength of the Religious life to resist them, the strength which Jesus gives? He bids us be strong, and He gives us the necessary strength.

The strength which comes from the consciousness of the presence of Jesus, watching us.

We must make our confessions for having frustrated the intentions of Jesus, and for having cast away the strength which Jesus gives. He requires more of us because He loves us more, and because He strengthens us more. Our strength in resisting any temptation must be in the consciousness of that great, that strengthening, love into which we are called. He bids us feel the pressure of His hand, as He holds us up. He bids us rest upon Himself, and never feel ourselves to be alone. There are some Religious communities in which individuals are never alone; there is always some one present to watch: we should feel that Jesus is always with us. Even though there be no outer eye, yet we are brought into the immediate consciousness of Jesus; our whole life is continually in His sight. But if in His sight, then in His strength. There is a moral strength in being watched by the eye of another person; but how great is the strength of knowing that we are watched by the eye of Jesus, whose very looking upon us gives strength!

We must, then, think of that eye as looking upon us continually. As we come to our confessions we must remember—'I have sinned against heaven, and before Thee' (*St. Luke* xv. 18). 'Against Thee, Thee only, have I sinned' (*Ps.* li. 4). If all the world has seen me doing an act of sin, it is as nothing compared with doing it in Thy sight, when I have promised to remember that I was in Thy sight, when I had come out of the world for this purpose. The world does not profess to see Thee always before it, as I do. Oh, then, let me always remember the greatness of my sin, of every sinful thought allowed within my heart, because it is a sin against a recognized, acknowledged, presence of Him, who loves us more than the world, and strengthens us with a strength proportionate to that love.

<small>The greatness of our sins, because done in the sight of Jesus.</small>

If Religious exist for the purpose of their own sanctification, it is not merely for their own sanctification, but to be the strength of the Body of Christ. As the priesthood is to minister gifts of grace sacramentally to the nourishing of the Body of Christ, so dedicated Religious are to gather up into their own lives spiritual strength on behalf of the Body of Christ, that the whole Body may be strengthened by our special self-sanctification. So we must remember the greatness of our sin, because we are thereby destroying the very purpose for which we exist in the Body of Christ; we are weakening the pillars of the house of God, which

<small>The Religious called to be the strength of the Church, as the Body of Christ.</small>

we ourselves ought to be. The house of God ought to rest upon our dedicated lives. How terrible was the ruin of old, when the Church fell down, not by the dissolution of Religious houses, but by the decay of the Religion within those houses, while they outwardly stood erect! How the Church fell spiritually prostrate! We must take great care to cherish the Religious life within ourselves, with the remembrance of this responsibility, that we are indeed called out of the world to be 'pillars in the temple of God' (*Rev.* iii. 12). We must not allow ourselves out of any false idea of self-depreciation to think that we need not be such, or that we cannot be such. We must be such, otherwise it is no use our having come out of the world. So how full of humiliation ought our confessions to be, that we do so fail of attaining to that sanctity which may indeed sustain, elevate, perfect the Church of God.

The deepening contrition of the true Religious.

Let us come, then, to confession with a deep sense of the special character of our sins as Religious; their special character as against ourselves, as against the special love of Jesus, as against the special grace and strength of Jesus, as against every purpose for which we exist in the Church of God. Let us seek to make our confessions with a deepening contrition.

A prayer for contrition.

Lord Jesus, teach us to know more and more of our sins, that we may truly humble ourselves before Thee!

CHAPTER XII

OF COMMUNION

IN our communions we must think what it is to feed upon Christ, to have our life nourished by Christ, to have our Christian profession brightened by Christ, to have our Rule lightened by Christ, to have our hope gladdened by Christ, to have any painful discipline which we may have to bear soothed by Christ, to have our temper sweetened by Christ, to have our intercourse one with another sanctified by Christ. The world at large comes to feed upon Christ with very little knowledge of what it is to expect from this coming, but we ought to come with a consciousness of those manifold gifts of Christ's presence which each communion ought to convey.

The manifold grace of our communions.

We ought to draw near to Christ with that tender love which befits Him. We ought to cling to Christ with that tenacity which knows Him as the one stay. We ought to make Christ truly one with us, as a healthy body incorporates with itself the nourishing food of which it partakes. Unconsciously the body takes in health and strength from the food whereon it feeds, but we are to feed upon Christ, not unconsciously, for He is the very wisdom of the Father, and we cannot take in wisdom except in the heart of wisdom. The

We must feed on Christ with loving intelligence.

natural food of the body is unconscious, and the body which is nourished is unconscious; but the food of which we partake in the Holy Eucharist is the food of the incarnate intelligence of God, and it can only be received into the loving intelligence of man.

The Religious called to a special knowledge of Christ. There must be a real consciousness of coming to Christ, if we are to look for a real manifestation of the power of Christ. Of course, that will vary according to different persons' capacities, and so we may well believe that the wisdom of God is communicated to many an unintelligent worshipper, who has no thought whatever of feeding thus upon God, and yet receives through that communion a gift of mysterious wisdom, sanctifying the life, uplifting the soul, stablishing the heart. But for us it is different. We have come to some knowledge of Christ, and though He can feed without knowledge those who know Him not, yet He cannot feed us to whom He has given knowledge of Himself, except through the instrumentality of that knowledge we have received. Take care, then, to come and feed upon Christ with an intelligent apprehension of the divine wisdom coming near to us. This is to come and feed upon Him, that we may have 'the eyes of our understanding' opened to behold the glory of the Father, in union with Him (cf. *Eph.* i. 17 ff.). We must take care, then, that we come to our communions with a true intelligence.

And also with a true love—for the intelligence can no more receive the being of Christ alone than we can take the Second Person out of the blessed

Trinity, and give Him independent existence. As the Second Person exists in the unity of the Holy Ghost, so we cannot receive the Body of Christ, except in the power of the Holy Ghost. It is the power of the Holy Ghost by which the Body and Blood of Christ are brought to be in that sacrament which we receive, and it is by the power of the Holy Ghost dwelling in ourselves that we must be brought to lay hold on that heavenly food, and partake of it. A mere act of our own intellect will not enable us to lay hold upon Christ. We can no more contain Christ within our intellectual nature than we can contain Him within our bodily nature. But it is the power of the Holy Ghost which enables us to feed upon the substance, and which enables the intellect to feed upon the wisdom, of the Son of God. Where the Holy Ghost is, there is love. So if we would really feed upon Christ, it must be with an intense love, proportionate to our knowledge of that fellowship of the Holy Ghost wherewith we are called to feed upon Him. It is of no use for us to say, 'I understand more about the Holy Communion than a great number of people who come.' No dogmatic knowledge will avail us. There are many with less accurate knowledge, with very mistaken apprehensions of Holy Communion, who yet feed better than we, for they feed with love. We must have love at least proportionate to our knowledge. It is by the power of love that we can come to know anything worthy of God or of Christ.

But knowledge will not suffice. We must feed on Christ by love in the power of the Holy Ghost.

The consecration of the Religious to Jesus Christ demands a growing love.

And so we must take care that we really are drawing near with that special character which should belong to a life that is consecrated as ours is to Jesus Christ. What is it to be consecrated to Jesus Christ, if we are not absorbed in His love? The power of the Holy Ghost must indeed teach us to love Christ more and more. It must be a growing love. We cannot rest still in love. We love more and more. The Holy Ghost draws us onward in the love of Christ. Year after year, as time goes by, must find us not falling away from the first love with which we entered upon our novitiate, but growing in that divine, supernatural, calm, mysterious love of Jesus Christ, in the acknowledgement of the power and of the glory of the wisdom of Jesus Christ. So, in the power of the Holy Ghost, we must really come with an intelligence and with affections both illuminated and quickened for the reception of the being of the Son of God. Then we shall indeed find that this indwelling of Christ is the foundation of our Religious life. 'Other foundation can no man lay than that is laid, which is Jesus Christ' (1 *Cor.* iii. 11).

Gathered into the being of Christ, our communions develop His indwelling which is the foundation of our Religious life.

And in every growth of the spiritual temple that original foundation is still the living basis of it all. As the building of Christ develops, so the foundation of the power of Jesus Christ develops also; and we must look to the being of Christ, communicated to us, as being the foundation of our Religious life. What would it be if God had united us as mere men to Himself, in our natural estate? What a terrible union that had been! But we have been taken into the being of Christ and regenerated, our bodily nature transformed by the gift of the divine nature, by the mediatorial power of the human nature of Jesus Christ communicated to us in our Baptism; and it is in the power of that transformed nature that we are united unto Christ. We cannot be united to Christ while He is in the risen body and we are in the body yet dead; we cannot be united to Christ until we have been taken into that risen body wherein He lives. So with His risen body as ours we can be united to Him. Thus it is for the purpose of cementing, stablishing, perfecting, developing this union that we come to the Blessed Sacrament, and each communion must be a fresh binding of ourselves in body, soul, and spirit to the glorious being of the risen Son of God. We must come, then, with that tender love which is due to Him with whom we are so mysteriously united. We must come indeed, as those who have passed through the grave in order to become one with Him with an entire consciousness of His holy love.

And then we must remember that our communions are to be our joy in keeping our Rule. Our Rule is to develop the life of Christ within us. All the restraint of our Rule, all that seems unnatural, is just for the purpose of destroying that wild nature which is at variance with the operations of Jesus Christ. Our communions must raise us into the gentleness, the tenderness, the refinement, the self-control, the disciplining energy

Our communions the source of our joy in keeping the Rule.

of the life of Christ. We are not to serve Christ with the impetuosity of natural zeal, but with the calmness of a being entirely united to Himself, and moving in accordance with all the breathings of His holy, undisturbed heart. The world at large may be disturbed by many things, but we ought to be so feeding upon Christ that the tranquillity of Christ may hold us in perpetually.

<small>Our Rule the safeguard of the life which our communions nourish.</small>

We must thus be feeding upon Christ continually, and find in our Rule the restraint of our nature, it being held in so as to co-operate with Him. Whatever we are checked in, therefore, there should be not only a negative sense—'I cannot do this,' but a positive sense—'I am not to do this, because I am to live in union with Christ.' Our Rule must hold us thus, continually, in this positive sense of co-operative union with Christ. So it is that our Rule should indeed be the safeguard of that life which our communions must nourish. And we should be looking upon each fresh communion as a fresh strength, in the joy of which we are to live closely united with Christ. So He will indeed be the gladness of our heart.

<small>The sense of community life developed by our communions, for we are bound to one another in Christ.</small>

At times we may find much that is wearisome and irksome, but the presence of Christ will fill our hearts with gladness and joy. We may be in some isolated sphere of work, and we may be tempted to say, 'What is the use of my belonging to a community, while I am so much alone?' The object of a community is not that we may be one with another, but that we may all by means of the community be held together in Christ. So, if one is separated by some local work in some distant mission, still we are living in the stay of the community, as if we were living in the chapel; as little separated as if we were staying in our cells. Our communions do indeed bind our isolated individualities to Christ, and to one another in Christ, but our community exists, not that we may be bound to one another, but that we may be the better individually bound to Christ. In all our communions we should seek for this real abiding union with Christ, and recognize this as being the very object for which we have entered into community life. What though we never see any one of our brethren? Yet if we feed upon Christ in consciousness of brotherhood, then we are one with the other. In fact, the sense of community is probably the strongest in those communities where the separation is greatest; as where there is total silence, and where the life has to be spent continually in the cell, yet there it is probable that the sense of community life is beyond all appreciation.

The more we are separated into the fellowship of Christ, the more we come to realize how we are one with another. And so we must be very careful that the sociality which the Rule of an active order commonly permits does not destroy that which, after all, is the real object of our union one with another. We must take care that the substance of our community life does not disperse itself, like a liquid that is poured into a glass, and then effervescing overflows. It seems to fill the glass, but after all the glass is left empty. So there is a danger lest in the effervescence of social inter-

In our community life we must guard that fellowship with Christ which is the object of our fellowship in community.

course this abiding, substantial character of community life should very much suffer. We are consequently to be constantly on the watch, to see that we are thus living closely in the fellowship of Christ, and in the strength of our communions. We are to realize that we are associated each with the other in order that we may be the more closely bound to Christ; and that although our mutual union and fellowship prepares for this union with Christ, nevertheless, upon the other hand, it is this union with Christ which really makes us have a community life at all, which really makes us to be living as members one of another. So we must see that we do come to our communions with a great sense of the power of the community life which these communions are intended to cherish and perfect.

Each act of communion should bring its special development of the life of Christ in us.
And we must look for the development of the life of Christ within us. Each communion should be, as it were, adding some fresh point to the image of Christ within our souls. As each touch of the artist adds some fresh feature to the painting, so each communion is a touch of Christ, which should develop some fresh feature of His own perfect likeness within us. And it is not that it does this merely in some one direction, but as each moment of the morning adds imperceptibly a fresh glow to the whole illuminated hemisphere, so each communion imperceptibly should add a fresh glow, a fresh brightness, a fresh colouring to the sphere of the soul which it penetrates; the whole nature should assume a fresh glory with

each communion. As the form and colour of the landscape come out with the sun's advance, so with each communion the form and colour of our spiritual life, not merely in this or that particular, but in all its complex bearings of form and colour, is to stand out with greater clearness and beauty, each communion bringing its own fresh illumination, and perfecting us in the glory of the Sun of righteousness.

Oh, we must see that we do thus really come to Christ, as those who are looking up to Christ, as those who rejoice to live in His power, and who know who and what He is. We must not be content to come to Him with the ignorance of the world, but with hearts illuminated and quickened with the power of the Holy Ghost. We must come in the fullness of the wisdom He has given, and seek those fuller manifestations of wisdom He has yet to give.

<small>Each act of communion must be quickened with faith and holy desire.</small>

Thus, too, we must take care that in every communion we are really longing for the end of all things. To come to communion is to long for all outer communions to cease, that Christ may come in the fullness of His revelation. To come to our communions, really longing to feed upon Christ, is to long for the veil to be done away, and for Christ to show Himself in His perfect abiding glory. We must come to our communions with this great hope, not thinking of many years that may be before our Society upon earth, but longing for ourselves and our Society to be absorbed in the ocean of the divine presence. We must come to

<small>In our communions we must long for the coming of Christ.</small>

our communions time after time, seeking really and truly to look forward to His appearing.

The Religious is set apart to watch for Christ's coming.

Are we set apart from the world in order to wait and watch for Christ's coming? Then when we come to the Holy Communion, we must come really waiting and watching with that inner gaze, which seems to take the measure of the very distance which Jesus has yet to traverse; with that eager expectation which seems to see Jesus close at hand. We must come to our communions remembering that we are set apart to watch for the coming of Jesus. We are looking for Christ to appear, like soldiers on duty waiting for the presence of their sovereign. They watch for that coming, keeping the ground clear. Every sound reminds them of that coming. And so our hearts must be continually waiting. We are here on duty, waiting for the coming of the Sovereign. And then when the Sovereign has come, there is the following on to the palace.

The coming of Christ is the end of strife.

And so it is for us to be waiting for the coming, and longing for the time of waiting to be over. We may have to be waiting out in the driving rain and mud, and amid the tumult of the world, but we must be longing and eager for the coming of Christ. There is nothing that can stay these storms but that coming. No shelter, that we can put over our heads, will avail us against these driving storms of worldly life; no shelter, that we can devise, from the noise and tumult and evil words of the mob round about, will avail to keep our hearts clear from the horrid suggestions of evil spirits continually coming and mocking. Oh, there is no end for it, until Christ comes!

So we must learn indeed to be longing for Christ to come, and we must come to our communions with this intense expectation of the coming of Christ; each communion must give us a deeper sense that He is near. And we must be longing for Him to come, that so we may follow Him into His royal home, and be delivered from all the weariness of this world's stormy intercourse. It is a stormy one, but it is a short one. Soon, soon shall He come whom we love! Let us come to Him in Holy Communion, and feed upon Him there. So shall we be strengthened to wait until His coming. Our eyes shall be opened to watch for His coming, and our arm strengthened to labour for His coming, and our understanding tranquillized, that we may bear all the difficulties of the time in the calm assurance of His holy advance. So let us delight to come to our communions, that we may gain some foretaste, some blessed anticipation, of the coming of Christ. Let us be careful that we come to our communions with that intense, tender, longing love, which befits those separated from the world to live with Christ here in obscurity, and to long for His appearing in His glory.

Our communions must develop our longing for His coming, and give us strength to endure.

CHAPTER XIII

OF THE DIVINE OFFICE

ITS NATURE AND DIGNITY

'*IN addition to the offices which are of obligation upon all clergymen of the Church of England, the Fathers shall recite the Day Hours.*'

<small>The remembrance of God in the saying of our office.</small>
When we say our offices, my dear brethren, how careful ought we to be; how careful to say them in real union with Jesus Christ, how careful to say them in the power of the mind of Christ, really lifting up our hearts to God. If there is not a real lifting up of the heart to God, a real consciousness that God is being addressed, it is impossible that we can say our office otherwise than profanely.

<small>All is spoken as before Him.</small>
We must keep well before our minds the thought that these offices are said to God, said for God, and said for His glory. Even those verses of the Psalter which are not formally addressed to God, they yet are spoken to Him. Although we appeal to our own souls, or to the objects of His creation, yet we do so, not for the purpose of appealing to ourselves or to them, but of expressing the longings of our soul and our relation to all before God.

There can be no attaining to God without this real effort. We cannot lift up our hearts to God, as it were, by accident. It requires the gathering up of every faculty of our nature in order to say our office aright—our memory to be true to the words, and our lips to give them their true expression. If we do not present the substance of our office, we are not to think we can present the spirit; our minds, and our lips, must be true in the production of those words we have to say. And then the understanding. We cannot present these words to God without some good understanding. True it is there are many phrases in our offices which surpass our understanding, many that we cannot understand at all, and all containing significations to which our understanding does not reach; but yet there must be none in which our understanding does not have part. Even if it be a verse of the Psalter so difficult of translation that we cannot determine what was the mind of the Spirit in writing it, nevertheless our understanding must rise up into the fellowship of the mind of Christ, as we present it to God. We must realize that it has its meaning; we are to accept that meaning with our understanding; we are to understand our insufficiency.

The remembrance of God in our offices demands the attention of all our faculties.

And there must be real effort of the will. The affections must bear our words, and our thoughts, up to God upon the steady wing of that pure Dove. The Holy Ghost must bear our will with all our affections up to God. We must see that our will goes along with our understanding, that our will is not hanging down upon earth while our words have reference to heaven, that our will is not satisfied with earthly primary accomplishments, while our words reach into the vast circle

The will must follow the understanding, as we lift up our hearts to God.

of an eternal fulfilment. No, we must take care that our will and our affections go along with our words while we say our office. We must find our will rejoicing in the very fact of speaking with God.

The office as the offering of our whole nature should be sung.

So we must be careful to present our office really and truly, substantially, intelligently, spiritually, affectionately before Almighty God. There must be a lifting up of every faculty of our nature to take part in this. And so our office is not complete unless it be sung, because there is a part of our nature which is not taking its share. Our whole nature must thus rise up to God, and we must deplore the incapacity of our nature to rise up to God as it ought to rise. Our saying our office must ever be accompanied with a very penitential spirit, because at the very best we say it so badly.

All slovenliness must be laid aside.

If we are really thus to gather up all our energies, we must take care that we do it to the very best of our power. We must take care that however much imperfection belongs to our office by reason of nature, yet no slovenliness is there by reason of will.

Our office must be said in union with Jesus.

And then we are to say our office in real fellowship with our Lord Jesus Christ. We cannot rise up to God except in His fellowship. It is only His mediation which can take us out of this lower sphere of being, and we must say our office with the constant thought of the Lord Jesus Christ enabling us to say it. We must say it as really being an act of union with Him. Just as in Holy

Communion we receive His substance into our bodies, so in the saying of our offices we bring forth the power of that substance, so that it may rise up to God. We are thus continually to approach to God in union with Christ. We develop the being of Christ in each one of our faculties while we say our office; without it the being of Christ would be dormant within us. The being of Christ cannot be developed in our nature except by acts of devotion, in which He acts through our faculties to God. The being of Christ is like the strong sap which rises up into the herb which has been trodden down, and as it fills the leaf, the leaf begins to resume its firmness and its erect position. So the being of Christ fills every one of our faculties which were crushed under the foot of the great enemy; the being of Christ lifts up our faculties erect before God. We must understand that we cannot rise up to God except in union with our Lord Jesus Christ, and if we are really to rise up to God in acts of devotion with Him, we must sink into the depth of His being, just in proportion as we rise to the height of His actions.

We must not merely look upon our Lord Jesus Christ as associating Himself with us, and helping us to carry out the purposes of our mind, helping us to perform those acts of devotion internally and externally which belong to the office; our devotion really and truly springs out of His. He does not perfect our thoughts, but we in our imperfection give expression to His thoughts. We must go deep down below ourselves into the mind of

Our devotion is the up-springing of His life within us.

Christ, in order that Christ may raise us up far above ourselves into the presence of God. So in our office we must be careful really to unite ourselves with Christ, and let His original devotional powers be the principle giving effect to all our office.

As a Society we are gathered into the being of Christ, and must say our office with His mind.

We ourselves may often be cold, dry, unwilling to go to our office, but we must remember that we do not go just for the gratification of our own desires, or for the attainment of some daily need, but because Jesus requires it of us. The soldier does not go to his duty because he finds himself inclined to go to this or that place, but because he belongs to a corps, and must be present there. We in like manner belong to the Body of Christ, and we must be found in our place, presenting the mind of Christ before the Father. A Religious community is gathered into the being of Christ, otherwise it would be no community at all. It might be a collection of persons, but it is the gathering into the being of Christ which makes us to be a community; without this there could be no union, no oneness. And so we have to contemplate our words of devotion as bringing forth this power of the mind of Christ. We have to recognize our place in the Body of Christ, that we are speaking to God, not simply as individuals who are anxious to lead a devout life, but as persons whom Christ has called into union with Himself in order that through them, as a collective body, He may speak unto the Father. The sense of our vocation as Religious must rest upon our daily saying of the office. So must we indeed enter into the mind of Christ, and seek that strength which comes from Him.

But if we do this we shall find how He will gladden our office with His presence. If we really think that we are speaking as between Him and the Father, how can we speak otherwise than in the fullness of joy? We are speaking between Him and the Father, and, therefore, we are speaking in the fullness of the power of the Holy Ghost. We cannot be speaking in the power of the Holy Ghost unless we are speaking between Him and the Father, for the very office of the Holy Ghost is to bind the Father and the Son together. Our very existence is sanctified by the Holy Ghost in Jesus Christ, and thus is gathered up into that mutual life of the Spirit which is the eternal life of God.[1]

And if in the mind of Christ, then in the power of the Holy Ghost.

So we must really try to have our office said in a manner worthy of this divine surrounding. Oh, when we say our prayers, how little do we realize what it is for Christ to be thus speaking through us to the Father! How little do we think of it as a real substantive truth, that in order to pray we are taken into the very being of God; that this is no mere philosophical idea, no mere metaphor, no mere phrase, but that more truly than we can speak with our lips, we speak with the utterance of the Second Person of the blessed Trinity, and more truly than our words go forth to vibrate on the lower air, our words go forth to fill the ear of the eternal Father with the utterance of His only-begotten Son. If we would but think what it is

Our office is truly the utterance of the Son to the Father through our lips.

[1] See Note I at the end of the chapter.

thus to be saying our office within the very surrounding of the eternal Trinity, in the power of the divine life, in the fullness of that love which binds together the Father and the Son, then we should come to value the joy, the solemnity of this work.

The offices of the Temple worship at last find their living utterance in us, as the members of the Body of Christ.

And we must realize that the saying of our office is a thing which could not be done for four thousand years of the world's history. Although these very same words which we say were so continually being said in the Jewish temple, yet they were said outside of God, for God was not yet 'manifest in the flesh' (1 *Tim.* iii. 16). They did not come within the sanctuary of the divine life; they were 'weak through the flesh' (*Rom.* viii. 3). The form of our office is well-nigh the same which was going on for many hundreds of years before Christ came, but the divine life now fills our office, whereas there was no divine life in that time of expectation. Our office must be said in all the power of the life of the new Jerusalem. Our office must be said in all the consciousness of the indwelling of the Holy Ghost. Oh, if we would bear it in mind, that all those solemnities, all the pompous ceremonial of the ancient temple, were only typical of the spiritual dignity of our worship! If we would bear in mind, that our worship springs out of our union with Christ, that it is, so to speak, the flowering of our Eucharist! Our Eucharists are a planting of the root, hidden within us, and that root must rise up and blossom in our daily office. We must realize thus how our Baptismal life, by which we are really and truly incorporated into Christ, and our Eucharistic life, by which that Baptismal life is nourished, rise up into the sublime dignity of our daily office—the Psalter, the anthology of God, the blossoming of the divine glory.[1]

Thus, then, we must try to consider the great dignity of our daily office, so sadly lost sight of by most persons in the present day; most people knowing it as nothing else than Jewish form, looking upon it rather as the dead leaves of last year still remaining on the ground, than using it as the putting forth of the fresh foliage, by which the summer's glory may dignify and sanctify all our present position. Let us learn thus indeed to take great delight in our daily office, as for the very act in which we especially, as a community, abide in the Father and in the Son by the power of the Holy Ghost. No wonder we do not understand much in our daily office! How could we understand words which ought to be worthy of this! We may understand litanies and hymns which we make ourselves, unless we are careful to frame them entirely according to the phraseology which is of heaven. That which comes out of our own heart and mind we may feel ourselves capable of knowing, but that which comes from the mind of God must be beyond our understanding. That which comes from the mind of God must demand the solemn surrender of our understanding, in order gradually to learn more and more what it means, and what that is which we have to do.

The dignity of our daily office, as coming forth to us from the mind of God.

[1] See Note J at the end of the chapter.

In our office we come before God in the truth of Jesus Christ.

So, then, let us seek to realize increasingly the great dignity of our daily office, whether in the church or in the chapel. Let us seek to realize that we do indeed thus come before God with the words, the mind, the power, the mystery, the love of Jesus Christ.

NOTE I

'That mutual life of the Spirit, which is the eternal life of God.'

'The Holy Spirit is the eternal flow of mutual love, wherein the Father and the Son dwell together, one undivided God.' So wrote Father Benson in a sermon for Whitsunday written in his old age (*Cowley Evangelist*, August, 1924, p. 171). In a retreat given at Aberdeen in 1877 the Father used a similar line of thought to that in the text, which may well illustrate his meaning. In one of the addresses, on the procession of the Holy Ghost, he said: 'The Holy Ghost is that love which comes from the Father to the Son, and returns from the Son to the Father, without any change of nature, without any difference of degree, or of form, or of grace in that transmission. . . . As we are taken up into the humanity of the Son we are taken up into the fellowship of the Holy Ghost, through whom that humanity exists, and it is the Holy Ghost who comes so to take us up, and to bind us in that unity with the same love whereby He is the bond of the Father and of the Son. It is the same love, wherewith the Father loves the Son; and with this same love He loves all the members of the Body of His Son. And so the same love, wherewith the Son loves the Father, must be in us as His members. If the Son does not love the Father in us, then we are separate from Him, separate from His love. As His own love is continually returning to the Father, so His love must return to the Father in us His members, for His love returns to the Father in its whole fullness' (*Cowley Evangelist*, August, 1919, p. 149).

NOTE J

'*There was no divine life in that time of expectation.*'

In the Epistle to the Romans St. Paul describes as the chief of the privileges of the Jews that 'unto them were committed the oracles of God' (*Rom.* iii. 2), and later in the same Epistle (*Rom.* ix. 4) he describes as their peculiar blessing that 'to them pertained the adoption, and the glory (the divine Shekinah, resting outwardly upon the tabernacle), and the covenants, and the giving of the law (the moral law), and the service of God (the sacrificial worship, the ceremonial law), and the promises (their spiritual inheritance.)' All these were ever pointing them to a gift of life still to come with Jesus Christ. They lived by this hope, and the divine oracles were 'to train the faithful soul to long for a salvation which the natural heart, even of the best, could not understand, and could only very imperfectly desire' (*Commentary on the Epistle to the Romans* iii. 2, p. 102). When therefore Father Benson speaks here of there being 'no divine life in that time of expectation' he means that the worshippers then had no gift of the life-bringing Spirit, such as is now poured out upon us.

In the *War Songs of the Prince of Peace* (Vol. i, p. 9) Father Benson writes: 'The daily Psalms ought for us to have a very different meaning from what they had for Jews before Christ came. They are no mere forms inherited from the times before Christ. They were then as the wood laid upon the altar, but waiting for the fire to descend from heaven. Now Christ has touched them and kindled them with a heavenly flame, and we are sadly profaning His great gift, if we do not use it with the utmost jubilance of faith.'

CHAPTER XIV

OF THE DIVINE OFFICE

THE SPIRIT OF CHOIR

'*THE psalms shall be said, not with excessive slowness, but with reverence ; and care shall always be taken that one side shall have finished saying one verse before the opposite side begins the next. A pause should be made at the colon in each verse.*

'*If any Father is hindered by business in the house or parish, he shall endeavour to recite his office in private, and shall report the reason of his absence to the Father Superior or his representative for the time being.*'

The external care with which we say our Psalter must be the outward token of that inward reverence and love which our hearts feel. We have not merely a mechanical duty to perform. We are not merely to get through the articulation of sound, in saying our Psalter. We are to lift up our hearts to God. And although we are to do this, not for the purpose of prolonged contemplation or meditation, yet we must do it with a real effort to contemplate Him whose praises we are speaking, and whom we are addressing. And this cannot be unless we do say our words with sufficient slowness to enable our making real acts of love in the saying of them. We must seek

_{The saying of our office demands external care and the reverent attention of our minds and hearts.}

to give to God a real gift of our understanding, and a real gift of our affections, in all the saying of our office. The letter of the Rule would be fulfilled by getting through the words, but it would indeed imply that all life was gone if we could assent to the theory of some persons that nothing more than a repetition of the words is exacted under penalty of sin. If it is a sin to omit the words, it is a sin to approach God with the words without bringing at the same time those affections and contemplations which the life of the words demands. Let us take care, then, that we do say our office clearly, distinctly, reverently, and with sufficient slowness to enable us to weigh well what we are doing in speaking with God.

<small>The office the utterance of the whole choir.</small>

So we must be careful not to clip the office. It is one office which is said by the whole choir; and if half the choir begins its verse before the other is finished, the whole choir has not said it. It should be so said that it would be possible for one voice to take its part in both sides. It is one continuous utterance of the choir as an undivided whole.

<small>The saying of our office a bond of union with our brethren, even when said in private.</small>

We should find a great encouragement to ourselves in meeting one another in our place in choir. We ought to realize the sympathy with which the office is said, as a great stay to our individual life; but if our occupations prevent our being in choir, we ought still to seek for union with our brethren in the saying of our office. Though we say it in private, yet we say it as a part of our responsibility to the brotherhood, not merely as a duty, or as an act of affectionate worship to Almighty God, but as an obligation we owe to the Society to say it, with such reverence as we can.

We are, then, to try and carry the spirit of choir about with us. If we are to do this, we shall certainly not absent ourselves from choir unnecessarily. It will indeed be our joy to come into the house of God, along with our brethren. 'I went with the multitude, and brought them forth into the house of God; in the voice of praise and thanksgiving, among such as keep holy-day' (Ps. xlii. 4, 5); and that no unknown multitude, but along with those whom God has called out of the world with us, to share in our inmost affections, and to approach Him along with us in openhearted devotion. Such ought to be our feeling when we come to choir, such our love of choir; and so we shall be anxious, if possible, to take our place there.

The spirit of choir abiding in our hearts.

'*When stress of business or any other cause makes it impracticable to say any office, then members of the Society shall at the least repeat the lesser litany and the memorials, which are usually said in the Society at the hour.*'

Thus, in the midst of any stress of business, however great it may be, we shall be able to keep up the spirit of the office; the Lord's Prayer supplying us with the special intention which belongs to the office, and gathering up in the most sacred formula all the various thoughts of the mind of Christ, and our memorials causing us to bring before God those special objects which awaken the intercessory charity of our Society at

When compelled to be absent from choir we may unite ourselves with our brethren in spirit by making a memorial of the office.

that time. And this we can do, however much we may be hindered. If, for instance, we are upon some mission work without having any interval of three minutes to ourselves, yet we can repeat these without having the book, and in the moments between some one person leaving and another coming we can repeat, if not all the memorials, at any rate first one and then another. So we must take care that we really do strive to identify ourselves with the full purpose of the Society; and we shall find that this close attention to our choir office, whether in choir or out of it, will have the effect of lifting up our lives into a real heavenly sympathy in the power of the Holy Ghost.

We exercise the special grace of the Society as we say our office.

So, then, let us consider well with ourselves the great joy of saying our office. Last time we met I was speaking of that grace of Christ which is involved in the saying of the office, that which is alluded to in the collect of St. Chrysostom. It is no mere human effort of the heart, no mere agreement of the human will; it is a real grace of our Lord Jesus Christ. He speaks in us. In us He addresses His Father; He speaks in us by the power of the Holy Ghost. It is a very expression of the life of grace, when we do thus come before God. We do rise up into the full intercourse of the eternal Trinity while we say our office, and we bear up our Society along with us. We do not come to our office merely as individuals, as individual Christians; we come as being linked with those who are under special obligation for the use of this divine grace. The grace by which we worship God is not in our case a mere individual grace, but the grace of the community in which we specially share. God has been pleased to call us out of the world to take part in the worship which the Society gives to Him, that so we may feel and experience in our inmost hearts that grace which belongs to the community life. And we shall feel this especially at such times as we are isolated, and obliged to say our office alone. We must feel the hand of the Society sustaining us, the Society guiding us. The details of the memorials take us out of our own will into the remembrance of the will of the Society, and so we become perfected in the worship of God.

Let us, then, be very watchful to say our office with all that care and completeness which befits so solemn an action. Let us avoid all hurry, all distraction of thought, all the impetuosity of natural disposition. Let us bring ourselves under due regulation. The very habit of getting to repeat our words one with another has of itself the effect of bringing our whole being into unity. Our outer organs of utterance, our very thoughts, become identified, while we grow in the habit of not merely reciting words at the same time, but reciting them with a real unity, so that syllable after syllable shall come forth as one utterance from all lips. <small>The saying of our office together with reverent love unites us one with another.</small>

And when we think of the voice of our Society rising up to God from various parts of the world, it should give an expansiveness to our prayers. The thought of those who have said our office before us, and of those whose day has yet to begin, <small>The continuous utterance of the Society in the divine office binds all our houses with one another, and with the past.</small>

should link us together in a thought of continuity. As our presence together in choir teaches us identity, so this succession of offices in various longitudes teaches us of the continuity of our life. We are ever living before God, bringing before Him the wants of the day. They are ever recurring. The earth is in one continual change, but our cry to God should go up with an unchanging perseverance. The cry of the Society should rise up before God, so as really to be heard of Him. If it is to do so, with what earnestness it must leave the heart, with what care it must go forth from the lips! Let us try to realize our office as a great bond between the various houses of the Society that are most widely separated.

<small>We say our office as the members of Christ ever freshly partaking of His life.</small>
And let us remember to say our office in the strength of our Eucharist. Let us understand that it is indeed the Body of Christ of which we are partakers, which speaks through our lips. It is as being nourished with Christ, it is as members of Christ, that we are to say our offices. We must be careful always to speak them in the freshness of the divine life; not to say them as though that life were extinct, or as though that life belonged to some other exercises, but to say our offices as being the true and proper exercise of that life of Christ of which we are made partakers. We live before God as the members of Christ; we beseech the mercy of God as the members of Christ. The holy Angels who watch round about—they also address God while they gaze upon Him, and they also tell His praises. But our praises should be

nearer to God than theirs; for in all our praises, in all our prayers, there is that substantial presence of Christ which is wanting to them.

Let us compare our saying of our office with the outward, formal utterances of the Israelites before Christ came; and let us compare it with the spiritual contemplation with which the blessed Angels gaze, and in that gaze speak to God. Let us compare our saying of our office with both of these, and remember that whether we give little care to it or no, it is more precious to God than either of these can be, because we do speak to Him as the members of His only-begotten Son. It is the mind of Christ which we have to bring before Him; it is the words of Christ which we speak. It is in the unity of the life of Christ that we have power to approach Him; and He, as He looks upon us, beholds His well-beloved Son, and is well pleased. Oh, let us think of the eye of the eternal Father watching over all those who come to Him saying their office truly in the grace of our Lord Jesus Christ. Let us think of that welcome which the eternal Father has for us, that so we may indeed continually rejoice to live in His praise.

Our utterance of the praise of God more precious than that of Israel of old, or of the Angels in heaven.

CHAPTER XV

OF THE USE OF THE PSALTER

<small>The Psalter expresses the sympathy with our needs which our Lord took to Himself by His assumption of our humanity.</small>

WE ought to use the Psalter as a special means of entering into our Lord's sympathy with ourselves. We should use it, not merely as being His words, which He having clothed Himself with our nature speaks in the power of the Holy Ghost, but we should use the Psalter as being His members, and as having His life within ourselves; so that its expressions are not merely the expressions of a want felt by Him in His ineffable life of humiliation and suffering many hundreds of years ago, but the expression of a want which He still experiences in His mystical body, He Himself really and truly bearing the burden of our life, really and truly feeling with us and in us. He does not unite us to Himself in order that we may subject Him to our will, but He unites us to Himself in order that He may subject us to His will. And therefore the saying of the Psalter should be a real instrument for bringing our wills into the control of the Spirit of Jesus Christ. Are we in want of words? There let us go, where the Spirit gives utterance.

<small>The words of the Psalter become a living utterance of the Spirit on our lips.</small>

For the utterance which the Spirit of God gives is not less truly His, not less truly divine, because it has been provided in ages far away. It is as truly the divine Spirit within us, when the words of inspiration come forth in the fullness of power from our submissive hearts, as if the same Spirit were now to call our minds to fresh utterances, according to immediate necessity. We shall certainly find how the Psalter does not merely exhibit the largeness of our Lord's sympathy, touching upon every feature of our life, but how it does indeed meet our own need. We shall find our own will rising into the experience of the will of God while we accustom ourselves to use ejaculations taken from the Psalter upon all the various occasions of life. For this purpose it is that we should very specially study the Psalter, learn it, and familiarize ourselves with it, so that it may indeed rise up to our lips upon every occasion.

Blessed is that heart which is continually approaching God in the words of the Psalter! Blessed is that understanding which does indeed find all the circumstances of life illuminated by the teaching of the Psalter! Blessed are those affections which find themselves winged by the words of inspiration, and not only find expression but expansion! They become larger as they become truer. They find words which may truly express their meaning, and while their meaning is expressed, they also look up to receive greater gifts from God than they themselves would have dared to anticipate. *The words of the Psalter illuminate, enkindle, and enlarge our hearts.*

So we should accustom ourselves to this practical familiarity with the Psalter, bringing it in so as to meet the wants of daily life, finding in the wants of daily life a real opportunity of sympathy with our Lord Jesus Christ. He calls us to watch *By familiar use of the Psalter the sympathy of Jesus Christ will enter into our daily lives, and we shall grow in sympathy with Him.*

along with Him, and He does not leave us alone. He does not leave us just to pray as best we can, but He seems to say, 'These are thy needs, these are the words I give to thee, these are the words in which thou mayest find repose, strength, light, and perseverance. Thus shall thy hope be enlarged, thus shall thy vision be clearer, thus shall thy heart be refreshed, thus shall thy life be sanctified, thus shall thy want be supplied.'

He will thus speak to us and unite us with Himself.
We shall in the Psalter find admonitions of loving sympathy from our Lord Jesus Christ, by which we may meet the various difficulties of life. We shall find them not merely as the dry teachings of the natural moralist, but we shall find them as the sympathetic teaching of one who has given them to us, and who bids us really unite ourselves to Himself while we seek to follow Him. Seek, then, thus to say the Psalter as a means of bringing forth the life of Jesus Christ into all the energies of our own heart, and on all the occasions of our own life.

We must utter the words of the Psalter in the power of the Holy Spirit.
If we are to do this it must be in the power of the Holy Spirit. The same Spirit by which David beforehand was inspired to write the words is necessary for us, if we are to speak them. We cannot speak them with the mere stammering tongue of earth. We cannot speak them with the finite power of our natural condition. We must speak them in the power of the Holy Ghost. 'The Spirit helpeth our infirmities' (*Rom.* viii. 26). He it is who will bring home to our hearts the meaning of many words. Commentators fail to do this.

They may explain them in a certain degree to our understanding, but the intellect is not capable of grasping the whole divine meaning; the Spirit must open the eyes, the heart, really to love the things of God, and really to recognize the features of the divine life.

And the Spirit of God is ready to do so, if we will thus look to Him. We invoke His presence constantly at our meditation, but we must be careful to act in His power, not only in our meditation, but in all our acts of worship. Without the power of the Spirit we cannot really draw near to God. We know not what we should pray for as we ought. Our natural faculties are too dull, blunted, earthly; they cannot rise up to communion with God. The Spirit does indeed lift us up, and the words, which otherwise would have but the mere flat meaning of earth, assume the true and proper meaning and proportion of the divine life. Thus are we indeed taught to speak the words of our Lord Jesus Christ, according to the mind of Christ. It were in vain to have His words without His mind. We have His words by the external tradition, but His mind we can only have by the teaching of the Holy Ghost. We must, then, live under the teaching of the Holy Ghost, so that, using the words of Christ in all the circumstances of our daily life, we may learn really and truly to desire the things which Jesus would have us desire.

The Holy Spirit will teach us the mind of Christ.

The Holy Spirit will guide us to the meaning of the words, and use them for our blessing.

It is the Spirit, and He alone, who can enable us thus to read aright the plainest passages, and it is He who will give many a meaning to passages which are obscure. Where the natural intellect fails to afford the sense, where criticism is at fault, in these passages the Spirit of God will often guide the heart to meanings which scarcely belong to the words, but yet He will use those words to develop such thoughts within our hearts. It will often happen that though we cannot analyse the passage intellectually, nevertheless the Spirit of God will make these words to shine out to our affections, and so will lead our affections onward thereby. We must not put away such teaching of the Spirit as if it were valueless, because it cannot be retained upon the regular rails of the earthly intellect. We must yield ourselves up to the teachings of the Holy Spirit. We shall find that He will keep us in safety, and guide us into truth. His holy suggestions will be of great power to the strengthening of our souls. The more we accustom ourselves to holy and reverent intimacy with Him, the more shall we find His power.

The Holy Spirit will bring to our remembrance the words we need, if we will trust ourselves to Him. And it is He who will bring words to our remembrance. It is very important that we should have the words of the Psalter stored in our natural memory by the natural effort of learning, but it is the Holy Spirit of God who will really quicken the memory, so that we may be able to call particular expressions to mind, just when we have most need of them. The Holy Spirit of God will make us to remember just that which at each time will be most helpful. We should trust ourselves to the fellowship of the Spirit, trust our memory to Him as well as our understanding, really bathe our memory in His holy love. And we should do so with a trustful faith. We should feel assured that He will not let us fail, if we do. Trusting ourselves to Him in this manner, we shall come to an experience of His personal care for us. It will be a delight to us, not merely to remember particular verses as being applicable, as the natural mind may remember the verses of some poem out of our own national classics, but rather we shall feel that it is the Holy Ghost really bringing up the words to our mind. If we look up to Him, and in the mystery of His glory see these words shining out, and hear these words coming forth into our ears, we shall rejoice in His love. Yes, to look to all suggestions as really coming from Him, to look to Him in order that we may receive such suggestions, will have a great effect upon our lives in really making us to walk in the fellowship of the Spirit.

Let us, then, be careful thus to use the Psalter in the power of the Holy Ghost, in the power of the Spirit of Christ, and as the expression of the will of Christ for us and in us. Let us say the words of the Psalter as the Holy Ghost dictates them, and in the consciousness that while we say them the eternal Incarnate Son is speaking with our lips unto the Father. There should thus be a real communion of soul with Jesus by the power of the Holy Ghost. The Spirit thus helping our infirmities (cf. *Rom.* viii. 26) will strengthen us to desire those things which Jesus desires, to know those things which Jesus knows, to love those things which Jesus loves, to hate those things The mind of Christ will thus become the law of our life.

which Jesus hates. In the Psalter we become identified with all the various movements of the mind of Jesus, and in the Psalter the mind of Jesus calls us to exercise those same functions amid the various circumstances of our own life. We cannot be just united with Jesus in some desires. Our whole law of life must be that which He teaches us by His holy inspiration. Our whole love, that is to say, our whole affectionate regard of all circumstances to be desired or shunned, to be approved or condemned, to be loved or hated, must thus be learned of Him. If we have the mind of Christ thus really operative within us by the power of the Holy Ghost, then we shall surely find how the Psalter will enable us to live at all times united to Him, to live always to the glory of God.

The spiritual use of the Psalter will bind us to Jesus, developing in us the sacramental gift of His life.

And our use of the Psalter in the public offices of the Church will gather up much reality and meaning from our frequent use of it in the various circumstances of daily life. We shall not find that we wear it out by using it. The more we come to ascertain the inexhaustible depths of its divine meaning, of its varied applications, of its intense love, we shall find how great the love of Jesus was to us individually. The more we sing it, the more we shall find how Jesus will guide us by His Holy Spirit, how He will bind us to Himself. There is nothing that should bind us in our daily life more truly and constantly to Jesus than this saying of the Psalter in the power of the Holy Ghost. And it is thus that our sacramental life is to be developed as a real operation. Jesus gives Himself to us, but if we have the life of Jesus stagnant within us, that life does not become our own, that life becomes suffocated at once. We find in ourselves that intense mental labour exhausts the bodily frame; but the more we exercise the mind of Jesus, the more we find the whole energy of Jesus developed within us. Oh, we shall find that the mind of Jesus, as He works within us, does indeed make the whole being of Jesus to fill our being. The spiritual use of the Psalter does indeed make the whole of our Lord's humanity to become diffused throughout our humanity. The various faculties of our nature become strengthened by the gift of Himself, just in proportion as we carry out His exercise, and say His words.

So, then, let us try to live in the power of the Holy Ghost, and in our Psalter. So shall we be perfected in the likeness of the only-begotten Son. *So will Christ be formed within us.*

CHAPTER XVI

OF MENTAL PRAYER

Mental prayer is the life of the soul, and must be practised regularly.

BESIDES the recitation of the Divine Office, the brethren will be careful to devote one hour daily, if possible, to the practice of mental prayer. This, I need not say, is of the highest importance for us. It is in mental prayer that the soul really enters into union with God. No revelation however clear, no familiarity however intimate with Jesus after the flesh, no sacramental union however complete, really benefits the intelligent soul without mental prayer. For all those minister to this capacity. It is this capacity which constitutes our individual life in the possession of all those gifts which God gives to us. While we are acting in mental prayer we are living; when we cease to act in mental prayer we are dead. Prayer, this interior prayer, is the very act by which the soul lives. It is the movement of the Spirit of God within the soul. It is the very act by which God calls the soul to listen to Himself, and to speak to Himself. And if we are to live in this life of mental prayer, it is most necessary for us to cultivate the habit of certain prolonged and regular exercises.

Mental prayer is communion with God.

So then in our hour of mental prayer, it is very important that we should understand that we are

OF MENTAL PRAYER 191

not merely considering abstract truth. We are not merely reviewing a theological subject. We are approaching a Person. We are speaking with God. God is truth. All the various forms of created truth which meet us are merely accidental: God is the truth whose glory is manifested in every one of His creatures, and we draw near to them as a means through which to approach Him, that in them we may gain some interior glimpse of His true being. His substance cannot be seen by the outward eye, but as we behold Him in His operations the gaze of faith rejoices in the contemplation of His glory. So we must come to our mental prayer definitely seeking to gaze upon God. Whatever the subject, it is God Himself who is the object of our contemplation; the subject that is proposed for us is to lead us to Him. If it does so lead us to Him that we are, as it were, caught away in the simple contemplation of Himself, let us praise Him for it. Do not let us think ourselves upon such an occasion bound to hold ourselves down to the limits of our prepared or appointed meditation. The appointed meditation is but a ladder, and if the power of the Spirit carries us into the presence chamber let us bow down and worship; let us worship with thankfulness.

We ought, then, to approach our meditation with a real hope that God will reveal Himself to us; not merely that He will enable us to acquire a clearer view of this or that truth which we have prepared, but that He will reveal Himself to us. 'O Lord, show me thy glory' (*Exod.* xxxiii. 18).

In mental prayer we seek that God will reveal Himself to us.

This must be our one desire in mental prayer; so that the soul almost seems to die, to die of very love. By the power of the divine love it is caught away out of this outer life. Such has been, we know, the experience of one of the Apostles— 'Whether in the body I cannot tell; or out of the body I cannot tell; God knoweth' (2 *Cor.* xii. 2). Let us remember that although we cannot dare to suppose that the same experience should be our own, nevertheless our experience must be homogeneous with this; our mental prayer is akin to it. As the imperfect stammering of a child is akin to the fervid eloquence of the accomplished statesman, so our meditation is akin to that of the Apostles.

We must persevere in mental prayer that the things of God may be revealed to us.

It is by carrying out our own work that we are to attain to those higher degrees of divine life, and it is in mental prayer that we are to draw nigh to God, and in mental prayer that we are to obtain revelations of God. As we give ourselves up to mental prayer, so will these revelations be given. We are not to say, 'I cannot practise mental prayer because I have not had these revelations.' We must practise in order that we may have them. We are not to put revelations away from us as if they did not belong to the ordinary Christian life. They do belong to the ordinary Christian life. The life which we lead in the present day, which has not got revelations, is not the ordinary Christian life. We must try to rise up to the ordinary Christian life. That is far above what the world contemplates; far above what we, taken out of the world, are too apt to contemplate. The ordinary Christian life should have its constant revelations. St. Paul bade the Corinthians 'desire spiritual gifts,' and he gives directions for those who receive 'revelations' (cf. 1 *Cor.* xiv. 1, 26, 30); and if he speaks of himself as having received an 'abundance of revelations,' yet in this very saying he implies revelations vouchsafed to those around him. So we ought to look up to God, seeking for and expecting revelations. We ought to feel as sure that God would give us revelations, if we look properly, as that when we take a telescope into our hands, if we hold it steadily and turn it in the proper direction, we shall see the object. It is our own unsteadiness of hold which makes the whole prospect of the veiled life so dense, but we must seek to cultivate the habit of mental prayer, so as to behold really and clearly the things of God.[1]

And God will reveal; He will reveal them to us by His Spirit. Yes, we must pray, and He will reveal. We are so apt to say, 'He has revealed.' But in the strict sense it is not true that He has revealed, because revelation is not a mere matter of past time. Revelation is the coming forth of the eternal God to the living soul. What is revealed to others may be written down on parchment, but the revelation of God cannot be conveyed thus; it must be the voice of God speaking in the soul, the hand of God lifting up the veil of eternity, the light of God shining into the inmost depths of the soul. And so the revelation of God is really a thing ever present. It is not

The revelation of God a perpetual, ever active, revelation of Himself to them that seek Him.

[1] See Note K at the end of the chapter.

accomplished once and for all, but what He has revealed He perpetually reveals, and He will go on revealing. So we are to live in the consciousness of that perpetual revelation which the living God is making to us, and to draw near to Him in mental prayer. It is as if there were some one holding a lantern to make the light shine upon some dark place where we could search. It is not enough that He has held the lantern for some one else, and for some one else to tell us what we shall find if we grope there; the same hand, the same lantern, is there to reveal the same objects to every generation of those who are really looking for them. So in our mental prayer we must realize the personal hand of Almighty God, holding the lantern which may shine upon us.

In mental prayer the love of God is ready to make His light to shine upon us.

That hand of the living, loving God! Oh, we must come to our mental prayer with a consciousness of the love of God as ministering to our meditations. We are not there simply to try and meditate by ourselves, as we may try and use some natural faculty to learn a language or to acquire an art, but in our meditations we put ourselves under the immediate care and guidance of the present and loving God. It is the love of God which must manage everything for us, and we have just to put ourselves in His keeping. The love of God will make His light to shine upon us, so that we need not fear lest we should not have light. We know the love of God gives us just that amount of light which is necessary. If He withholds from us the light, it is because He knows we shall attain what we want better by being without it than by having it. We must not come to mental prayer as if God were very far off and we had to make an effort to reach Him. God rather comes near to us, and takes hold of us, to see if He can really bring us so simply to love Him and trust Him that He may reveal to us His glory. So should we draw near to mental prayer with a real confidence that God Himself is taking part in it.

And the great matter of our prayer is speaking with God, developing certain affections. Certain intellectual points are given to us, but they are comparatively matters of indifference. It matters but very little by what gate we enter into the heavenly city, if only we enter in; it is the speaking with the great King which is the real matter. And so we must speak with Him. And when we speak with Him and He with us, what is the result? If God speaks with a soul, does He speak with it as we may speak one with another? We may speak one with another and our words fall upon the outward ear, but leave the nature unchanged. The word of God is the word of the Creator, and so the word of God never comes forth from God without a creation following it. When the word of God comes into the soul of a man, it creates a consciousness within that soul. It is not a mere passing articulation of sound; it is the abiding presence of the creative word which has come to that soul. *As we pray God speaks within us with His creative word.*

And what does He create in that soul? He creates some affections, for God is love, and God creates in the soul that which is akin to Himself, *The life-giving breath of God recreates the faculties of the soul, that we may enter into the fellowship of His love.*

faculties in which He Himself may live and act. So He creates affections within the soul, and forms them anew. Even as He took the dust of the ground and made it in the new form of man (cf. *Gen.* ii. 7), so now He takes the faculties of human nature, and lifts them up into the love and fellowship of Himself. When the word of God comes into the soul He does not come to find affections; enough if He find the soul waiting for Him with those natural affections, however imperfect they may be, which He has suffered to remain in spite of the Fall. But when He comes, and speaks within the soul, He wakes up those affections into a divine life. It is as if His breath, passing over a garden that had been entirely destroyed by the frost, suddenly made all the fruit trees that were therein to germinate, and stand out in all the promise of a rich crop. So over the frost-bitten soul of man the breath of God passes, when we come near to Him in mental prayer, and all those frost-bitten faculties rise up with a new life, and germinate and burst into a new fruitfulness they had not before: that which God gives them now is better. So it is for us to come to God in mental prayer, really giving ourselves up into His power and His love, that we may be formed again according to the fullness of that holy love.

We must hear the voice of God within, ere we can speak aright to Him.

Seek, then, in your mental prayer, seek above all things, this colloquy with God, putting yourself into communion with God to hear the voice of God, that hearing that voice you may live with the life of God. That voice it is which, coming into souls, makes them speak with God. We cannot speak with Him by any natural faculty, but when He has breathed into us this new life, His own love, then we can speak with Him. We may bring with us words of utterance and repeat them, we may form words by our own intelligence, we may at certain moments have such an excitement that we can speak the words without difficulty; but the word, which is really to reach to God, must be a word which God inspires. And so God teaches us to speak with Him, not merely in the excitement of an earthly sentiment, but in the calmness of the divine love. This is what we have to seek for in our mental prayer—to live with God in this fellowship of calm, divine love, by which we may hear the voice of the living God speaking within ourselves, and we ourselves may speak with Him in the power of the Holy Ghost.

This life, of prayer in the Holy Ghost, is far removed from the ordinary life we have to live in the world, and therefore we must be very careful and watchful to cherish it in every exercise of devotion. But if we do so, then our mental prayer will communicate its divine life to the saying of our office. It will communicate its divine life to all our most ordinary actions, to all our intercourse one with another. Oh, that we could attain to live so stablished in the consciousness of the presence of God that His holy love might indeed fill our whole being at all times! How watchful, therefore, should we be to keep off everything that is at all at variance with this calm stability of holy love in fellowship with God!

<small>The habit of mental prayer will give life to all our actions.</small>

This is the object of our enclosure, that we may live in this revealed fellowship with God. Let us take care, as we come to our daily meditation, that we really are always seeking to have this fellowship with God perfected in our hearts.

NOTE K

'The ordinary Christian life should have its constant revelations.'

When Father Benson speaks of the 'ordinary Christian life,' he means the Christian life as it should be in us if we were living true to its real character in Christ. It is a life in the Spirit. And the 'constant revelations' of which he speaks are the ever renewed light that is granted us upon God's ordering of our daily lives, and upon His purposes and gifts for us in Jesus Christ, if we are constant in prayer. We only know God as we hold converse with Him.

There are 'revelations' of things to come, but these are spoken of in Holy Scripture rather as oracles or warnings received from God by particular persons for special purposes. The word 'revelation' in the New Testament commonly means the unveiling of that which hitherto has been hidden, whether in the course of human history, or in the spiritual experience of the individual. This is the sense in which St. Paul prays for the Ephesians, that 'a spirit of wisdom and revelation' may be given them, 'in the knowledge of God,' that the eyes of their heart may be enlightened to know the hope of their calling as coming from God, and the riches of the glory of God's inheritance in the saints, and the exceeding greatness of His power working in them, the very power that wrought out the resurrection and glorification of Jesus Christ their Lord and head (*Eph.* i. 17 ff.). In this way new 'revelations' of the truth 'as it is in Christ Jesus' would come to them, not for intellectual satisfaction, but for their growth in Christ in their 'ordinary' daily life in the world.

Father Benson spoke similarly in the Society's Retreat in 1875: 'He comes to speak to us in our daily life, and that which He shows is hidden, until it is revealed by Him. He will unfold Himself to us, as we meditate upon His word, and draw near to Him, in answer to His voice, Come and see. . . .' So will come 'the development of spiritual illumination, not as an illumination catching a new view of truth, but as the morning dawning upon the mountains—the earth is the same, yet transformed' (*S.S.J.E. Retreat*, 1875).

CHAPTER XVII

OF THE DAILY MEDITATION

Discretion to be exercised in using the notes given for meditation.

IN regard to your daily meditation and the notes which are given, I wish it to be understood that it is not expected that every person should follow each of those heads that are put down in the meditation. There are more thoughts than would suffice, or be desirable, for any one meditation. It is better, therefore, just to take a general conspectus of the subject from the notes put down on the paper, and to select some two or three heads upon which specially to dwell. The three heads will tend towards a clearer understanding of what is the general drift and teaching of the meditation, but it is better to give a sufficient time to those points which you do select for your own immediate prayer, and not to traverse the whole ground.[1]

We come to meditation not for intellectual gratification, but to learn to behold the goodness and the glory of God.

We should dwell for some time on any point on which we wish to speak with God. We are not to think that because we see it clearly, therefore we can pass on to another. We do not come to meditation merely that we may see, but that we may learn to gaze in holy love. So we must rest upon the point until the loving affection of our heart is really drawn towards it by the inspiration of the Holy Ghost. We must speak with

[1] See Note L at the end of the chapter.

the Holy Ghost respecting it, consult as it were with the blessed Spirit dwelling in our hearts, and ask Him to teach us how we may best love this manifestation of divine truth. God is to be loved in every truth respecting the higher world that we contemplate. God is to be loved, and recognized, in all the works of the outer creation; but if by the visible things of God His invisible goodness is manifested, much more will it be so in the contemplation of heavenly things. We must see varied manifestations of the divine goodness. That essence, which we cannot approach in itself, is manifested completely in the Person of Christ, and the perfect manifestation which is in the incarnate Son of God makes its rays to shine in all that belongs to the economy of the Incarnation. All the varied surroundings glow with the traces of the divine glory, and it is for us in our meditation, not simply to rest upon that object which we are contemplating, but as we see it shine with its own special brightness we must follow on, and track that ray to its source. And so we need time to dwell on any particular point, time for us really to speak with God respecting it, to speak to God and to listen to God, to hear what God has to say concerning it.

But God does not merely speak to the intellect, teaching us to apprehend some new statements; God, who is love, speaks too in our affections, teaching us to love. So it may be that we have long apprehended some statement respecting some theological verity, and we have intellectually nothing more to learn, but our affections need

As we are taught of God, we learn to love the revelation made in Jesus Christ.

to be 'taught of God.' 'Every man that hath heard, and hath learned of the Father, cometh unto me' (*St. John* vi. 45). No mere human learning brings us to Christ. We may be profound theologians, and yet have no desire to come to Christ at all. That is because, although we have been taught about God, we have not been taught of God. Every one taught of God is taught with the attraction of holy love, and he who has been so taught cannot stay away, cannot hold himself back from Christ. He is drawn to Christ by a necessary impulse. The knowledge he has of God is not mere head knowledge present to his intellect, but it is the attractive knowledge by which his whole being is drawn towards Him in whom this truth is revealed.

We must wait on God in our prayer, abiding in His presence.

And we are not to be surprised that our intellect may gaze upon divine truth without being moved. We must wait until our affections really are moved by the Holy Ghost. We may have to wait some time. We are not to think it a strange thing that our affections do take a long time really to become disciplined. What multitudes there are who just fail of attaining the object of their meditation because they go away hastily, and impatiently, without giving themselves really time sufficient to experience the influence of the Holy Ghost. If we put a large lump of ice in the sun, we do not expect it to disappear in a moment; if we put our chilled hearts in the presence of the Sun of righteousness, we are not to expect that they will be melted through and through in a moment. We must abide under the influence of the Holy

Spirit. So we must not be wandering over too many thoughts in our meditation, but we must just rest in the divine presence, convinced that God who is truth, is also love; and as He brings the truth home to our intellect, so He will, if we will wait for it, bring that truth home to our affections.

We must give a certain amount of time to each point, and it may happen that we feel drawn to rest upon some certain point. We may have proposed to go over more ground; but it may be that God will draw us to some one thing, so that our whole time is occupied by that point. Instead of being fretted that we have not carried out our original purpose, we ought to be thankful that God has brought us into this communion with Himself. If God has guided our meditation, we ought to be very thankful to Him for it; and then any remaining points we may make the subject of meditation later on in the day, if there is time, or at some future time.

If we have found communion with God on some point of our meditation, we must rest upon it thankfully.

And then when we have made our meditation, we are not to think the meditation is over. We ought to be very careful to cherish it from day to day, and hold thereby a continuity of life.

The fruit of our meditation to be cherished from day to day.

> The Child is father of the Man;
> And I could wish my days to be
> Bound each to each by natural piety.
> *Wordsworth*

In this filial succession of times of meditation, it is not as among the generations of mankind. Old generations pass away and are forgotten; yet they pass away into the being of God. Our meditations are not to pass away as mere earthly things, but to live on, and be a continual bond of union between our souls and God. 'Thou shalt remember all the way which the Lord thy God led thee these forty years in the wilderness, to humble thee and to prove thee. . . . And he humbled thee and suffered thee to hunger, and fed thee with manna, which thou knewest not, neither did thy fathers know, that he might make thee to know that man doth not live by bread only, but by every word that proceedeth out of the mouth of God doth man live. Thy raiment waxed not old upon thee, neither did thy foot swell, these forty years' (*Deut.* viii. 2–4). Well, so it must be with us in our wanderings through the wilderness. We ought to dwell upon the spiritual food wherewith God has nourished us from time to time.

<small>The repetition of our meditations deepens our communion with God.</small> So we must keep our past meditations before our remembrance as much as we can, and therefore it is good for us to recur to our old meditations. On those days when there is no meditation given you can generally take up the meditation of the preceding day, or of some recent day, and recur to the same thought, and seek to find some fresh communion with God in its use. The repetition of our meditations is indeed a matter of great importance in our spiritual life. We are too apt perhaps to dwell upon the intellectual truth, to be satisfied with having apprehended it, and to let it go. But we ought to delight to revisit the same truths, to look upon truth as a real object; for indeed it is the object we have to visit. We have to visit God in that particular truth. That truth

is the form in which God comes near to us, and so we are not to let it go, as if it had been a mere cloud that had risen up into the sky and had passed away. We are to delight to revisit it. It is not even as a mere picture in a gallery. We must delight to turn back to it as a living being, as a mother delights to see each of her children from day to day. She comes morning after morning to see each one of them in their beds, to visit each, to pour out to each the fullness of her love. So we ought to delight in revisiting those truths on which our minds have dwelt, and in which we have found communion with God. And the repetition of our meditations may be one great means of giving stability, continuity, permanence, and vitality to our divine communings with God. We should seek in this way really to find God in all our spiritual exercises.

During this week you will be having daily meditations given in the Retreat for secular clergy, which I hope most of you can attend, and turn them afterwards to account as the substance of your own meditations. As we hear Retreat addresses, we should always remember that the great matter is the turning them to account afterwards; not the mere hearing of them, but, while we hear them, gathering up some points on which subsequently to meditate, and hold communion with God for ourselves. We are not merely to think of God as speaking to us through the Conductor as in a sermon, but as drawing near to us, and when a meditation has been given He seems,

When God speaks we must treasure His word, and recognize His presence.

O

as it were, to come before us in the form of that thought, and in the form of that thought to be waiting for us to dwell upon Himself. Thus as the manna fell like dew round about the host, and waited to be gathered up, but, when the sun was hot, then it melted and passed away (cf. *Exod.* xvi. 21), so after a meditation has been given there is this dew of the divine presence which we are to gather, and after a while it will melt and pass away. It is for us to recognize it as a real coming forth of the divine presence, in such a way that we may gather it up for our own selves and feed upon it.

<small>As we rejoice in that presence of God, we shall be perfected in the love of truth.</small> So let us be careful in the use of all meditations really to seek the presence of God, and to recognize the abiding character of that presence; and to recur to our past meditations, so that we may continually cherish and grow in the love of the truth. We shall find how that love of the divine truth will perfect our lives in the fellowship of the divine mystery. God will strengthen us more and more as we constantly and patiently recur to seek Him, and rejoice in His abiding presence.

Note L
'*The daily meditation.*'

It was the custom of the Father Founder, in the early years of the Society, to give out daily heads of meditation for the brethren to use, as a means of developing the spiritual life of the Society by common meditation on the same subject in an ordered scheme. This was the origin of the volume of meditations called *Benedictus Dominus*, which was drawn up at first for the members of a devotional guild, called the Society of the Apostolic Rule. These were given out for the use of the Fathers and Lay Brothers, and were afterwards published in a form that covers the whole Christian year, and so were made available for general use. In the preface to this book Father Benson writes: 'These brief heads of meditation were at first drawn up for the use of a small Society, in order that its members, though outwardly separated from one another and living in the world, might feel the bond of union which is formed by such devotional agreement. The meditative life is that whereby the soul abides in union with God; and the practice of meditation upon the same subjects daily is one great means of binding together those who are held back by the necessities of external society from much personal fellowship. . . . The law of sympathy in contemplation was given us by God for this very purpose. Mankind was formed to find delight in truth, not merely after the manner of individual intelligences, but with the consciousness of common joy in one life-giving object. And thus we were not only to find our life in the knowledge and love of God, but in the love of one another, which that knowledge sustains and purifies' (*Benedictus Dominus*, pp. v, vi).

CHAPTER XVIII

OF FASTING AND MORTIFICATION

Our need of humiliation of spirit, because of our weakness of both body and soul.

THIS is a subject which we must approach with much humiliation in the present day. For indeed, when we think how holy men of old spent their time in prayer and fasting with God, and then think of our own bodily necessities and our own spiritual weakness, we must indeed acknowledge that we are scarcely worthy to be numbered in the same company with those who used thus to serve God. And if it is a subject of humiliation, at least we must humble ourselves upon this account. We must come to God with a sad confession of weakness, not of His doing, but our own; a weakness indeed that is not even His penalty, but the fruit of our own continuing sin; weakness of body brought upon ourselves by years of varied forms of evil indulgence, and weakness of soul, incapable of gathering up for God's service that remnant of spiritual life in which we might still worship Him.

We must take our food with reverence and penitence when we remember our vow of poverty.

We must humble ourselves before Almighty God, and if we cannot fast in any sense that is worthy the name, at least we must take our food in such a way as befits penitence. We must take our food in thankfulness that He does still give us life, though we have done so little that is profitable to Him. We must take our food for the real maintenance of this life, that we may live to His glory, and not for our own self-indulgence. We must take our food according to the regularity of appointment, not according to the impulses of natural appetite. We must take our food with that reverence of demeanour which befits those who are conscious that they are submitting themselves to one of the necessities of nature, who are conscious that they are acknowledging thereby their subjection to the evil world, yet who acknowledge also that life must be used to God's glory, since it is supported by His bounty. We must take our food with indifference, whatever it be that God gives us, ready to receive at God's hand both that which is common or distasteful, as well as that which is pleasant to the taste. We must take our food with holy charity, mindful of those who have not got the same. Oh, when we think of our own vow of poverty, and turn to consider the poor! When we think that there are many who are glad to take even that which remains from our own table, when we send the remains of our table as a dinner, how we ought to feel the reproach, if we are not rising up to the fullness of that poverty to which we might attain, if we had more steadfastness of purpose. Thus must we make our feeding at least a matter of humiliation, if we cannot find in our fasting a law of virtue.

Why did men of old fast? They fasted that they might bring their bodies into subjection. Alas, we cannot fast, because, if we fast, our bodies *Fasting is for the subjection of the body to the spirit.*

instead of coming into subjection are apt only to gain greater power of evil over us. Men of old fasted, and brought their bodies into subjection to the will of God. They had their whole nature so entirely under control that in their fasting they attained more and more to capacities of spiritual perfection. We must try at least to make our feeding subserve this purpose. We must try at least to find spiritual perfection in the mode and manner and quantity in which we take our food. Men of old fasted in order to bring their bodies into subjection. They had one continual desire. The soul intent upon communion with God strove to assert itself continually over the mortal body. They were aware of that struggle that is coming on, how 'the corruptible body presseth down the soul' (*Wisd.* ix. 15), and being aware of this they abode in such steadfastness of will in communion with God that as they fasted their spirit triumphed.

Only by communion with God can fasting be profitable to us.

Our bodies are so much out of harmony that over-fasting develops in them every evil, and our souls are so wanting in steadfastness that they are unable in seasons of weakness to exercise that supernatural control which those of old used to have. Oh, if we could but live lives of more equable communion with God, how should we then find a holy power in the practice of fasting! It is not merely bodily weakness, such as belongs to all the race of man apparently in this age. It is not this which is our great difficulty. Our great difficulty is perhaps that want of spiritual equanimity, of spiritual repose in God, which would develop a holy energy from the divine presence to fill our bodies, and hold them safe from the uprising of evil desire, and sanctify them more and more for the struggle which they have to bear. Holy men of old knew that their bodies were indeed the seat of an evil which had to be mortified; but we, when we speak of mortification, speak of that which indeed we may praise in words, but which, alas, the moment it comes to us we put aside. It never seems the right time to die; and all the discipline of modern times seems to have its end rather in the sustaining of bodily comfort, than in the mortification of bodily enjoyment.

We look back thus to holy men of old; we see what their law of life was, and what their purposes were, and their practice; and as we compare this with our own, we feel ashamed to think that we can in any way profess to lead the life that they lived. These thoughts continually come home to our mind, and upon days of fasting we ought to think whether we are remembering the purpose of fasting, which is to bring the body into subjection, or whether we are merely observing them as a rule without a thought. If we have a thought of it, we shall also live in prayer for its accomplishment. The day of fasting will be a day of prayer that the Holy Spirit may so nourish us and all good thoughts in us that by His power all thoughts of evil may be purged out. Is it not the case that our fasting often turns to our hurt, not by reason of its merely natural results, but because it is not accompanied by the equanimity of holy prayer and repose in God, which ought to be the continual atmosphere of the Religious soul? On

Days of fasting must be days of prayer

our fast days we must see that our souls are really thus feeding upon God; so shall our fast day be a spiritual feast.

The fast of penitence full of joy, and power, in the following of Jesus.

The less we gratify the body, the more we shall find of divine delight, pouring itself into the soul. Holy men of old gave themselves up to fastings and severe fastings, and yet they were not complaining; their penitence did not make them querulous, did not make them gloomy. On the contrary, the deeper their penitence the greater their joy, for it was true penitence, which springs out of the abiding consciousness of the love of God; and so the more they gave themselves up to the work of penitence, the more they found themselves sustained by the divine power. Their fasting was indeed a continuance of our Lord's fasting in the wilderness, and by it their being was continually weakened, but their soul was never swerving from communion with God. So when Satan came to tempt, for he tempted them as he does us, they met him, but not as we meet him. How easily does he get dominion over us! How terribly tempted they! Yet in all these things they were 'more than conquerors through him who loved' them (*Rom.* viii. 37).

The fast of the wilderness a conflict with Satan.

But they were fasting, not merely to bring their bodies into subjection, but in order to help in the work of the Church in casting Satan out of the world. They were putting on their armour for the great conflict; this they knew, and they were not surprised when he assailed them. It did not seem to them a thing unforeseen. Not only did

OF FASTING AND MORTIFICATION

they know it was what they must look forward to, but they were prepared, and therefore strong, when the tempter came. They knew that when a saint is fasting, Satan will be sure to come up with his temptations, and that the life of the wilderness must be the life of the Religious; and it were no wilderness unless Satan were there to tempt. Therefore, their peace was not destroyed by those mocking devices or foul fancies with which Satan met their eye; their hearts remained undisturbed in communion with God. In their fasting they had been disciplining themselves; it was not a mere effort of moral endeavour. Then indeed they would have been weak, but in their fasting they were laying hold upon God, and so Satan found them strong with the strength of God.

It is for us, then, to remember in our fasting that we must expect Satan to assail us, and our fasting is for the very purpose of casting Satan out. We cannot cast Satan out except by a hand-to-hand fight, that is to say, by a spirit-to-spirit fight. Our spirits must come into collision with that foul spirit. Our spirits must indeed feel the terribleness of his grasp; but he must also feel the power of that fire of the divine presence with which our spirits are enkindled. *By our fasting we are to cast Satan out.*

We cannot drive Satan away by the flame of mere natural impulse. We may seek to drive him away by the strength of our own self-will, bursting out as it were in fitful flames; but as these flames burst out that foul spirit mocks at us, for it is a fire which does not touch his being. The flame of natural impulse dies powerless, like the flicker- *Satan can only be cast out by a soul that has learned to repose in God.*

ing of a flame in the midst of smoke, and he remains triumphant, yea, rather, turns all to his own purposes. But if the soul has been really reposing in God, sustained in God, not by the violence of natural effort but by the calmness, the tranquillity of supernatural repose; if it has been really resting upon God, so as to be nourished by the inbreathing of that divine Spirit wherein it rests: then Satan finds the soul incapable of being disturbed. He mocks the soul with foul visions; he assaults the ear of the soul with evil words; he tries to stir up every evil thought to which the soul has ever yielded itself, but all in vain. The calmness of the power of God holds the soul in the divine keeping, and that same divine power burns the spirit of the enemy, and torments him. Yea, that foul spirit cannot touch those souls in which the fire of the divine Spirit is found.

The power of the Church weakened in proportion as the spirit of mortification has been lost.

So it is that we should understand that our fasting is indeed the preparation for spiritual warfare. 'This kind goeth not out but by prayer and fasting' (*St. Matt.* xvii. 21). No wonder that, as we have lost this power of fasting through so many ages of the Church's life, the missionary work of the Church has retrograded for so many years. No wonder that those countries where men fasted of old, and believed in Christ of old, should now be given up to the darkness of Mohammedanism. Now that Christians have ceased to fast, Satan naturally becomes triumphant. And no wonder that throughout Christendom, although the name of Christ remains, yet the power of Christ is not felt, and Satan is able to lay hold of entire popula-

OF FASTING AND MORTIFICATION 215

tions. And why? except that the Church has ceased to live in the spirit of mortification, and deadness to the world. The Church has sought rather to feast upon the good things of the world than to die to the world that it may know the blessed feast of Paradise, and may win that feast by exercising the strength of God.

It is for us, then, as a Religious community, as a missionary community, to remember that we have a very special duty in this respect; and if we cannot fast in any way that is worthy the name, at least to do what little we can, and in the best way we can. *The responsibility of the Society.*

After all it is more the way in which the thing is done than the amount we can do. Men of old did fast for strife and debate, and God did not accept their fasting. Their fastings rather brought Satan in than kept him out. We must feed in humility, in penitence; feed for the simple supply of nature in a real spirit of mortification, as those who have to live in the world, but long to die to it, thankful if this were the last meal we were to eat; feed as those who are waiting for the better feast to be hereafter, as the only feast which can be a real satisfaction to us. *The spirit of fasting more important than the degree of fasting.*

So let us learn indeed to take our food in a true spirit of fasting, remembering that we owe this to our profession, to our work, to the Church of God, to ourselves at home if we would be a community fasting in Jesus, and to our brethren in distant parts that they may be partakers of our fasts and prayers; that souls may be won to Christ *Our duty to the Church and to the world demands the cultivation of the spirit of mortification.*

by our strictness in this respect. We owe it to the Church of God, for if we who make a profession are not careful to live lives of mortification, what will the world do? How shall we be able to speak to the world if we allow the softness and ease of the world to become the law of our life? We must be very watchful to be true in all these respects, watchful to carry out the law of our life, watchful to carry out the will of God. If we cannot rise up to the mortification of the Saints, we must at least find a mortification in our own weakness, a real mortification, a real humiliation of spirit, a real avowal of how little life we have of God, since we are so sensitive to the life of the world.

<small>The little we can do must be a law of humiliation to us.</small>

True, we must not attempt more than we have strength for. That would indeed be pride, and not faith; that would not bring with it any blessing from Almighty God. We must accept the position of humiliation in which we are, and be true, and take care that we do not forget to be humble, in the carelessness of ease, under the thought that as we cannot do much, God therefore does not expect us to do anything. No, God wants us not to forget this holy law of fasting. It must be the law of our life. We must serve God as living under this law, but as unequal to its true and proper fulfilment.

<small>We must seek for grace to accomplish more.</small>

And we should ask God to give us grace to enable us to observe this law better. We are not to think that because we may not be able to fast now, therefore we shall never be able. God has gifts of grace in store for us. Do we look to have

OF FASTING AND MORTIFICATION

great illumination of God, to be great in theology, great in meditation, great in eloquence, great in wisdom, great in missionary power? Is this the kind of spiritual advance to which we look? Oh, then all is wrong! For all these things are God's gifts, not our virtue. God may give them for what purposes He pleases to whom He pleases, to those who have no virtue, no spiritual life at all commensurate with them. But we must look for gifts of grace to enable us to fulfil these exercises, to be enabled to pray to Him in the simple faith of continual repose, to be enabled to fast and bring our bodies into subjection. We must look to Him for grace to do those acts of discipline which now we cannot do, to strengthen us to bring into harmony our bodies, to stablish our souls in the steadfastness of His grace, so that in due time we may be able to serve Him with that devotion which at present is beyond us; not merely that He should give to us what others have won by hard struggle, but that He should give us grace to win them as a true reward.

We are very apt to look upon the decorations of the spiritual life as if they were its essence; and therefore we are apt to desire them. They have a showiness and attractiveness, even for the natural heart. Even a natural man when he reads the lives of great Saints, and hears of their rapturous devotions, and their ecstatic feelings before God, is enkindled with interest in such things; but when the natural heart hears of their mortification and fasting, it does not understand

The great achievement of the Saints lay in their fasting and mortification.

it. It seems time thrown away to fast, and strength wasted, and so the natural heart does not appreciate those exercises by which alone we can become great before God. It is for us not to seek for those spiritual decorations, but to accomplish those spiritual exercises, and to seek for grace. As in a gymnasium, where many are performing feats far beyond us in agility and strength, we should hope by gradual and steady discipline to attain to these: so in the spiritual athletics of the Religious life we cannot do these things now, but we ought to hope to be able to do them. It is by divine grace that we are to be strengthened for them.

The soul filled with the Spirit of God is able to bring under the body with all its impulses.

The more our body is brought under control, the more we shall be able to bring it under. We cannot now wound our body without injuring our spiritual life, because our body and soul are so closely linked together, and the soul is so much the slave of the impulses of the body; but as the soul becomes more and more filled with the Spirit of God, it becomes more dissociated from the movements of the body, and the body will become to the soul as an encumbrance, a dead-weight, well-nigh dead; so we shall be able to beat it down. As St. Paul says: 'I browbeat my body, and bring it into slavery' (1 *Cor.* ix. 27). So in due time by the grace of God if we are diligent in our perseverance, humble in our penitence, steadfast in our endeavours, careful not to go beyond the mark in anything; if we are watchful in these ways, we may look to be at last able to take our share in the work of Saints.

And if there is that great outburst of Satanic darkness which does seem to be threatening the world, how is it to be met but by those who are thus disciplined? Will the quiet homes of the world be able to rise up to that warfare when Satan cannot be cast out but by prayer and fasting (cf. *St. Mark* ix. 29)? We must look for some little band of faithful Religious souls—it may be the only Christians in the world, but lingering on in the spirit of the ascetic life—to take their solitary battle with the powers of darkness, and in the power of the Spirit of God to drive Satan finally out of the world, and welcome the coming of Jesus Christ. Yes, we must look for the great single combats to be fought in the last days, by which the *spolia opima* may be won. They must be royal souls who shall win this prize; it can only be won by bringing the prince of darkness into subjection.[1]

We must look on to the necessities of the last great conflicts, that shall usher in the coming of Jesus Christ.

We must, then, realize our fasting, whatever our rule of food may be, as a means of regular bodily discipline by which we look for the grace of God to make itself more and more manifest within us; and in due time we must look to be able to do more than now we can, content now to humble ourselves, and to do what we can without striving more than is God's will, but looking up to Him to give us grace that we may have our share in casting Satan out, or at least in holding him back. There will be no place Satan will attack so much as a Religious house; there we may be quite certain there will be a gathering of the powers of

A Religious house, above all, must prepare for conflict with the powers of darkness.

[1] See Note M at the end of the chapter.

darkness such as nowhere else. We must see that there is divine strength to drive him back. And it is a great privilege to be in any way called to this conflict. We must esteem it such. So must we be careful in our training for the great conflict. We are just as much training, physically training, for the great conflict as when the members of a crew are training for a race on the river; it is just as much a matter of habitual, steady, regular discipline. We must not think, 'When it comes I will do great things.' We must be doing little things now. If we cannot do great things now, we must be careful to do little things well. Our aim must be to bring our body into subjection, and to help to cast Satan out of the world.

Note M
'The "spolia opima."'

The *spolia opima*, the spoils of honour, were the arms taken, or the armour stripped off, from the body of the general of the opposing forces on the field of battle. Strictly the phrase was applied only to the commander-in-chief, who after conquering his rival in single combat had thus despoiled him. In a subsidiary sense, however, it was also extended to the victory won by a soldier of lower rank, but it was still only used of the result of a personal conflict with the leader of the enemy.

CHAPTER XIX

OF INTERIOR MORTIFICATION

IF we are unable to do much in the way of external fasting we must see that we take great care that we have the interior fasting spirit. 'The soul may keep her fast within' (*Keble, 'Christian Year,' Ash Wednesday*). We must take care that we hold ourselves back from those gratifications to which our spirit naturally tends. The ordinary self-restraint of the Christian must be something severe in the soul of the Religious. The Religious soul must exercise self-restraint, not merely in matters that are sinful, not merely to avoid excess or to carry out a discipline with a view to some immediate end, but he must practise the fasting spirit, by which he holds himself back from the various gratifications which the outer world presents, in order that his soul may really be dead unto the world and alive unto God (cf. *Rom.* vi. 11). It is for God to determine when our bodies shall die, but it is for us to see that our souls are dead to the world, even while here. *[The interior fasting spirit in the Religious soul.]*

This is what we must be continually remembering, continually exercising ourselves in abstaining from the various gratifications by which the activity of our sensitive nature becomes excited. It is one of the great values of acting in obedience, *[Restraint under obedience brings greater good than the gratification of our own will.]*

that we are acting not under the impulse of our own nature, but in tranquillity, in detachment, in self-denial. When we do act according to our own natural impulse, there is an evil associated with it in the development of our natural will. But we need to fast continually from all gratification of our natural will, and so when we have various opportunities of good withheld from us, we are still to realize that we are gaining a greater good in that abstinence than might have been obtained from that indulgence. So much so that however great the good may be from which at any time we are held back, the abstinence shall always become a greater good. Whatever it shall be that holds us back, if we are able to hold back from that which we see to be good, in a real spirit of deadness under the law of Christ, there is a good of abstinence which surpasses any goodness in the act of performance.

We are called into Religion that we may learn to die to the world.
This must be our constant aim in the retirement of a life more or less cloistered. We are shut out from the world in order that we may exercise this virtue of holy abstinence, of detachment—that we may become dead. We are not shut out from the world, merely as if we were too feeble of nature to be able to live safely in the world. On the contrary, to the vast majority of persons life in the world is safer than life in the cloister. There are many dangers into which we are drawn when we are withdrawn from the world. But we are drawn into the Religious life, not as a matter of security, but as a matter of virtue and of excel-

lence, and as an opportunity of rising to higher exercises.

So the continual abstinence by which the soul is held back from that in which it naturally delights, from its gratifications, is a great act of self-surrender to God. And we must be very careful to form such a habit of holding back, that we never allow ourselves to be given up to anything except in obedience, except in accordance with a divine providence; never because such an act falls in with our taste or liking, never because it will be a gratification to our ambition to excel or to get forward in some prominent place, or what is more dangerous, to know that we have been specially useful in accomplishing such a work. We must see that we never give ourselves out in this way. We have given ourselves up to God, and therefore our whole nature must be held back from finding any enjoyment for itself in its dealing with the world. Its own enjoyment must be through the medium of the divine nature. It will indeed find an enjoyment in earthly things, but never as coming from them. It will see earthly things only as being reflected in the divine predestination. It will reach out after earthly things while it turns its back to them, while it reaches into the glory of God. It will be hungering and thirsting after earthly things, not like a man of science, a statesman, or a miser, but as reaching out after everything simply in God. As God gives us everything, and we find everything in God, so shall we find in everything a true satisfaction of our higher nature, and we shall be

A habit of self-restraint is the law of life for a soul surrendered to God.

the more satisfied as we are the more held back.

Living in the world we must hunger and thirst after God and His righteousness.

So this fasting of the soul from the fussiness of the outer life is necessary for the true Religious, that we may be able to live in the world, in the midst of the excitements of the world, and yet to be restrained as if we were dead. To have the whole energies of the soul directed towards the one true object—this is real hungering and thirsting after righteousness (cf. *St. Matt.* v. 6). There are multitudes of people hungering and thirsting for usefulness who have no idea of righteousness, hungering and thirsting after things most excellent in themselves, and yet only gaining evil from them. The soul which is really disciplined hungers and thirsts after God, after the righteousness which is found in God, hungers and thirsts, and knows that unless it has this hunger and thirst it never can have satisfaction which shall really be with benefit. We must be careful, then, to exercise this continual self-control of all our desires.

It is our Religious state which binds us to this constant exercise of the mortification of our natural desires.

It is our Religious vows which constitute this law of fasting. Poverty makes us content to put away all the means which naturally seem to be necessary to success; chastity bids us put away those gratifications by which we might be naturally led outward after the desire of various earthly aims; and obedience leads to that fasting which holds itself back from every yielding to the cravings of natural impulse and becomes simply enslaved to the sovereignty of God. As days of fasting come round we ought, if we cannot do much in the way of strict fasting, at least to examine ourselves whether we are living under this law of spiritual fasting, whether our Religious life is becoming perhaps a mere routine, whether perhaps it is not after all rather a means by which the many angles of worldly difficulty are rubbed off from us; or whether indeed we are so living under the restraint of the divine power that we are directing to God, in hunger for His grace, those desires of the natural heart which otherwise would be hungering for intercourse with the outer world. So with regard to all the anxieties of natural curiosity, all the claims of natural benevolence, the exercise of those various faculties which people living in the world direct, not improperly, to natural objects—we must see that they really are so held back as to be truly and worthily given to God. We must see that we really are keeping ourselves back from earthly gratification, in order that we may seek the grace of God.

And as fasting is not starvation, so must we understand that self-restraint is not spiritual starvation. If we were to think we were suffering great loss because we could not have an indulgence, whether of mental curiosity or of affectionate sensibility, of strength, or of cleverness; if we felt that we were suffering loss by this fast of the Religious life, then we should not be dying by it, but under it. It is not to die under it, but to die by it, that we are drawn away from the world into that Religious death by which we live for God. As in time of fasting we are not merely to feel the hunger, but are to look for the grace, so

We are not to die under our Religious vocation, but to die by it.

in this spiritual fasting we must not feel the outward restraint, but look for the great grace which God has to give.

<small>The soul that empties itself to receive God's grace will be filled.</small> If we do thus really and intensely look up to Him, then we shall be filled with righteousness. God gives His grace to the empty soul that really looks to Him. Not to the soul because it is empty, but because it has emptied itself in order to look to Him. So we must be very careful always thus to be really looking up to receive grace from God. Whenever there is any thwarting of our natural inclination, when we are held back by some consideration of divine providence, or of Religious Rule, or of authoritative decision, from something we should long for, we should immediately look up to God to receive from Him the corresponding gift. We are not even to look upon it as a matter of possibility, but of certainty, that He will give. The grace of God as necessarily flows into the empty soul that is really fasting for God, as the air fills up the vacuum that has been made in the way of nature. We must regard the grace of God as coming to us thus by the necessary truth of the divine covenant. Every such opportunity will be thus an opportunity of life by which our spiritual nature will be nourished.

<small>Fasting must develop in us an intense love of God.</small> We see, then, how fasting, whether it be of body or of soul, should develop in us an intense love for God. We must be looking with an intense love, for we cannot see God otherwise than by the gaze of an intense love. 'God is love, and

he that dwelleth in love dwelleth in God' (1 *St. John* iv. 16). He that looks up to God with love sees God, and he that looks up to God without love sees not God. And so our fasting must bring that intense joy which belongs to this divine love, while we look up to God and seek to have our need supplied by Him.

So we gain a real strength, even of body, for the fulfilment of our outward fasting, if we have this impulse of divine love. It is so even with natural excitement; it will make people forget their hunger, but that excitement leaves them exhausted in the end. But the love of God, while it does indeed raise us out of the thought of outward necessity, is a most true support to the faithful soul. It is thus that great Saints have attained to their great fasts, by their great love. It was not that they were able merely to endure pain which we could not endure. They were raised out of pain by the greatness of their love, to live in the simple enjoyment of God. They were raised above nature by the infusion through love of supernatural strength; and we in our poor little way must be looking after this. We must be seeking to be raised in like manner. If we would be raised thus materially by the grace of God, we must take care that we be raised spiritually. Our bodies are in God's power, but our souls are in our own power. We cannot practise bodily self-denial more than according to God's providence; it is not a matter dependent upon our own will. But spiritual self-denial we can practise. In proportion as we do so, we shall find that this infusion

The love of God, perfected in self-denial, will raise both body and soul to supernatural powers of endurance

of supernatural strength will fill our whole being; and when it has perfected the soul in the love of God, that same infusion of divine grace, that fullness of love, will become the very life of the body, so that in this love of God we shall be able to attain to endurance which in our present state we might think altogether impossible.

In the power of the divine grace we shall enter into the spiritual exercises of the Saints, and their experience of God's love.

We must be looking for this continual illumination of divine grace. We must be continually exercising this supernatural virtue of hope while we abide in patience. We must be waiting for God to manifest His power more and more within us, and He will assuredly lead us on. He will strengthen us in all holiness, and will enable us to do that which now we cannot. And as He enables us to enter into the exercises of Saints, He will also give to us the revelations of Saints, filling our hearts with that love wherewith the Saints have served Him, and with that delight whereby they found a foretaste of eternal reward in the midst of their suffering.

God reveals His will to them that look away from all earthly things to Himself.

See, then, how truly we are to be watchful in the practice of fasting. If we cannot fast much in the way of the body, at least we can practise that fast of the soul by which it holds itself aloof from earthly enjoyments to gaze upon God, and finds its strength, its satisfaction, its joy, in the communication of the divine will.

CHAPTER XX

OF THE BURIED LIFE OF THE RELIGIOUS

'*THE cell is the grave in which the Religious is buried to the world, and the Paradise in which he finds heaven begin. On entering the cell look to the form of the Crucified, realize your union with Him, and say: "Here will I dwell, for I have a delight therein."*

'*The more true we are in keeping our cell, the more shall we find its joy. Spiritual exercises become wearisome just in proportion as the heart is deadened to spiritual things by being absorbed in the world.*

'*Go forth from your cell, whether it be to work, or to teach, or to visit, with a consciousness that you are going forth from the house where God dwells with you, and that He goes forth along with you to your external occupation.*'

On Saturday, the eve of All Saints, we do well to consider the buried life. It is the day of our Lord's burial, and all Saints come out of His grave. There is no Saint upon the other side of that grave. All are Saints whose life begins from it. All Saints are those who have died to the world along with Jesus Christ. They have been buried with Him, and while their bodies are in the world they remain buried with Him. The world is for them not a home of delight, but a dark prison-house,

The Religious life a life of burial with Christ, passing through His grave to the fellowship of His risen life.

230   THE RELIGIOUS VOCATION

although it be full of hope (cf. *Zech.* ix. 12). While we wait for the stone to be rolled away (cf. *St. Mark* xvi. 4), nevertheless the world is but a place where we are imprisoned for a little while, and the only longing of the saintly life is to enter into the joy of the risen Lord. The Saints are those whose life, as far as concerns outward things, is buried with Christ. So the Religious life is a help towards saintliness, because it is a life of burial. The cloister, whether it be more or less strict, and in proportion to its strictness, is a help towards realizing the grave of Christ. We come into the Religious life in order to be united to our Lord, and there is no union with Him who has passed through the grave, except by ourselves passing through it. The grave is the great separation between those who have not yet entered it and those who have passed through it. Jesus has passed through it, and no soul that has not died can be living in the fellowship of His joy who has risen. We must take care that the Religious life is producing in us this effect, that it is helping us on to the life of holiness in the risen fellowship of our risen Lord.

The one joy of the incarnate life of Jesus was the contemplation of the eternal life.

And so we must think how the body of Christ came into the grave. While He was in the world, what was His life? It was a life of suffering; the world had for Him no pleasure. Among the continual sorrows of His life one joy there was that ever filled His mind, and that was the contemplation of the life beyond the grave, the knowledge of the life in which He was ever living with the Father. This was His one joy. This joy He

OF THE BURIED LIFE OF THE RELIGIOUS 231

experienced for Himself when He looked forward to the glorification of His body. 'Father, glorify thy Son' (*St. John* xvii. 1). And this joy was His joy as He looked forward to the glorification of those around Him. 'Father, I will that they also, whom thou hast given me, be with me where I am; that they may behold my glory, which thou hast given me' (*St. John* xvii. 24). If, then, we are really drawing near to the grave in fellowship of spirit with our Lord Jesus Christ, if we are drawing near to the grave as befits those who know, and understand, and appreciate their substantial union with Jesus Christ, we must be as He was, separated from all the joys of this world. There must be but one joy which alone fills, which alone satisfies, the soul, and that joy eternal life—life, not yet revealed, but life which is given to us in earnest, and which shall be our own when we come to the manifestation of the sons of God. 'It doth not yet appear what we shall be: but we know that, when he shall appear, we shall be like him; for we shall see him as he is' (1 *St. John* iii. 2). If we are to be like Him then, that likeness must be begun now. There can be no possibility of likeness with Jesus Christ, unless indeed we are living the buried life.[1]

So, then, we must be careful to cherish all the practices of mortification by which the various energies of our natural being may be put to death, 'put to death in the flesh, but quickened by the Spirit' (1 *St. Pet.* iii. 18). We must see that all our dealing with the outer world is such as natur-

We must be true to the law of the Passion of Christ, sanctifying all joys of heaven and earth.

---
[1] See Note N at the end of the chapter.

ally comes out of the Passion of Jesus Christ. Whatever joy we feel, we ought to remember— this joy has been purchased for me by the suffering and death of Jesus Christ: if I did not come to this through the participation of that Passion, then this joy had been my curse. Every joy, not only of heaven but of earth, has been purchased for us by the death of Jesus Christ, and we come to it as the children of our Lord's suffering, bearing within ourselves that body wherein He suffered, and acting towards the outer world in that body by which He suffered the world's opposition. Let us cherish this principle of strength, the indwelling not only of our Lord's body, but of the very body which suffered, bringing with it the continuance therefore within us of the reasons of that suffering. That suffering must really sanctify all our dealings with the world; that suffering is really violated when we deal with the world, and are content to forget it.

<small>We become sanctified and well-pleasing to God as we ever act in the remembrance of the Passion of our Lord, and in the contemplation of heaven.</small>

Let us dwell upon the thought of our Lord's suffering body being thus given to us that we may live in its merits. The merits of our Lord's sufferings are as blessed incense, making our acts to be fragrant and acceptable before Almighty God. What we touch with the touch of faith, in the remembrance of His passion, becomes immediately fragrant and pleasing to Almighty God. What we look upon in the faithful remembrance of that one true object of contemplation which is ever before the mind of Christ and His people, what we look upon with eyes that are really disciplined to the suffering of Jesus and the gaze of heaven, becomes sanctified to us. What we look upon, forgetting the heavenly vision, becomes an object of sin.[1]

What we look upon, and what we speak. We must remember that our words are to be mortified, that they may be brought into real union with the incarnate and crucified Word of God. Our words gain their power in dealing with mankind, not by reason of their vivacity, their eloquence, their learning, their vigour, but by reason of the indwelling of the incarnate Word. It is that Word, which has died and is risen again, which must live on in our words, if our words are really to be effectual. Therefore our own words must be mortified; our law of speech must be a law of mortification if we are indeed to allow the fragrance and power of the word of Christ to go forth. The word of Christ which comes forth from a mortified soul is a word indeed powerful, for there is nothing in that nature to hold back its power. But the word of Christ when it goes from unmortified lips, however many may be the gifts of nature with which God has endowed them, will be unavailing to bring heavenly truth home to the hearts of men. The truth can come home to no heart, except through the grave of Him who is the truth. Our nature, if it serves as an envelope in which that word is wrapped, becomes also a casket by which its virtues are enclosed, and its power destroyed. Our nature must be as that alabaster box of ointment, which was broken in order that the fragrance might fill the house (cf. *St. John*

The law of mortification must rule our words, if the word of Christ is to go forth with power from our lips.

[1] See Note O at the end of the chapter.

xii. 3); so our whole nature must be done to death, in order that the nature of Christ in His holy energies may go forth in all our words and acts.

<small>Our outer nature must be disciplined to live true to the nature of Jesus Christ.</small>

So we must be careful to cherish this life of mortification, that our outer nature may have no sensitiveness, save only to the approval of Jesus Christ; that our outer nature may no longer respond in its natural elasticity to the varying circumstances of the outer life, but may be simply the medium through which these outer circumstances pass into the inner, the higher, the better nature, the nature of Jesus Christ, in whom our true life is found.

<small>If we cultivate our outer faculties, it is that they may become the instruments of His action.</small>

If we cultivate our outer faculties, we must cultivate them not for ourselves, that we may live in their superficial enjoyment, but for Him, that they may be worthy instruments of His actions. All the faculties of our outer nature have to be given up to Him, and we in the cultivation of body or mind are like servants, making ready the drawing-room in which the royal presence may be manifested. So we are to cultivate our nature simply for Him. And in our inner self we must be absorbed in the contemplation of His supreme indwelling glory, that so He may act in us, and we may be lost to our own consciousness, and lost to the sight of others, that He in all things may be glorified.

<small>We cannot be mortified in our lives, unless we practise mortification.</small>

We must take care, then, really to practise mortification in all the acts of our daily life, really to live as those who are truly dead, who have a certain outer nature around them which has to die, but whose life becomes more and more joyous as that remnant of the outer nature dies away. In order to do this we must be continually practising mortification. We must be living a mortified life, and we cannot live a mortified life unless we are practising mortifications. It is an old saying, 'The Religious that is not mortifying himself is already dead.' His Religious life is dead if his life is not in the continual practice of mortification.

We must take care, then, that we are mortifying all the various faculties of our nature; and therefore, in dealing with the outer world, that we are shrinking from the indulgence of mere idle curiosity, of mere natural eagerness, of thoughts about things which may be in themselves of the greatest interest. We must learn to consider the important interests of the Church, as we would conceive those blessed ones think of them who look down to see the outward phenomena of earthly life from the presence of God in Paradise. Our cell must be to us a Paradise from which we look forth to the world; and though we must be interested in watching the world's history, as it tends to the development of the work of grace, nevertheless it will be with calm tranquillity, with absence of eager passion or of sensitive care. It must be with that abstractedness of prayerful hope with which the blessed ones in Paradise with Jesus look upon these things. We must check all eager curiosity, and be content to know, or not to know, things that are passing in the world. What we know, that we must know not simply for the purpose of

We must look upon the things of the world as do the blessed in Paradise, mortifying our natural feelings,

and lifting our souls in prayer to God.

the gratification of knowing; but every knowledge that comes into our soul must immediately breathe itself forth in prayer to God. Every knowledge that does not nourish the life of prayer is like undigested food in the natural body, the source of spiritual disease. We should thus learn to mortify all natural curiosity and those various forms of interest which belong to us in the world.

<small>The spirit of mortification in work desires only the manifestation of God's grace, whether by ourselves or others.</small>

And so we must practise mortification as to our plans. We must be ever living in holy, tranquil prayer for the manifestation of divine grace. We must be carrying out God's will and work in the exercise of the gift of prudence as He instructs us, and of all the virtues both moral and intellectual. We must be carrying out God's work in the power of the Holy Spirit of counsel; and at the same time we must be living in that perfect charity which loves the whole Body of Christ, and which therefore finds the same interest in the work of others as in our own. Deadness to our own work; gladness that the work of others should succeed rather than our own, if both cannot; thankful self-surrender to our Lord Jesus Christ—this is that life of deadness, in which we are to try by God's grace to be cloistered.

<small>The mortified soul will wait patiently on the Lord.</small>

And then we must mortify the eagerness of our own minds. We must be content to wait God's time. If it does not seem possible for us to carry out plans which suggest themselves to our minds, we must be content to wait. 'They that wait upon the Lord shall renew their strength' (*Isa.* xl. 31). Unless we have mortified all hastiness of the natural disposition, we are still but sources of weakness. Until we have learned to be still and silent, waiting upon God (cf. *Ps.* lxii. 1), we cannot learn to be 'strong in the Lord' (*Eph.* vi. 10), and to do God's work.

And so also in the utterance of knowledge. We must be careful that as we listen for edification, so we speak for edification, and not for the mere communication of knowledge that suits us. We must mortify ourselves in the telling of things; not merely abstaining from idle and evil speech, but putting a restraint upon ourselves, even in matters that are legitimate for secular persons. We must be practising self-restraint in all our intercourse with others, and so a holy silence must rest upon all the faculties of the soul; the soul absorbed in God, listening for God, seeing for God, speaking for God; or rather, becoming itself neither listener, nor gazer, nor speaker, but becoming the mere instrument through which Jesus in His glory lives upon the earth, and hears, and sees, and speaks. *The mortified in speech become the true listeners to God, and the true speakers for God.*

So let us seek to attain to the life of real mortification, the life of holy joy. For there is no joy like to this. The excitements of earth weary but for many an interchange of gladness and sorrow, but the life of one dead unto the world is one continuance of holy joy in the perfect fellowship of Jesus Christ. *The joy of real mortification.*

O Lord Jesu Christ, grant that we may be thus indeed dead unto the world, as befits our holy calling; and in the fellowship of Thy life, in the *A prayer for mortification of spirit.*

participation of Thy action, and in the sanctification of Thy grace may yield up all the faculties of our nature for the fulfilment of Thy will towards this outer world, and in our energies may ourselves rise up to live in the joyous contemplation of the glory of God, to which we hope to attain through Thy boundless merits.

NOTE N
'The world had for Him no pleasure.'

When Father Benson says that the one joy which filled the soul of Jesus on earth was the contemplation of the life beyond the grave, the joy of the eternal life, he must not be taken as meaning that life in this world had no interest to the soul of Jesus, and that He only longed to be free of it. He had come to do the Father's will, and that will involved the complete identification of Himself with all our life in all its aspects. But He is ever looking to the end. He has not come to be at home with us in the world. He has come to bring us to be at home with God in the world to come. This is the new world that He creates by the continual oblation of Himself on earth, His very sympathy with us involving suffering at every point, and by His rising from the dead. This is the victory through suffering to which He looked forward, who 'for the joy that was set before Him endured the cross' (*Heb.* xii. 2); and it is a victory which He wins for us whom He has loved, and for whom He has given Himself. His joy is to bring us to share in it, and so fulfil His Father's will, and manifest forth His glory. This is the joy that He prayed might be fulfilled in His disciples (*St. John* xvii. 13).

We are too apt to think of eternal life in simple contrast to this brief life that is here our portion. But Father Benson is speaking of eternal life in its true sense of perfected fellowship with God, a full participation in the life and the love of God. This was the joy of the Father, in which Jesus ever lived. But He had the fullest sympathy with the pure joys of earth, as when He speaks of the mother, who, when her child is born, 'remembereth no more the anguish for joy that a man is born into the world.' But He uses the phrase to lift up the minds of the disciples to the joy that would soon be coming to them in the sight of the glory of God in His own resurrection from the dead, and this would be a joy that no man could take from them (*St. John* xvi. 21, 22). This was the secret power of His own life on earth, 'the unconquerable gladness of the life of God,' as Father Benson called it in a Retreat given in 1874, sustaining in suffering, purifying all earthly affections, and raising all things to the purposes of the divine glory. We are buried with Him, that we may be absorbed into the full energy of His life.

NOTE O

'*What we look upon, forgetting the heavenly vision, becomes an object of sin.*'

By an 'object of sin' Father Benson means an object that awakens sinful desire, which becomes an occasion of sin in ourselves; as we speak of an object of thought, or of desire. There is no suggestion that the world itself is evil; rather 'God is to be loved and recognized in all the works of the outer creation' (p. 201). But it is God that is to be thus loved, and we are not to rest in simple enjoyment of our own intellectual or sensual gratification; and it is Religious, vowed to the complete surrender of themselves, of whom he is speaking.

Father Benson throughout these instructions speaks of 'the world' in the familiar language of St. John's Gospel and Epistles, a usage which is as clear as is the language of St. Paul when he speaks of the old creation which has been 'subjected to vanity,' and which looks 'to be delivered from the bondage of corruption into the liberty of the glory of the children of God' (*Rom.* viii. 20, 21). Sometimes it is the world in this Pauline sense of a creation marred and cursed by sin in the spiritual world; sometimes it is the world of human life, organized apart from God and occupied only with the affairs of this life, and lying 'in the power of the evil one' (1 *St. John* v. 19). It is this world in both senses that was made to reflect God's glory, that was the object of God's love, and that Jesus came to redeem. But it was to redeem it that He lived and died and rose again, and ceaselessly works still. And we are 'to learn to love and work for it,' as He did (p. 129), even to love it 'with an intense longing to bring it to share in the same knowledge which we possess' (p. 260). But we must be no more 'of it,' than He was (*St. John* xvii. 16), and it is the Religious who by his Profession is called into this closest fellowship of life and work with Him.

CHAPTER XXI

OF DEMEANOUR

'THE demeanour of the brethren should be at all times grave and religious.'

We must remember that we are separated from the world, and our outward demeanour must show this. It is not that we are to be forced or unnatural, but there must be a habitual restraint upon us. We must cultivate a habit so that restraint shall be natural to us, that we may grow into the deportment of holy Religion; a deportment that shows that the inner nature is really purged from the passions by which others are moved; a deportment that shows that in what we do we act, not upon our own impulse, but in obedience; a deportment that shows that in all we do we are living, not for ourselves, but for another object, that is, for the glory of God. The deportment of the Religious should therefore always be grave, recollected, and worthy of the object of our life, in all our dealings with one another, in all our dealings with the world outside, and when we are alone.

A habit of restraint should mark the deportment of the Religious.

Our life of Religion is a dedication to the real fact of Christian life. The world is ignorant of the fact. The businesses, the occupations, the recreations, the passions, the interests of the world,

The inner sense of God's presence apprehends the true fact of the Christian life.

distract men so that they cannot see God within themselves, cannot feel God within themselves, cannot experience that change which Baptism has made in their nature. But the Religious is set apart on purpose that he may realize this; that he may live for this, and that he may know this, not merely as a doctrinal but as an experimental truth, not merely as a dignity but as a power, not merely as a power but as a law. We must understand that we are set apart as Religious to bear the presence of God within ourselves in continual remembrance. As others bear it by sacramental gifts, so we ourselves by our avowed profession; and the remembrance of this gift should be the constant habit of our lives. Blessed are they who do live in this continual remembrance of God, abiding by covenanted fellowship within themselves! Yes, such souls, even though they are in the world, are truly Religious, and unless we are cherishing this remembrance, although we may have put on the garb of Religion, we have only put it on as a witness against our reality in regard to the true purpose of our life.

The life of the Religious, if it is to be worthy of God, must be purged from self-assertion, that the indwelling presence of God may be truly manifested.

We must see, then, that we do cherish this reverence of demeanour which is really worthy of God. The old word which the primitive Christians used for godly was 'worthy of God,' a life 'worthy of God' (cf. 1 *Thess.* ii. 12), and we must see that our life is worthy of God, that our deportment is worthy of God, such as God Himself, if He were living in the house, would show. Our life must be as much as possible transparent, having nothing of ourselves to come between the manifestation of God within ourselves and those who are round us. Our natural being ought to be just like a piece of glass in which something is imbedded, and you see that which is within, but see nothing between your eye and it. So should our life, purged by holy discipline from all the defilements of earthly corruptions, simply allow the presence of God to be seen within us. Any natural gifts of our own do not add any glory to this. No, this is seen most truly and most perfectly when nothing of ourselves is seen. He is the best Religious, not who adds some gift of cleverness or any other faculty to the Religious life, but who adds nothing whatever of himself to the life of God within him; on whom as we gaze we seem to lose all thought of the individual, and to behold God. Our desire and aim must be to purify ourselves from all thoughts of ourself, so that there may not be anything of our own to mix itself with the manifestation of God within us. This is a truly recollected life, in which all the faculties are so intent in gazing upon God that they really and truly allow the life, the light, of God to shine out, and be seen through them. Such is the deportment which we are to seek to gain.

And it will necessarily be grave. It will be reverent. It will be in a certain sense abstracted; and yet it will not be abstracted in any such sense as to make us unfit for that which we have got to do. This inner recollectedness of God within us is not an absence of mind which makes us

The recollection of God's presence a very practical reality.

incapable of attending to natural duties, but quite the reverse. We may give ourselves up to a dream, and be what men call absent-minded, but this is not being with God; for being with God is being intensely present, present where we are as God is present where we are, present to things round about us with that intense consciousness that belongs to God. Recollectedness with God, therefore, is no dreamy unfitness for natural duties, or for simple actions of ordinary interest.

<small>The recollection of God's p r e s e n c e brings virtue to all we do.</small>

This recollectedness of God's presence is an exercise of God's indwelling grace by which we do all things for all that are round about us with an infinitely greater power. There is a real virtue in all we do. The garment of Christ shines whiter than any fuller on earth can whiten it (cf. *St. Mark* ix. 3), and our life must really partake of the glory of the life of Jesus by showing forth the virtue of the life of Jesus in every undertaking. See, then, how the deportment ought indeed to be grave, recollected, worthy of God who dwells within, reverencing the presence of God within the sanctuary of the heart, and yet not leaving the outside uncared for; not leaving external things as if they had nothing to do with us, but acting towards them in the power of that indwelling presence, loving as God loves, hating as God hates, acting as God acts, speaking as God speaks. If we could thus really be transparent temples of the most high God, what a blessed life would ours be, a life far greater in dignity and honour than that of the holy Angels, a life worthy of God!

Now we need a very great deal of care in order

to attain to recollectedness of demeanour, and our habits of silence, our habits of reverence one for another, our punctuality at various acts, all these are just modes of discipline by which we may be dislodged from self and live for God, modes by which self-will may be set aside, modes by which the impulses of self may be restrained, modes by which the interests of self may be checked. All our rules as Religious thus tend to detach us from ourselves in order that we may live really and truly conformed to the being of Christ. St. Paul was living in the world a life of intense activity, yet he says, 'I live; yet not I, but Christ liveth in me' (*Gal.* ii. 20). Christ in-living was the strength of the Apostolic life. We retire from the world in order that we may be able to cherish this presence more than in our poor fallen state we should be able to do amid the distractions of the world. One most devout Religious has written, 'I never went out among men without feeling myself to return less of a man, than I was before' (*Imitation of Christ*, Bk. I, cap. xx). So we may be sure that the associations, the distractions, the conversation, the aims of the world do make us less of men than we were before. We think we are getting greater, our minds getting enlarged, our hearts widened, and our sympathies enlarged, but we forget that our divine life is becoming dim. We are learning to live for the world and less for God, to gain powers such as the world can nourish, and lose powers which can only be exercised in complete detachment from the world.[1]

The rules of Religious life and conduct are framed to bring about detachment from the world and life towards God.

[1] See Note P at the end of the chapter.

The observance of external reverence among ourselves the exercise of a loving restraint.

Our deportment, therefore, should be a deportment thoroughly grave and Religious, and such as may really and truly cherish and shelter this divine presence. So in our walking alone or with others; so in our postures at home. And if we feel some restraint it must not be felt as irksome, but be a loving restraint, not a mere slavish restraint in obedience to a rule, but a loving restraint in obedience to the remembrance of God. We must remember that the Rule is given us that we may remember God.

In the necessary times of recreation we must not lose the recollection of God.

So also we must be careful in our recreation times in the Common Room, both priests and lay brothers; we must be careful that our recreation is really such as befits us as Religious, that it is not what the world calls relaxation, that it is not a relaxation of ourselves from the presence of God. We may require relaxation from the tension of natural study, of intellectual study, or of hard work; but we must be careful never to relax from the presence of God. For that is indeed not to become strengthened, but to become weakened. If we become relaxed from our hold upon God our whole being becomes flabby, and becomes incapable of being rectified without going through much discipline to recover what it has lost. There is no such thing as relaxation in the loss of God, but there is great relaxation in losing self. We must seek our truest relaxation from the thought of self in the losing ourselves in God.

'*The customary tokens of reverence shall be shown by all to those who are their Superiors in the community,* uncovering the head when passing them or speaking to them; thus, laymen before priests, Novices before Professed.

'*All shall rise at the entrance of the Father Superior, or, in his absence, at the entrance of the Father Assistant, and when he leaves the room.*'

All these tokens of reverence in the community are tokens of reverence to the covenanted presence of God, who has chosen the community for Himself. They are not given to individuals as such, by reason of any gifts they may possess, nor are they withheld because such gifts may be fancied to be wanting. All reverence is due to the presence of God. So the title 'Reverend' was primarily and specially an attribute of Religious Orders, not of the clergy at large. It was given with a view to the special acknowledgement of the conscious, recollected presence of God in a dedicated person, whose presence, wheresoever he went, should recall the thoughts of the presence of God. They thus were given up to this remembrance; and others were to remember it when they saw it. So indeed the Religious ought to be a witness to the divine life wheresoever he goes in the world. *Acts of reverence towards one another are given as to those dedicated to the recollection of God.*

'*Recollectedness of demeanour must be carefully cherished when out walking, but there must be no appearance of gloom. The whole deportment should be consistent with the reverent joy of communion with God, in which the Religious is constantly invited to dwell. Let this interior Religious spirit be carefully cherished, and the exterior Religious demeanour will easily be preserved.*'

Our external demeanour must bear witness to the joy of communion with God.

People must not think that the Religious life is a gloomy, sad one. No, they must see the joy of God depicted on our very countenances. If the heart is habitually living in the joy of God, the joy of God will form a halo round about the whole nature. We must then take great care that we are witnesses to the life of God in all its sacredness and in all its joy. If we are so, we shall indeed experience the fullness of joy in our own selves, and our life will be more and more hallowed, strengthened, perfected by the presence of Him whom we are thus careful to remember in all our ways.

'Haste and noise must always be avoided. In moving about the house and at meals much pains should be taken to be as quiet as possible.'

Haste destructive of the Religious spirit.

Care in this respect springs from, and develops, gentleness of spirit. If the mind is well under control, if there is real self-forgetfulness, if we are mindful of what we are, we shall be sure to do everything with that quietness, stillness, and composure which so eminently belongs to the Religious. We must not even let activity bring us into haste. Although our minds may have much to occupy them, we must take care that that which occupies them never destroys the occupant, that is to say, never makes us lose our self-possession. We must be ourselves the inner occupants of our consciousness, and hold all that we have to do thoroughly in control, so that the variety of things to which we may have to turn may never involve our mind in confusion, nor our outer demeanour in disorder. We should be careful that all our actions are done with real steadiness.

We have to learn—it takes a lifetime to learn—really to control our impulses. We have to learn to act, not upon impulse, but with steadfastness and regularity, and we shall be greatly helped in this by being watchful in this steadfastness of demeanour. Sudden impulses carry us away hither and thither by fits and starts, but if we are acting really and truly in the illumination of the highest reason—that is, reason sanctified by the power of the Spirit of God—then we shall always be doing that which we have to do at its own proper time, giving to each thing its own proper measure of time. We may even destroy that which we have to do by just cutting it a little short; an interview upon some religious matter may often lose its value, a courtesy may altogether fail of being recognized as such by reason of some little hastiness. We ought to be seen to be really occupied about that which we are doing, as really occupied by it as if we had nothing else to do. If speaking with others, we should be as if we were wholly at their disposal, not betraying to them that we are in haste to be off. The Religious will act, not by natural impulse, but in the power of the Spirit.

In moving about the house all ought to be as quiet as possible, not only with silence of the voice, but there should be as little noise as possible. This is a part of the reverence which we owe to a Religious house, a reverence to the presence of God as having claimed the Religious house for Himself. We know how the footstep is hushed in the chamber of death, and if we are dead in this The stillness of a Religious house.

Religious house there should be the hushing of the other actions in homage to the inner and hidden world to which we live. A death in a house seems to put the house in immediate communication with the hidden and higher world, but not so truly as our Religious vows put our house; for ours is an habitual deadness to the world in order that we may live unto God.

The overshadowing cloud of God's presence.
So our mode of going about in the house should make us feel that it is not our own home. It is God's home, in which God is to be reverenced. It is to us the home in which our Father's presence is to be manifested to us. In returning to our home, we are to think of coming under that overshadowing cloud. As the pillar of the cloud in the wilderness spread itself like a tall palm-tree, and overshadowed the camp of the Israelites, and softened the glare of the eastern sun, so we ought to feel the shadow of the divine cloud resting upon our house, and our actions ought to be tranquillized, solemnized, sanctified, in accordance with this presence (cf. *Exod.* xiii. 21, 22, and xl. 36 ff.).

All the work of the house thus becomes sanctified.
So also in doing the menial work of the house, it ought to be done not as a mere matter of discipline as a menial work, but in the thought of the divine glory sanctifying the whole place. And at meals, we must take care to observe quietness both in the manner of eating, and with the furniture of the table, glasses, plates, knives, forks; taking care that all are moved in quietness and regularity. It is this habitual care which expresses the reverent habit of the soul, and which also tends to impress that reverence upon the soul.

'*In chapel there should be devotional composure, and any obtrusive exaggeration of voice and gesture should be avoided. All should kneel upright, and abstain from leaning back when seated at office.*'

All should endeavour to observe the same posture during prayers in chapel, kneeling upright, either without support, or with the wrists resting upon the book-board, and with the palms of the hands straight, not resting upon the elbows, nor turning to the east, nor prostrating themselves. All should sit upright without leaning back. By observing this rule we shall become as much as possible assimilated to one another in our manner of worship. 'There is one body, and one Spirit' (*Eph.* iv. 4) ; so there should be one composure of body. Anything that marks strong individual feeling is at variance with the true sympathetic devotion of a community. Any peculiarity of individual devotion breaks us up into chaos. As the individual becomes developed, the community is lost sight of. We see this exemplified in the very external characteristics of some nations. How the great nations of the East, generation after generation, have remained the same, with so little individuality in them: we see how the very countenance of all seems to be one and the same. Whereas in Europe with its manifold individualities we have the variety of forms and expressions, and characters, and countenances, and bodily configuration. But in a Religious community we ought to be gathered back into the oneness of the Body of Christ.

We are not to think that the absence of in-

[margin: The sense of the corporate life of the Society will check individuality in the manner of our worship.]

Individuality of devotion will be developed by this care for corporate unity. dividuality of demeanour will at all destroy individuality of devotion. It will be quite the reverse. The more individuality of external devotion is repressed, in order that we may conform ourselves to the general bearing of the Society, the more intense will be the effort of the soul in its devotional approach to God. By repression we do not destroy but deepen the real energies of the soul. Superficial devotion puts itself forth in various outcries, groans, distortions of the body; but intense, habitual, abiding devotion, a real absorption of the soul into the fellowship of the eternal life, on the contrary gathers up all the energies of the soul in one, and the individualities of bodily expression will be checked.

'In speaking to strangers there must be cheerfulness and courtesy, and all appearance of haste or annoyance must be carefully eschewed.'

Interruptions do not hinder our work for God. They become part of it. I have already referred to this in speaking of courtesy. Upon many occasions no doubt the visit of a stranger will be an annoyance, an interruption. It will seem that we are hindered in something much higher. But if we are careful to give ourselves to this act of courtesy, as an act of divine love, then at once we raise it up to a proportionate dignity. Then it becomes an act of greater spiritual import than whatever it may be that we give up for it. It may be a small act of courtesy, but we should, as it were, let it be placed upon the stepping-stone of our previous engagement. We have not to step down from the work of Christ to attend to it, as a trifle; rather let it be put upon the platform of the work of Christ. Then whatever it be that we are obliged to suspend in order to pay this act of courtesy, it will be an elevating power, and instead of losing we shall gain.

We must always show this cheerfulness, whatever may be our work at the time, or our own state at the time. We must be careful not to let any spiritual depression, or parochial anxiety, betray itself in our outward demeanour. We are dead to the world, and we must meet all those with whom we have to do with the brightness of the life of God. It is important that all who see us should see us to be living in the joy of the divine life; not merely that we have given ourselves up to God, but that that life is a real delight, joy, pleasure, gladness, brightness to us. So they will come to apprehend its reality. If they see us to be in any way gloomy or unnatural, then they will think we are given up to a mere ideal; but if they see that there is indeed a brightness to our life such as they do not find amid the excitements and pleasures of the world, then they come to learn that our life has a reality; they will know its reality by seeing its result. *Cheerful courtesy must reflect the joy of our life in God, independently of our passing dispositions.*

If, however, visitors or others want to speak with us, we must be very careful to let the conversation be as brief as possible, to check them in the frequency of their coming if they come too frequently, and to take care that the conversation is really on a matter of business. Talk on matters of business is very apt to degenerate into talk, not matter of business at all. We must be careful to *In conversation with externs who seek our help we should be mindful of our true life.*

R

check all such conversation, as far is it can be done with courtesy and charity. But we must be careful never to get into a mere short, snubbing manner, as if we had no regard for people's interests, but to speak to them as having the mind thoroughly absorbed in higher occupations, and therefore not becoming distracted, or separated, from the higher life by converse with them.

The danger of respect of persons.
And we must take care not to indulge ourselves in worldliness, that is to say, in any respect of persons, in finding pleasure in speaking with this or that person in the world because of their station. We are separated from the world. We must be very careful not to let the world come back again into our hearts. It is very apt to do so, perhaps all the more because of our separation from the world. When we see few persons, we think more of some person who has some little distinction than we should if we were living in the full throng of society. If we were seeing a vast number, and a variety, of persons from day to day, the thought and name of one would blot out the thought and name of the other; but the tendency of the Religious life is just to exaggerate any little importance of earthly distinction, because these matters stand out upon the dead level of its ordinary existence.

'*When strangers are in the house, and either through ignorance or carelessness lead to a violation of any rule, as that of silence, they may be courteously attended to ; and when the necessary attention has been shown, they must be reminded of the rule, if necessary.*'

We are not to think of them as having committed a breach of Rule, but we are to be careful to let them know what our own Rule is. And all must be done with courtesy. It must be felt that our Rule has all the elasticity of life about it; that it is not a mere matter of dull routine, unfitting us for intercourse with the world, but elastic, filled with life, and therefore giving us a greater capacity for dealing with all sorts of persons round about. The Religious is separated from all in order that he may be identified with all. He is separated from all, but he is gathered into the heart of Jesus Christ which encloses all. Living in the heart of Jesus, he must find all worldly associations transfigured, glorified. It is a far greater thing to regard any one as a soul, a brother or sister 'for whom Christ died' (1 *Cor.* viii. 11), than as distinguished by any characteristic of mere outward life.

Courtesy and charity must rule our attitude towards visitors in the house.

'In all companies the brethren shall be as unobtrusive as possible, and unless called upon to speak in the interests of religion, they shall remember that silence is the best preservative of the religious spirit.'

We are not to be anxious, if in company, to shine by brilliancy of conversation, or by display of learning, or wit, or eloquence. We are to remember that our Religious life is death, and in whatsoever company we are, the deadness of our outer life should be perceptible, and the glory of our inner life should be manifested. We should never seem, in society, as if we had any rights, as if we were slighted by any want of attention, or

In society we are to be mindful that we have died to the world.

as if we were looking to receive any attention. We are there, as though we were dead to all these things; not there for the purpose of helping forward the natural brilliancy of society.

We are to shed abroad the light and joy of the Holy Ghost..

But we are there for the purpose of not only having within ourselves, but shedding round about us, a holy joy. And so it should be felt, not merely that we are shut out from some of the ordinary pursuits of the natural man, but that we are indeed filled with the better gifts of the Holy Ghost. The power of the Holy Ghost ought to be perceptible in what we say, or do. And it will be so, if we are really living in that power. We cannot of course show forth the Holy Ghost by any effort of our own. We might as well attempt to make a dull day bright. We cannot make the sun shine; and so, we cannot bring the Holy Ghost into prominence in our conversation. But if we are walking in the light of the sun, then the surface of our body is warmed with the heat thereof; and if we are walking in the light of the Holy Ghost, then our inmost soul will be warmed. We cannot do this, except by living in that fellowship.

When called upon to speak, we must speak as those who are living continually in the fellowship of Jesus Christ.

We are, then, to seek in all ways we can to commend our Religion, our faith, our vocation. If we are called upon to speak, then we should speak with all the ease, and forethought, and wisdom, natural as well as supernatural, which may be needed. We are not to be anxious to speak, but when we do speak, we must be careful that what we do say is really worth the saying. We must speak not for the purpose of exhibiting ourselves, but for the purpose of winning others to Christ. We are to remember that at times, if through silence we lose a certain estimation of learning or brilliance or whatever it may be, yet we gain much more; and if we are accustoming ourselves to silence, out of love to God, we gain these gifts of the Holy Ghost, and we shall find that, when speech is necessary for us, the same blessed Spirit will help us to speak. How does conversation frequently undo the public and authorized teaching of the preacher! We speak in one way in the pulpit, in another way in society. People see that our private life is our real self; we must take care that our private life is really absorbed in the power of the Holy Ghost. Then our demeanour, our behaviour, our conversation, will all show that we are living in the continual fellowship of Jesus Christ.

NOTE P

'*I never went out among men without feeling myself to return less of a man than I was before.*'

These words, occurring in the *Imitation of Christ*, appear to be adapted, or loosely quoted, from one of the letters of Seneca the Stoic, who lived at the beginning of the Christian era. See the note in the translation by Dr. Bigg, published by Methuen, p.76: '*Avarior redeo, ambitiosior, luxuriosior, immo vero crudelior et inhumanior, quia inter homines fui.*'

CHAPTER XXII

OF SPIRITUAL INSTRUCTION

THE WITNESS OF A RELIGIOUS COMMUNITY IN THE CHURCH

A Religious community exists to be a means of spiritual instruction to the Church.

WE must remember that we live as a Religious community in the Church of God, not merely for our own sakes, but for the sake of others. Our Society ought to be one of the great principles and powers of spiritual instruction to the Church at large. And this it is to be, not by any special natural gifts of individuals among us, for we do not want a community for the purpose of exercising such gifts, but because we are a spiritual community, gathered round about the Incarnate Word of God for the participation of the spiritual life, so that He may speak through us as a body, and through each individual among us as belonging to that body. So, however wanting we may be in any gifts, however obscure in any position, however little called to take part in any of the controversies of the Church, nevertheless our very life may be an instrument of divine truth. 'Grace and truth came by Jesus Christ' (*St. John* i. 17). They did not come upon Him at His baptism; they were enshrined within Him in the silent years of His infancy; and we must seek to recognize our own calling as depositories of that grace and truth which are come by Jesus Christ.

We are called into the spiritual fellowship of the Incarnate Word, in order that He may use us as His supernatural organs. He has His various forms of self-revelation to the world. He has the sacraments, by which He communicates grace. He has a priesthood, which has the call to the exercise also of the prophetic office by which He would appeal to the human intellect. But He calls us as a Religious community to enshrine within ourselves certain spiritual affections, in order that in the manifestation of those affections by which we live He may influence men's hearts. He does influence mankind by the various external operations of the Holy Ghost, but He calls a Religious community into existence to be, as it were, a visible manifestation of that supernatural, affectionate life.

<small>The influence of a Religious community rests on the spiritual life enshrined within it.</small>

Some communities have been known for their intellect, but intellect without love is of little value. Others may have comparatively little intellect to distinguish their annals, and yet may have been among the most powerful instruments for the conversion of souls to God. It is for us, living as we do in an intellectual age, to cultivate the intellect; but as a spiritual body we must take care that we cultivate intellect, after all, only as one of the forms of divine charity. We must see that we approach all intellectual matters, and all those various subjects which strike upon our ears from day to day, not with the mere eagerness of the natural understanding, so prone to shipwreck

<small>The intellect must be cultivated, as one of the forms of divine charity.</small>

itself in individuality, heresy, and pride, but in the full power of divine love, loving Him whom the world hates, and loving the world with an intense longing to bring it also to share in the same knowledge which we possess, that it may love by that same power of the Holy Ghost by which we are drawn to love God.

A Religious community, like the primitive Church, must exhibit to the world the love of God.

A Religious community, therefore, is called out of the world to do a very special work in the world, as enshrining various energies of divine love. It was so with the whole Christian body in the earliest days. What was it, by which the world was converted to the faith of Christ? It was not the great intellect which was ranged upon the side of the Church; the Church was rather ranged against the great intellect of the day, than acknowledged as the head of it. It was not the great writers and apologists of the Church who really won the victories of the Church. It was the divine life of holy love which was the instructing power to the world; and it was an instructing power which none could gainsay nor resist. Hatred may invent arguments by which to overcloud the clearest enunciations of truth, but hatred can only make itself more visibly hateful by putting itself in opposition to divine love. It is the life of love, in which we are called to live with God, which exhibits the Incarnate Son of God to the world. It is this which must overpower the world. It is this which is invincible.

The truth of God, as it passes through the human intellect, always gathers some of the weakness of the instrument through which it passes. Though its own inherent life remains eternal, yet it is liable to a continual discomfiture; it seems to be overthrown by powers much weaker than itself. But love is an energy which nothing can possibly overcome; the more it is opposed, the more it triumphs; the more it is opposed, the more it asserts its own imperishable life. As our Lord Jesus Christ wasted away with fasting in the wilderness, exhibiting by that very wasting of hunger the immortality of being which belonged to Him, so the powers of divine love, working in the faithful, show themselves all the greater in proportion as they exist in circumstances which seem to render them impossible. Give us such circumstances, in which no human heart can love, and then let it be seen that our love is truly divine. This is that witness against the world which the Church of the early days bore, and which as a Religious community we are specially called to bear in these days. We are to remember, then, that our life is indeed a life of power, a life of witness. *The truth of God is established by the witness of divine love prevailing in our hearts.*

And if we do live in this holy love, if we live in consciousness of the responsibility of making the life of Christ manifest to the world, it will indeed enable us to carry on many a work of instruction. It is one thing to argue, it is another thing to instruct. Argument may supply external information; but there is no spiritual instruction without the conveyance, the communication, of the holy, life-giving, truth-speaking Spirit. No man can be instructed in the things of God, except by *Instruction is the work of the Holy Ghost revealing the things of God, and speaking through us as we abide in His fellowship.*

coming under the power of the Holy Ghost. Flesh and blood cannot reveal the things of God, but the Spirit of our Father who is in heaven (cf. *St. Matt.* xvi. 17). So it is by having our whole being filled with this power of divine love that we must take care to instruct in the faith. Our whole life must partake of this character, and our acts of teaching, in whatever way we may be called to teach, must never sink from the fellowship of this blessed Spirit. Whether it be the teaching given in missions or retreats, or the quieter teaching of the school or the class, or of the individual catechumen, or of any child who may be coming to us—in whatever way we may have to instruct, we must always approach our work in the Spirit of divine love. We constantly repeat our *Veni Creator* before our own meditations, but we must remember that we need that He, who comes to us to teach us to meditate upon divine truth, should abide with us, and anoint our words. Otherwise they will be altogether wanting in any real power to persuade, to convert, to animate those whom we teach.

The Holy Ghost a fire, which alone can purify or soften the natural heart.

How great a gift it is—this utterance of the Holy Ghost which is thus given to us in the fellowship of the life of Christ—really to approach individual souls in the fullness of this divine love! Often, no doubt, we have experienced the great barrier there has been between us and some whom we have been teaching, barriers of various degrees of stolidity, of incapacity, of want of interest. We probably know that there are certain prejudices working strongly to keep back from us those to whom we are speaking, so that our words fall upon unwilling ears, and can gain no admission. Well, we must remember that this power of the Holy Ghost is a power which is superior to all of these impediments. The power of the Holy Ghost is a supernatural illuminating power, which does not need clearness of the natural intellect in order to receive it, but purifies the heart, so that it may receive the truth. And as it purifies the heart from the darkness of ignorant abasement, so it purifies the heart from the greater darkness of stubborn prejudice. We must remember that we are given up to live in the life of God by the special call of the Holy Ghost, as members of a Religious community, and that therefore the Holy Ghost has pledged Himself to work along with us, and burn the way before us, so that there is no power which ought not to yield to His influence.

Thus, then, let us seek to recognize the power of the supernatural life which we seek to cherish in a Religious community. Let us always remember this power in order that we may act in it, in the various ministrations which we have to perform, whether as priests or laymen; whether it be upon what men call some important occasion, or whether it be in some very simple act of daily life. Let us be careful always to be not merely intellectual teachers, but spiritual instructors in Christ. How often is it found, that persons of comparatively little education effect much more in the way of overcoming prejudices, and winning souls to Christ, than persons of much greater gifts!

On all occasions we must act in this supernatural power.

And why? It is because of this power of the Holy Ghost.

The active presence of Jesus is pledged to us.
Oh, let us consider well how great our power ought to be, if we are really seeking to cherish this gift, as a Religious community. 'Where two or three are gathered together in my name, there am I in the midst of them' (*St. Matt.* xviii. 20). And for whatever purpose we are gathered together, for that purpose our Lord Jesus Christ comes to be in the midst of us, and with a special advent. He comes with a special power of His Holy Spirit to sustain, to illuminate, to enkindle the life of each member of a Religious community.

We must act in the power of the grace of the community of which we are partakers.
We ought, then, not merely to think of what we owe to a Religious community, but of what we derive from it. We owe to our community, and to the vows that we have made, that we will do all we can; but we must remember what we have received as belonging to a Religious community, and we must do that which we have to do, and accomplish what our vows involve, in the power of that community grace which we have received. However we may be isolated, though we may be in some distant country all alone, yet we ought to feel the power of this grace of community, setting us there to be indeed the instructors of those hearts in the gifts of the Holy Ghost.

The duty of witness to the world of the divine life and gifts that we have received.
Seek then, dear brethren, seek to dwell upon this great work which comes to us, to witness to the world. We are to be witnesses to all, whether they are willing to receive us or no, witnesses of a power which they cannot understand, witnesses

whom they seek to resist, but whom they cannot stay or check. No external pressure of the world can really find its way into the being of a Religious community without its consent. The external operations of the Church may be very much hampered by various external circumstances, but the life of a Religious community, in the simple cherishing of the gifts of the Holy Ghost, is a life gathered into the very being of God. God gathers us thus into Himself in order that, when He has replenished us with His gifts, He may, as it were, project us into the world, and make manifest what He is by what He has done for us. 'I will tell you what he hath done for my soul' (*Ps.* lxvi. 16). This is the saying of the ancient Psalmist; and this must indeed be the continual saying of the Religious community. 'God is in the midst of her, therefore shall she not be moved; God shall help her, and that right early' (*Ps.* xlvi. 5). God has put His Spirit upon us, in order that we may accomplish His will.

We must see, then, that we are really living in this fellowship of God, waiting for God's opportunities, knowing that He will call us to speak, whenever He pleases. We are not to think we can gain these gifts of God and exercise them when and where we will. We must be waiting upon God. The ancient prophet went to ask God where he should go, went again and again (cf. *Num.* xxii. 8, 19). But it is not for us thus to force God. If we will yield ourselves up to the influence of His Holy Spirit, He will Himself suggest, as well as control, that which we do at His bidding.

<small>We must wait upon God for His guidance and control.</small>

When He Himself has suggested it, we shall do it in a manner worthy of Himself; but when He holds us back, we are to remember that He is holding us back in order that He may fit us for, and fill us with, fuller gifts.

<small>While we wait upon God, we must wait with God.</small>
And so we are never to think that we are impeded by any times of waiting, or of hindrance, or of setting aside. We must never think that it seems impossible that we should ever be able to carry out God's work because it may be impossible at the present moment, or for many years. The years St. Paul spent in prison were no impediment to his missionary work. On the contrary, God was filling him with graces for the time of action. So must we also remember, 'The word of God is not bound' (2 *Tim.* ii. 9). If we are really to instruct the world in the word of God, we must be living in the power of that divine word, and we must understand that there is no external power that can possibly hinder us, that can possibly bind us. The world may at times seem to hold us back, but in due time the world's grasp will be relaxed, and the intensity of the power of God will be shown. It matters not though we be kept at times hidden from the world for many years. What though we were kept, as our Lord Jesus was, thirty years? It matters not if we are kept back, so long as we are kept back with God. But we must remember that we are at all times to be looking up to Him, as Himself the instructor of all who will be filled with His grace, so that, whensoever we speak, we may speak in His power. 'In a multitude of words there wanteth not sin'

(*Prov.* x. 19), but God can make the fewest words powerful, with the infinite power of His divine love, to effect consequences which shall abide for ever.

So let us realize that we are indeed called into a Religious community to carry on the work of spiritual instruction, but that that work is not at all to be measured by the mere extent of opportunity, nor are we to find any discouragement, if it is thwarted by the impediments of outward necessity. We are to be living ourselves in fellowship with Him, who is the incarnate truth; and He who comes to dwell in us will make Himself manifest in our lives in such a way as He pleases. Our society will thus indeed be a witness to the eternal truth of God; and in its witness all of us are called to share. Yes, we must remember that we are all of us called to share in it, and if we are not ourselves careful to be living in the eternal truth of God, and in the joy of being taught of God, then it is not merely that we, as individuals, fail of the privilege and the power which we might have possessed, but we injure the community to which we belong. We are 'many members, yet but one body,' and all of us 'members one of another' (1 *Cor.* xii. 20, and *Eph.* iv. 25). We have each one to contribute our portion to the glory of the community, whether as priests or as lay brothers; we have each of us to help forward the community by the spirituality of a life 'hidden with Christ in God' (*Col.* iii. 3); or else, whether as priests or as lay brothers, we cause a spot to be

The effectiveness of our witness, not dependent on earthly opportunity, but on the truth of our fellowship with God individually.

on the surface of that which ought to be bright, and we paralyse the action of the Holy Spirit of God.

The failure of one may injure the witness of the whole Society

You know how it was when the Children of Israel went up against Ai. It was one of no great importance or station who treasured up some little thing of earth within his tent, yet the whole army of Israel suffered thereby. So any little worldliness, any little selfishness, any little pride, any little irritability of temper, or the like, may just be the thing that holds back a Religious community from carrying out the work of God. God cannot work by a community unless the whole community is, as it were, in a state of spiritual instruction in the fire of the Holy Ghost. Any one of us remaining cold or worldly, although we may fancy no one will know it but our own self, or may fancy that it does not matter after all what we are, because we are so insignificant and so separate from the spiritual life of the community that after all we might as well not be there, and that it cannot therefore matter whether we are what we are or not—although it may seem to be so to us, nevertheless we must remember that we do thus hold back the work of God, God's witness, that witness which He would have this community give, unless we are in our inmost beings and with the whole integrity of our nature, and in heart and action, yielding ourselves up to the transforming power of the illuminating Spirit. It does not matter whether we have this or that natural gift, but, if we do retain this or that natural temper, we hinder the supernatural manifestation of the work of the Holy Ghost.

Let us then consider the greatness of our calling as a Religious community, a greatness which is even in one sense proportionate to our insignificance. For a Religious community may in one sense be doing a great work for God, that is, it may be a great and influential community even though it have but little spiritual life, and its work may be a great work, with great results; yet it is probable that it will be manifested in those results that there is an absence of spiritual life. We see such communities at work in Christendom. But we are very small, and very insignificant, and our whole being is just in the greatness of our spiritual gifts, otherwise we are nothing. But our insignificance does not really impede the greatness of spiritual gifts, if we really look for them. So, then, let us take care that whatever we touch, we touch with the finger of the fire, of the power, of the Holy Ghost. Let us, if we are as insignificant as a spark, be powerful with that which makes a spark powerful, a capacity of kindling whatsoever it touches, and of multiplying with the force which it contains within itself. Let it be manifested that our life is not merely a spark of human kindling, but a spark of divine fire which the deluge of the world's storms cannot extinguish, and that it is capable, according to the fullness of divine love, of spreading itself far and wide in the energies of that life from whence it originated.

Our insignificance no hindrance to the fire of the Holy Spirit kindling all around us.

O blessed Spirit of divine love, teach Thou our hearts, and enable us to teach others also. Kindle our hearts, that we may kindle others also; and

A prayer to the Holy Spirit.

in whatever way Thou callest us to have dealings with the world around, grant that we may never approach any in the mere coldness of earthly nature, but that we may indeed in every action make manifest the fire of Thy divine presence, and find the blessedness of Thy holy fellowship.

CHAPTER XXIII

OF SPIRITUAL INSTRUCTION

WITH ESPECIAL REFERENCE TO THE STUDY OF
HOLY SCRIPTURE

WE have to consider this subject both with reference to our own selves, and with reference to our work, the instruction to be obtained by our own selves, and the instruction to be given to others.   *The double character of our study of Holy Scripture.*

We must remember that as Religious priests we are set apart on behalf of the Church of God. We do not live for ourselves, or for our own salvation, or for the glorification of God in ourselves; but we live both as individuals and as a community— as individuals by reason of the grace of the community, and as a community by reason of the diligence of individuals—to be centres of a spiritual light and intelligence for the Church of God. The Church has our Universities for the cultivation of theological learning,[1] but a Religious community has something more than this to do. We have not merely to acquire, to accumulate, and to communicate theological learning, but theological intuitions, the wisdom of the Spirit,   *Set apart for the instruction of the Church, we must learn the wisdom of God.*

[1] There was more truth in this when it was said, about the year 1874, than there is under present conditions of theological teaching in the Universities.

that wisdom of which St. Paul speaks as 'speaking wisdom among them that are perfect' (1 *Cor.* ii. 6); that wisdom which cannot be known by the natural heart, and which is not found in the schools of learning; which takes all learning into itself, and yet in one sense needs it not; that wisdom which rises above all learning, and quickens all other learning with a power that learning in itself cannot possess.

<small>We must gain the knowledge of wisdom as St. John gained it, by abiding in the fellowship of the Incarnate Word.</small>

It is the duty of a Religious community to be really set apart for theology as a life, to live in the wisdom of the Incarnate Word; and all our acts, being done in the power of union with Him, should develop the brightness of the light of heaven. Especially is this incumbent upon us by reason of our dedication. He who reposed upon the bosom of Jesus at the Last Supper is essentially the divine of the Church; and we must have that light living on in ourselves if we would honour his memory and share in his grace. We must gain that knowledge even as he gained it, from personal closeness of fellowship with Him in whom all wisdom resides. Our whole life must thus be a real drinking from the fountain of eternal wisdom, that so we may know divine truth in all the fullness of its own spiritual power.

<small>The truth thus becomes a principle of life, and lifts us above controversy into the higher intuitions of faith.</small>

We must, then, be careful about our own spiritual instruction; careful that we are indeed instructed in the mysteries of God, instructed, informed by the fullness of the truth, instructed with the fullness of substantial truth; having the truth dwelling within us as a real living substance, so that our natural being recognizes truth by a supernatural habit, and faith, corresponding with the divine revelations, seems at last to anticipate them, and becomes a faculty not merely for receiving that which is handed down, or of weighing well that which is contained in the original deposit, but is continually beholding more and more of God in that which it has received. How different is divine truth, grasped by the intuitions of spiritual faith, from what it is in the mere hands of the orthodox controversialist! How does the world fight about that which it has already killed! It is for us not so much to fight with the arms of controversy, as to have the truth fighting for us, and making us free, because it is within us, a power of glorious life (cf. *St. John* viii. 31, 32); enabling us thus to rise above the region of the world's controversy, as we gaze upon the Lord of love. So must we seek to have ourselves really instructed in the mysteries of God by the power of the Holy Ghost. There must be this continual seeking after the power of the Holy Ghost to teach us; and we must seek with confidence that we shall not seek in vain.

We must, therefore, be very careful to become thoroughly imbued with the principles of spiritual instruction. As we read the early Fathers, we see how their minds were filled with certain principles of spiritual instruction, principles which guided them at once to a conclusion. In reading passages of Holy Scripture, they needed not to inquire what was the mystical interpretation which had been set upon them by those who had lived

The principles of the mystical interpretation of Holy Scripture carried forward, on a higher level, the teaching of the Prophets.

before; the laws of this spiritual instruction guided them at once, so that they could reach the same conclusions in the power of the same Spirit. And thus, in effect, they were only carrying on what had existed before Christ came, although before Christ came it had been little more than a mere natural faculty. The schools of the prophets were schools of spiritual instruction by which the laws of the divine utterance were recognized, and in which those who were duly trained came to the apprehension of hidden verities which lay underneath the symbols in which God delighted to speak. And these schools of the prophets, all that prophetic intuition which belonged to the old Covenant—we are not to think that it has passed away; rather, the half-awakened eye of the old Covenant gazes now with a clearer vision upon the glory that is revealed in the new. Yes, we are to recognize this prophetic power as underlying all the true teaching of the Church, so that any teaching which has not this prophetic power is really wanting in one of the great elements of Christian teaching. Our preaching must not be with the mere words of human argument, but must be the utterance of hearts and intelligences duly awakened, and quickened with the fullness of spiritual truth.

We must know the truth as a living power by the Spirit, and become identified with it.

It is for us, then, to be very careful to acquire a familiarity with the principles of the spiritual interpretation of Holy Scripture, that so we may be indeed instructed in the things of the Spirit. We cannot know them by our natural faculties (cf. 1 *Cor.* ii. 14). If we attempt to know them by the lower faculties they become crystallized in our hand, and we can no longer deal with them. They even become harmful rather than helpful, because their own tenderness, and fragrance, and gentle influence, has been shut up in the hardness of mere intellectual transmission. We must take care, then, that we are having our own selves really filled with these principles of spiritual instruction, that we are really becoming more and more identified with divine truth.

For here is the great difference between spiritual and intellectual apprehension of the truth. The intellect takes into itself the truth which it is taught, but it does not become one with that truth. It takes that truth into itself rather after the manner of a book, which should have the capacity of uttering the things imprinted on its pages. But spiritual apprehension does not merely receive, recognize, and utter truth; it lives in the truth. And this is what we need to seek, to become really identified with the truth, taken up into the being of God, so as not merely to contemplate Him as an external object, but to behold the glory of the divine life within ourselves. We are to repose upon the bosom of the Incarnate Word, and there we are to be taught the mysteries of God, taught in the fullness of divine sympathy; the truth of God, in a mystery of divine transfusion, being poured into our being until our whole nature is glowing with its glory. This must be the great purpose of our life, to become identified with the truth.

The difference between intellectual and spiritual apprehension of the truth.

> By habits of external reverence, and of interior contemplation, we must delight in the truth, and seek to be conformed to it in our lives.

And while we seek for this by the acts of outer service, so also by the interior acts of spiritual intelligence. We have to bring our outer being into conformity with the truth, and we have to bring our inner being into intellectual conformity with the truth; and the Spirit of God must move both our body and intellect, restraining the body with habits of devout reverence, and inspiring the intelligence with habits of spiritual thought. We must thus repose in the divine truth, and become identified with divine truth; we must breathe the very divine truth, so that the word of God becomes sweeter to us than our necessary food, sweeter than honey unto the throat (cf. *Ps.* cxix. 103). There must be real delight in divine truth—that which is so continually expressed in our cxixth Psalm, which is the utterance of the heart recognizing the glory of being instructed in the law of God as a living power with which it becomes identified, and finding in it the fullness of its joy. We must seek this in all our repetition of the Psalms, in all our study of Holy Scripture, in all the study of the mystery of the sacred language, and in all our theological researches; we must ever be seeking to have our minds filled with this power of divine truth as a principle of supernatural life.

> We must be taught of the Spirit.

We are not to wonder that the world at large does not recognize divine truth; how should it? When we feel a wonder that the world at large does not recognize divine truth, it only shows how little we ourselves appreciate it. For if we did appreciate it, we should know that it is just as impossible for a man born deaf to appreciate the laws of sound, as for the arguments of the natural intellect to bring any one to the acceptance of the truth of God. We must have the ears supernaturally opened; otherwise we cannot hear that voice of God, which only can teach him 'which hath an ear' (*Rev.* ii. 7), by the power of the Spirit. We must seek to be thus ourselves continually instructed more and more in divine truth, in all the fullness of its divine power.

And as this should be the law of all our study of Holy Scripture, and of all our private meditations, so also we must be very careful to avoid all that is not really identified with the truth. We must be very careful to avoid all false sentiments, not thinking that it is possible that the clouds of sentiment should come round the truth as a veil or decoration. They always come to destroy. How much power of divine truth has been destroyed by the mere speculation of the natural intellect, and the mere cloudy sentiment of the natural imagination! We must take care that all the faculties of our souls are kept well under the supreme dominion of the laws of divine truth. Better far is it to see nothing, and to feel nothing, than to see something which seems to fill up what otherwise would be a blank, and seems to solve what otherwise would be a contradiction. We must be very careful to keep ourselves clear of all false speculations and sentimental imagination, in order that we may live in the clear gaze upon divine truth. As the eagle gazes upon the sun,

Merely natural speculation, and sentimental imagination, can only destroy the truth.

so should our eye be fixed upon the divine truth. We must behold the Sun of righteousness in all the fullness of His own simple glory. The clouds of morning and evening may be bright objects for lower souls to dwell upon, but they hide the sun. They shine with rays from it, and they seem often to the soul as if heaven would be blank as they cleared away; but they must clear away, either before the clearness of the noon-day, or else to leave nothing but the dark behind. We must be very careful to keep our speculations upon divine truth, our imaginations, and our religious sentiments, thoroughly under the check of the substantial glory of the Incarnate Word, and the law of divine revelation.

<small>Simplicity in the contemplation of God, as He reveals Himself in the Incarnate Word, will establish us in the truth.</small>
Thus must we accustom ourselves to the austere contemplation of God, as He is pleased to reveal Himself, and to feel quite sure that the more simply we do thus know the truth, the more truly, the more perfectly, the more lovingly we shall know it. Though we may seem at times to forfeit much that is added in various tints of external beauty to divine truth, nevertheless it is for us to realize that the outshining of the divine truth, in its own living splendour, is something far more than any of the gorgeous surroundings which after all only testify to the uprisings of the damp fogs of the earthly nature, and only make manifest a heart which has become to some degree estranged from the simplicity of God. Let us be careful to live in the simplicity of the earliest days, when the brightness of Jesus Christ was quite sufficient to stimulate every energy, and

satisfy every longing of the intellect. Thus let us learn indeed to seek the fullness of spiritual instruction, that we may be ourselves thoroughly instructed in the ways of God, in all the simplicity, in all the brightness, in all the warmth, in all the glory of the divine life of the Incarnate Word.

O blessed Word of God, Thou light who lightest every man that is in the world, shine Thou forth in all Thy glory in our hearts. Enable us to see the fullness of Thy mystery. Open Thou our eyes, that we may indeed gaze upon Thee with steadfastness and devotion. Fix our gaze upon Thee, that we turn not away to any clouds of earth, however bright they may seem to be under the glow of Thy shining. Let the brightness of Thy shining penetrate our inmost being, and so wake the glory of Thy life. Thou hast taken upon Thyself our nature that we may repose in Thy truth, and hast given us Thy divine nature that we may gaze into the mysteries of Thy truth. Thus bind us to Thyself. Grant that we, instructed in the fullness of Thy power, may live and speak according to the perfection of Thy eternal glory. Keep us from the wanderings of a transitory imagination, and bind us to Thyself in the revelation of that eternal truth which has been our only joy during the lapse of earthly years, and shall be the fullness of our joy and glory when we behold Thee, as now we cannot. Grant that every gaze upon Thyself in this our pilgrimage

A prayer for perseverance in the contemplation of the fullness of truth in the Incarnate Word.

may be indeed the anticipation of that which is to be hereafter, and may not be forfeited; but may be a principle of eternal life, whereby we shall in Thine eternity contemplate Thy glory for ever.

CHAPTER XXIV

OF CONVERSATION

THE LAW OF SILENCE AND THE LAW OF SPEECH

'*SILENCE must be strictly observed at all times and in all places where it is enjoined by the rule of the house.*

'*Silence is one of the chief joys of the Religious, and imparts to all his actions strength, tranquillity, and perfection; for in silence the soul holds blessed communion with God, feeds upon the grace of past sacraments, contemplates the true hope of the eternal reward, and rises up to the demands of the divine will, in the joyous correspondence of grateful love.*'

The true life of the Religious is speaking with God. Silence is the habitual law of our outer life. It is but in compliance with the necessities of our present exiled condition that we speak with one another. We live in expectation, we live in anticipation, we live in the earnest desire of the time when all, abiding in the presence of God, shall pour forth their inmost soul in one unceasing utterance of praise to Him. The joy of heaven is to hear the word of God filling our being, and as we live in the power of that word, to utter it, and to breathe it forth back again to Him from whom it comes. The soul glorified in Jesus, the

Silence the habitual law of the Religious, because living in the anticipation of heaven.

body perfected in the life of the resurrection, gazes upon God, and gives itself forth in undivided return to Him.

The joy of heaven is the consciousness of God, shared by all alike.

The joy that binds together the Saints in the blessed community of eternal life is a joy of perfect sympathy, since all are pouring forth their whole being to Him who is the centre of their conceptions, and the common principle of their life. They turn not aside from Him to speak one to another; their whole being is rapt in the thought of Him; and they live in the knowledge of the mutual love which binds them all because that love binds each to Him, and the very power of love whereby each is bound to Him is an undivided power. They live there, not as separate individuals existing according to the law of their own consciousness; but there they have a perfect life as members of one living body, living with one undivided act of life. There they live for ever perfected in one, and their whole being is but the temple of the eternal Word. All their movements are hushed, all their words and thoughts have ceased, everything that is transitory has passed away for ever. Their common consciousness is the changeless and eternal consciousness of God, as the central principle of life; a consciousness eternal, that never can be exhausted, and changeless, for it knows no accident, but in its eternal changelessness ever knowing itself with a freshness of perfect delight; changeless and free from all the novelty of changeful time, changeless in all the perfect freshness of the never-wearing life of God.

And so in a Religious community that which should really bind us together is not the mere accidental interchange of thought, with reference to mere transitory things, but the fixed interchange of the consciousness of divine love, reciprocating the glory of the divine life; each of us having received a vocation from God, and all of us living in the mutual consciousness of the vocation which we have received in common, and which, as it binds us to Him, binds us also one to another. We are not bound together by some external bond wrapped around our being, but we are bound together by the intense power of the attractive principle, which unites us in a common flow of life, because it draws us towards Himself.

The consciousness of a common relation to God binds all the members of a Religious community in one.

So let us realize that unity of life, of consciousness, of love, in which we ought to be bound as a Religious community which in its highest intensity lives in the deepest silence. It is perfected in the gaze of God. It is perfected in the removal of all consciousness of the perishing world. It is perfected in the common joyous anticipation of the life in which we are to take our place among the blessed. The Religious gazes through the grave, and the grave is but the gate of light and life to the Religious soul. There is nothing for him to leave on this side of it. As he himself passes through it, his whole being is already stripped of all that is accidental, of all that belongs to the world; the power of God has taken possession of him, and the grave is but to him an open door through which there is access for him to the

The silence of the Religious, who has passed through the grave of Christ and responded to the voice of God speaking within.

throne of light which he sees beyond. The true and perfect Religious gazes through the open door of the grave, through all the regions of silence which belong to the dumb creation, and hears a voice calling him onward; and feels that voice to be speaking with the lips of his own inner being. He responds to that call, and his onward motion is but his response to it. He gazes through the open door of the grave, and finds himself drawn onward by this mighty attractive power in all calmness, without any jar or jerk, having nothing that needs a shaking off, in all the quietness with which the heavenly bodies move through the vacant regions of space by the silent powers of the material universe. As those powers are the reflection of the utterance, the communication, of the word of God, so by a power which acts upon him in perfect calmness, in perfect equality, in perfect continuity, without jar, or jerk, or break, or cessation, he finds himself drawn onward through the grave to the blessed multitude of the redeemed, and there he finds his place. Needing no preparation, he rises into it, as truly as flame mingles with flame; he is borne onward in the power of the divine life.

Gathered into the being of the Incarnate Word, the glory of God draws him onward in loving response.

And that divine life is not a dead and stationary object, so that as he moves into it he finds the shock of entering into something which is stationary. His life of love is but a progress; and his life in heaven is but the same blessed progress of continual knowledge, and is absorbed into the being of God to behold God more perfectly than he could behold Him here, to hear Him more

OF CONVERSATION 285

perfectly than he could hear Him here, to breathe himself forth to Him more perfectly than here he could respond to the call. So he is taken into the perfect energy of the glorified being of the Incarnate Word of God, and in perfect silence of thrilling joy he becomes aware of the glory of God, as God exists within Himself; he becomes aware of the glory of God, as God in His infinite love makes His bright being to spread around to be the life of all His Saints. Silently he enters into the new thrill of changeless delight; and the soul that has contemplated the progress of the spiritual life, the life of the Religious dead long ago to the world, is gathered onward by stages of divine attraction into the abyss of the heaven of the Saints.

Thus we see how the being of each of the Saints pours itself forth to God, and all are conscious only with the consciousness of God. Accidental things are passed away; they are bound together in one perfect and eternal love, and that love is the knowledge of God.

Knowing God, the Saints are perfected in the love of God, and find therein their delight.

And so, dear brethren, we are in some sort to anticipate this. This is the law of our silence. This is why the Religious life is a life of silence, because it is the anticipation of that final repose of holy energy responding to God. But in this our state of imperfection we need to speak one with another also. Our consciousness is not yet such that we can gaze fully upon God, and gazing upon Him behold all things, and see all hearts, derived from Him and existing in Him; we need to speak one with another. Our nature is not yet per-

Our speech one with another on earth, must be consistent with the calmness of our life towards God.

T

fected in that surrender to God which permits of our having this perfect utterance. We speak one to another, but we must be careful that our words one to another are worthy of this law of divine attraction to which our whole being is subjected. We must take care that our words, applying to the accidents of time, are not at variance with that calm mighty impulse which bears us onward into the joy of eternity.

'*All must be careful that their conversation, whether amongst themselves or with others, shall be of a kind tending habitually to edification.*'

The inspiration of the Spirit will not be lacking, if our lives are true to God.
Our conversation, therefore, needs to be very guarded. It cannot always be truly and properly inspired, but it must always be consistent with the divine inspiration. Oh, that our lives and lips were so true to God, that our words might indeed be constantly uttered with the power of the Holy Ghost giving them life! Would that our lives were so stablished in God, that this divine life might spread itself forth, and communicate itself from one to another with the manifestation of our consciences, and the interchange of our intelligence, and the embrace of our affections! Oh, that all might thus indeed be inspired of God!

Our speech must be consistent with the requirements of the truth, the love, and the glory of God.
It is for us, then, to be careful that nothing is at variance with this. There must be nothing at variance with the divine truth; there must be nothing at variance with the divine love; there must be nothing at variance with the divine glory. Our conversation must be ever consistent with

the divine truth, carefully avoiding all the errors which spring from the blindness of human nature, human poverty, human prejudice, and human ignorance; and consistent with the divine glory, avoiding all that is unseemly, all that is unworthy of the dignity of our position as really pressing onward to God. Would that we could bear in mind that with these lips, with which we speak to one another, we shall be in eternity ever speaking the glories of the Word of God! Would that we could be therefore careful that our conversation may indeed be dignified with the holiness of God! And so with the divine love. Our words must ever be free from earthly bitterness. Oh, how apt we are to think of earthly words as deriving their brightness from the keenness of some natural sentiment, and we forget that those natural sentiments which do so powerfully stir man's being belong to this state of exile, and are thus a part of its misery and sin. We are so prone to forget that all those sharpnesses of language which win the admiration of mankind are just apt to be the very opposites of that pure, calm, self-forgetful love in which the soul of the faithful pours itself forth to God. Our words must be words of mutual love, otherwise they are words which are inconsistent with the inspiration of God.

Whatsoever it be, then, of which we are speaking, it may tend to edification, and it will do so if it is spoken really in harmony with the divine love. It is not merely words of a dogmatic character which tend to the edification of the speaker or the hearer. Our words must always be spoken with

Our words, spoken in the consciousness of God, will tend to edification.

such consciousness of God as their true end that in ourselves in speaking, as well as in those whom we are addressing, they may help forward the consciousness of living in God. No doubt many a word would remain unspoken which perhaps we think to be harmless; but words that are harmless are often very superfluous, very often much at variance with the purity of divine inspiration, and very often they draw the mind down to the mere momentary things of life, without regard to any eternal interests, or any sense of moral duty or perfection.

Our words with one another must spring from our love of God.

It is for us to seek in all the converse of life to build up one another in the life of God, so that it may indeed be felt by all that are present, that we are speaking for the purposes of divine love. All words of interest in transitory things must have their interest with a view to the divine love. We must have a real interest in one another, because God would love us through one another, and because God would be loved by us in one another. Yes, all the slightest words of affection should bear upon themselves the glow, the warmth, of the divine love. And so we must be careful always to speak to edification.

God will speak through us words of edification, if we abide in Him.

And as this will often lead us to silence, so it will often lead us to speech. We shall be watchful not only to see what we must not say, but what it is our duty to say. If we are really careful only to speak in God, and for God, we shall find that God will continually speak by us, so as to help those that are round about. Oftentimes we find ourselves unable to speak words of edification, because we only look into the shallow receptacle of our own minds, and we cannot find there scope enough to get an impulse for the words of divine truth. But if we are really living in the fellowship of God, we may rest assured that God will give an impulse to our words. God is ready to speak by us upon many occasions; yes, upon all occasions we shall find that God is willing to speak by us. Man cannot indeed edify his brother, but God through man builds up the divine life of the Incarnate Son of God in those who thus speak to one another. We may speak words of piety, and words of religion, and they may be merely human words, superficial, perishing; but words that tend to edification are words of life, words which God speaks through us, words which we speak because we are abiding in God. So let us be watchful, dear brethren, to yield ourselves up to God that we may be instruments of His utterance, and speak such words as shall indeed edify.

'*Any matter which would cause unnecessary pain to any person present must always be avoided.*'

As our words are to be the words of divine love, they must bear the impress of divine love upon them. As anger is God's 'strange work' (*Isa.* xxviii. 21), so rebuke is a form of speech strange to the lips of those who live in God. True we may have to speak words of rebuke and censure at times, but we must be careful always to do so in the fullness of divine love. We must take care that they are not the result of human passion, of party spirit, or of any earthly prejudice, and that

In giving rebuke our words must yet spring from divine love.

they do not bear upon themselves any of the tokens of earthly separation, and individual private interest, such as belongs to mankind. We must see that our words are really words of love, full of love to God, and therefore glowing with a blessed power of love from one to the other.

The evil of censoriousness and bitterness of speech.

And as they are to be full of love one to the other, so they must be full of love also to those that are absent. We must be careful to avoid that censoriousness which is so great a characteristic of all modern speech. We must be careful to avoid all unnecessary sharpness, even in speaking of that which is evil. We should tremble, as we speak of that which is evil, with all the tenderness with which we should handle some sore, or painful bodily wound. So it should be a pain to us to speak of another's fault, of whatsoever kind, by whomsoever committed, whatever his position in the world may be.

The restraint of love upon our words will be a sacrifice well-pleasing to God.

Oh, let us take care that our words are really perfected in love! It is very difficult thus to repress our own earthly nature, and to keep ourselves purged from all the violence of earthly passion, and immediate desires, and the conflict of various wills; it is very difficult to keep ourselves purified from all of these, and we often find it one of the hardest forms of self-sacrifice to stop the sharp word which would fall from our lips, and perhaps awaken the laugh, or stir the passion, of those around. But we are to strive to yield our speech a sacrifice to God, and we are to realize the power in such a sacrifice, the blessedness in such a restraint, the acceptableness to Almighty God of such a law of conversation.

So, dear brethren, let us see that our words tend indeed to edification, because we are members of the Body of Christ; and let us see that our words are ever words of love, for nothing but love can come from the lips of Jesus Christ.

<small>We must speak as with the lips of Jesus Christ.</small>

CHAPTER XXV

OF CONVERSATION

THE SANCTITY OF THE GIFT OF SPEECH

Speech the glory of man, as created in the image of God.

WE were considering the importance of reverence and dignity and love in conversation, that all our conversation should bear the impress of the divine life. We should remember that in conversation, in the use of the words of ordinary language, we are exercising the great faculty by which man is in the image of God. The faculty of speech is not the mere upgrowth, the development, of a power found in the lower brute creation and gradually perfecting itself for mankind, but it is the faculty which distinguishes mankind from all other creatures of the animal race, the expression of the mind by which he was formed in the image of God. The organs of other animals may occasionally be trained to imitate the mechanical sound, but as it comes forth from their organs of utterance, the sound which they produce mechanically is no word, because it does not come forth from the inmost mind, by which alone the word has its life. Our words must be living words, coming forth from the living intelligence, coming forth in the fullness of the life of love which belongs to those who are conformed to God. The word must be the expression of wisdom in the power of love, as the Word of God is the wisdom of the Father coming forth in the power of the Holy Ghost.

We should constantly dwell upon the sacredness of this gift of speech by which man is formed in the image of God, and by which we as Mission Priests are specially called to carry out the work of God. We have not merely to transmit an accumulated store of information for other generations to deal with; the word of our ministry is a word of life—a word not about life alone but the word that gives life. 'If any man speak, let him speak as the oracles of God' (1 *St. Pet.* iv. 11). How we should consider the sacredness of that gift of speech, by which the word of God comes forth from our lips to do a greater work than of old, when the rays of the sun were made first of all to spread the external light through the darkness in which our earth was enveloped! We have to speak the word, and say, 'Let there be light' (*Gen.* i. 3), by which the power of the Sun of righteousness shall make His light to shine within the darkness of the naturally fallen soul. If we would consider the sacredness of this gift of speech, we should learn indeed how sparingly it should be exercised, how cautiously it should be kept free from all that is unworthy of its divine application.

The life-giving word of God coming forth from our lips.

How reverently do we treat those objects which are in use upon the altar, but of all these there is none so sacred as the lips of the priest, by which the sacrifice is constituted and offered. The lips of the priest should indeed, therefore, 'keep know-

As the vessels of the altar are holy, so much more the lips of the priest, by which the sacred mysteries are consecrated.

ledge' (*Mal.* ii. 7), since from the lips of the priest comes forth the very Wisdom of God, to be the sacrifice in the sanctuary of the Christian Church. We should be very watchful to remember that we always do carry about with us this instrument of the altar. And it never can be anything else but the instrument of the altar, and that of the highest altar—not merely as the paten and the chalice associated with the external oblation, but itself the very link between that which is external, which is of earth, and that which is spiritual and divine. Whatever society we go into, whatever we may have to speak about, we cannot take other lips to speak of earthly things. We must speak with those lips with which we utter the words of consecration; as St. James says, 'Therewith bless we God, even the Father; and therewith curse we men, which are made after the similitude of God' (*St. Jas.* iii. 9).

As we guard our lips, the more the sanctity of our inner life is preserved.
If all Christians are to be watchful in the use of speech, because of its sacredness in approaching to God, much more must we, whose lips are, so to speak, the common property of the whole community, so that the Christian Church, the Body of Christ, approaches God and is nourished, and God approaches His people, through our lips. We cannot dwell too much upon this, for the more carefully we watch this organ of utterance, remembering its sacred character, the more we shall indeed find that it is the link between ourselves and God. The more we allow our lips to be profaned by common things, the more our inner life loses its sanctity. If, then, we will cherish the

faculty of speech as a thing thus solemnly sacred, we shall not become gloomy in our unworldliness, but we shall indeed retire from the world into the blessed stillness, tranquillity, peace, love, and joy which characterize the heavenly life.

The word that comes forth from our lips is after all only the utterance of that which is already found within the heart, and that which is repressed does not cease to be. If we are careful of our lips we shall be careful of our thoughts, for the thought is the yet unspoken word. The thought is the reproduction of the true self, becoming conscious of its own essence, whether in its purity or in its vileness. The unspoken word is within, in the heart; and though the lips be the outward register of thought, yet the thought is the inward substance of the life. Our thought is of one substance with ourselves, even as the eternal Wisdom of the Father is of one substance with the Father. As far as our imperfections serve to portray the expression of that spiritual invisible glory wherein God dwells, so do our thoughts testify to our truth.[1] *As our thoughts are, so are we; and as we think, we speak.*

We must, then, be watchful over our outer words, and over our inner thoughts; and the watchfulness over the one will tend to make us watchful over the other. We are not to think that the thought of evil is evil, because it strikes upon the ear, but remember that the utterance of the evil is God's special provision to make us watchful against its production in the soul. God makes us shudder at our thoughts, by making us *Our words and our thoughts react on one another.*

[1] See Note Q at the end of the chapter.

> It is God's good pleasure that through man's lips the oblation of Christ should be made before Him.

shudder at the words. We must, therefore, be careful to recognize the sanctity of speech because our lips are instruments of the altar, and because our outer words show what those hearts are which we are bringing near to God. By our lips God speaks to the people in words of admonition, and with words of mysterious power for consecration. He would have us purify ourselves, as far as is in our power, so that we may be worthy of taking part in the oblation.

> The Religious priest is set apart specially to be mindful of this mystery of divine action.

It is for us, dear brethren, to remember how specially we are pledged to this as being Religious. For what is our Religious profession, if we are not to be constantly contemplating the mystery of that divine life in which we have to live before God? Many are the people of the world, many are the secular priests, who in the activity of outer life have scarcely time or opportunity to turn within themselves and consider the greatness of the work in which they are engaged. But God calls us apart from the world in order that we may consider, in order that we may 'see this great sight' (*Exod.* iii. 3), a sight not external to ourselves, but a mighty result of creative power coming forth through our own organs. We must consider well what is due to that special acknowledgement of our divine calling which our Religious vows indicate. We are not to think that we are to be as the priests of the world. Our profession does involve us in separatedness, in a special spirituality of aim, of thought, of knowledge, of watchfulness of action. It does involve us in a life of special obligation to the word of God, for otherwise our Religious life is a superfluity, and if it is a superfluity, it is also profane. So it is our duty not only to cherish with special care the lifeless furniture of the holy altar, but to cherish with a special care that living furniture, our own speech.

At all times we should be recurring to the thought of this, and see whether our words are really worthy of God. That old designation of the Christian life, which we lose sight of in modern conversation—godly, godlike, like to God. It is no godly life that has not the divine likeness, or, as it was in the Greek phrase, that is not lived ἀξίως Θεοῦ (1 *Thess.* ii. 12), worthily of God. Nothing can be worthy of God that is not like God, nor can anything be like God that is not worthy of God. We should indeed seek, then, not to be like man in his fallen state, but like man in his true character as the image of God, for that is truly man-like which is God-like, since man is God's image. If any one is not God-like, then he is not man-like; he is only like the ruin of man, and not like man. So much of the upgrowth of human nature is but as the ivy and the weeds growing about some ruin. Their roots are struck in the soil that has accumulated in the crevices of the building, and though they are beautiful to the eye, they are but the destruction of that whereon they live. And so much that is now considered manly, and beautiful, and worthy of man, is after all only the very eating out of that divine mortar of holy life by which human nature should be cemented together in its perfect beauty and fitness as the habitation

Our words must be worthy of God, as spoken by those created in His image.

of God. Much that is most admired, and which the world delights to pluck for its beauty, and for its fragrance, is after all no part of man's real, true nature; it is but the upgrowth, which is destroying the thing from whence it takes its nourishment.

The words we speak are the formative principle of our nature, conforming us to God's likeness, or degrading us.

So let us be watchful, constantly watchful, to consider whether our words, which are the true formative principle of our nature, are really words worthy of God, and whether they are words such as become man, because he is formed in the image of God. Our great poet spoke very truly in those words, which he puts into the mouth of a man standing upon the verge of the commission of a great crime:

'I dare do all that may become a man;
Who dares do more is none.'

Shakespeare, 'Macbeth,' Act 1, Scene 7.

We must understand that those things which the great bulk of men do, and dare, are not the result of human development and growth, but of man's degradation and decay; manhood is annihilated when man is not conformed to the will of God. Blessed indeed is that life in which the speech is so carefully watched that indeed it may be manlike and God-like. The whole character of man will then be developed. For as a musical instrument loses its tone if it is not properly used, and the jarring discords destroy the very capacity of pure sounds, so it is with the faculties of man; if they are used for the mere strumming of the world's accents, or of unholy passion, the whole nature of man loses its capacity of correspondence with the divine voice. We must take care, then, to cherish our union with God by watchfulness over speech and over thought—the word unformed and the word uttered.

And if we are thus watchful, then the power of the divine truth will indeed become itself the form of our life, for truth is natural to man. Man's being as naturally grows in conformity to the divine truth, as his outer nature grows in conformity to its anatomical structure. Man's mind has indeed lost God's truth by reason of the Fall, but it does not come by the Fall into a condition that is natural. Its true, its natural condition is its unfallen condition, and, if the power of the divine truth be really reverenced within the soul, that power will begin to make itself felt as a living formative principle more and more. If we really are watchful to speak words such as befit God, and to cherish thoughts such as are worthy of God, then the word of God will, as St. Paul says, 'dwell in us richly' (*Col.* iii. 16). It will be indeed a living power that dwells within us, and does become the very form of our new life, as he says again, 'Be ye transformed by the renewing of your mind' (*Rom.* xii. 2). The word of God, given us in our regeneration (cf. 1 *St. Pet.* i. 23), finds in us a real capacity of adaptation to its own needs; it does really take possession of us; it does form us anew so that we may be perfected in its own image. Our laws of thought will be perfected in the intuitive capacities of 'the engrafted word' (*St. Jas.* i. 21), and our aims, and desires, and all our life will glow with the results of this indwelling power.

The divine truth expressed by the word of God will transform our nature, as it is received in living power.

The word is not merely the instrument of the will; it is not merely a faculty of our nature; it is the central and forming faculty, and the whole nature takes its shape in harmony with it. So, if we have the word of God as the real central faculty and power of our nature, our whole nature will indeed correspond with that divine impulse and form.

The sovereignty of the eternal Word within us.

We ought thus to be very watchful to cherish this divine faculty, which is truly the indwelling of the eternal Word, and always to speak in such a way as is consistent with the affectionate and intelligent acknowledgement of His present sovereignty. This will indeed cause holiness, and power, to surround our life. We shall then speak to God, and God will hear our words. How often must we in our prayers wonder that God can hear our words, when we know of the thick fog of sin which comes between our utterance and His hearing! Wonderful it is that God does hear the voice of His dear Son speaking in our official utterance as priests of the Church, although there is this thick, this miserable envelope of evil shrouding our whole nature. But if we are really careful to live in the power of the divine life, then we shall find the power of the divine word; then God indeed will rejoice to hear His word in our words; then He will indeed rejoice to give answer to our prayers. We speak in the name of the Son of God, but that name is uttered beneath such a dense covering of evil that it is marvellous that it should be recognized. If we will come before God really living in the name of Jesus Christ, really living as those whose lives are formed by the power of the divine word, then indeed we shall 'ask what we will, and it shall be done unto us'(*St. John* xv. 7). But our outer life must bear the token of submission, of entire submission to Him who is the Word of God; otherwise the word of God cannot rise from our lips to be recognized by the ear of the eternal Father. Let us then be constantly cherishing this indwelling in us of the Word of God, and remembering the obligations, and considering the great powers, which arise from this indwelling.[1]

If we would really dwell upon the thought of the power which belongs to the priest whose life really allows the word of God to shine forth and to be heard in its clearness, if we would realize the power of this life, how all other powers would sink into insignificance! But, alas, we merely look upon the word of God as an occasional adjunct of our lives, instead of recognizing it as the perpetual interior principle of our lives. St. John Baptist was 'the voice of one crying in the wilderness' (*St. Matt.* iii. 3). He lost all thought of himself in the acknowledgement of his mission as the voice sent from God; but our life is something more than his. As when the voice of the Lord God was heard in Paradise in the midst of the trees of the garden (cf. *Gen.* iii. 8), so the voice of the Lord God is heard in the priesthood of the Paradise of God, in the priesthood of the Christian Church. The voice of the Lord God is heard, and it is for us to lose all thought of any other

<small>As the word of God abides in us, the priest becomes the very voice of God.</small>

[1] See Note R at the end of the chapter.

form of life than that which we derive from this. We must seek to lose ourselves altogether, to be nothing but the voice of God; and that voice, not a mere external moving upon a dissociated frame, but an internal exercise of the organization which it has assumed. The Godhead and the Manhood are joined together in the Person of Christ, never to be divided. Our manhood and our divine life are indissolubly one, the power of the divine life being continually ready to assert itself through our organization. Whithersoever we go 'the Spirit of the living creatures' (cf. *Ezek.* i. 20), the Spirit of the incarnate Saviour, must be within us, our life and His indissolubly bound together in an organization of changeless life.

<small>The utterance of the priest is identified with that of the Incarnate Word, as the mediator of blessing to all mankind.</small>   Thus must we strive to realize how our speech is not merely an article of altar furniture, and the most sacred of all the vessels of the sanctuary, but it is indeed identified with the utterance of Him whom we worship. The blessing of God comes forth from our lips in all the fullness of the power of God. The blessing of God that is given through us is not like a charge of electricity which being once discharged leaves that wherein it resided vacant; but it is a power which is continually responding to the needs of mankind, and keeps our whole being continually replenished with its divine virtues. Virtue goes out of us (cf. *St. Mark* v. 30), and the more it goes out the more is our nature filled with its energies.

Thus must we strive to realize increasingly the great sacredness of that gift of speech which belongs to us, as men formed in the image of God, and chosen from among our brethren to be filled with 'the fullness of God' (*Eph.* iii. 19), that we may speak to God with a perfection of nature worthy of His acceptance, and speak from God in the participation of a power capable of effecting all His will. We may thank God that we are withdrawn by our Religious calling from the idle associations of the world, which are so apt, in spite of the greatest watchfulness, to fritter away and destroy the spiritual life of the priest. But we must be careful that, being thus separated from the world, we also cherish the sacredness of that which is thus enclosed. It is nothing that we fence round the garden of the priestly soul by the rules of an external enclosure; we must see that we are cultivating this garden with all the fullness of divine growth, and that we are keeping it from the upgrowth of those weeds which no enclosure will avail to keep away.

The sacredness of the gift of speech to be guarded, because we are set apart to speak to God, and from God, in the fullness of divine grace.

In all our intercourse one with another, therefore, we must seek to cherish in ourselves and in our brethren this habit of reverence worthy of God, remembering that we are indeed set apart to draw near unto God, not merely on behalf of our brethren, but in the fullness of a nature worthy of God's acceptance, by the renewing power of His Incarnate Son; and that we are to speak from God to our brethren, not merely by the involuntary inspiration of the prophets, nor by the learning of an earthly teacher, but in the fullness of divine blessing, in the power of the Holy Ghost. Our lips are thus to be channels of

The intercourse of Religious brethren must be governed by this law of reverence for their vocation.

grace between God and our brethren, and therefore must be kept worthy of God, free from all the pollution of the merely natural heart, cleansed from all the trivialities of the earthly life. They must be kept pure, and worthy of Him whose anointing Spirit has been pleased to rest upon us in order to make us partakers of His life.

Note Q

'Our thoughts testify to our truth.'

Father Benson appears to mean that the truth or untruth, the faithfulness or unfaithfulness, of our souls to that image of God in which we were created and which is renewed in us by our new birth, is revealed by the thoughts which we harbour in our minds. For we thus reveal ourselves. The glory of God is His perfect unity of being; we are to express that unity in ourselves as our thoughts, finding expression in our words, reveal that we are of God, and that we abide in Him. There is to be no discord between our thoughts and our words, and the true law of our life as begotten again of God in Jesus Christ.

Note R

'If we are really careful to live in the power of the divine life, then we shall find the power of the divine word.'

In what is said of the 'word of God' in this paragraph, and throughout this instruction, it is often impossible to determine whether Father Benson had in mind the personal Word of God, or the spoken or written word of God, whether mediated by prophetic utterances in Holy Scripture, or by our own selves, through the Spirit. It is probable that he had both in mind, for 'every word that proceedeth out of the mouth of God' is an utterance of the eternal Word, the mediator of all creation. This ambiguity in respect of a precise distinction belongs also to Holy Scripture. The language of St. James in the first chapter of his Epistle—'Of his own will begat he us with the word of truth . . . the engrafted word, which is able to save your souls' (*St. Jas.* i. 18, 21)— and the similar language of St. Peter—'Being born again, not of corruptible seed, but of incorruptible, by the word of God, which liveth and abideth for ever' (1 *St. Pet.* i. 23)—read in the light of the prologue to St. John's Gospel, can only be interpreted fully in this double sense.

The living energy of the word of God in our hearts arises from its coming forth from Him who is the eternal Word, in the power of the Holy Spirit. It is through His indwelling, in the power of the same Spirit, that we are enabled to speak, and bring forth in our own utterance a word that is God's, and not ours. It is ours, as proceeding from our lips; it is God's, as the utterance of His Son in and through us. We bring our understanding, our recollection, our reverence; but we speak as we have learned to hear and see in the power of the illuminating and enabling Spirit. We speak then as we are 'taught of God' by His Word.

CHAPTER XXVI

OF CONVERSATION

OUR SPEECH ONE WITH ANOTHER

'*THE brethren must not speak to strangers of any matter relating to the state or condition of the Community, nor to one another without serious reason, unless it be to the Superior General, the Assistant General, or the Provincial Superior.*'

Avoidance of discussion of complaints in the community makes for its peace. They should be referred to Superiors.

This is of great importance in preserving the real peace of any community. Complaints whenever they arise should always be carried to their proper source, and not lead to disparaging conversation amongst one another. One word that is spoken to one in authority will often suffice to get some matter set right, whereas many words spoken to one another only tend to make anything that is wrong very much worse. We are not always capable of judging how far a matter is a fault, and therefore persons are very liable to be condemned unjustly in conversation: but if we speak to those who have the responsibility of government, then, if it is a fault, it will be set right.

The danger of external gossip.

And while we are careful in this way among ourselves, we are to be careful not to discuss the affairs of the Society in any way with strangers. Persons will often be taking a certain interest in the house, and getting a certain amount of gossiping information about the house, and it is very undesirable that they should be able to fasten this on any one of ourselves. Those persons whose opinion is really worth having will never be trying to get such information. We should therefore be careful not to speak about the concerns of the Society to others.

And this, not merely with reference to matters that are at fault, but with reference to all matters. People often are anxious to know the numbers of the Society, and what works are being undertaken. It is of no concern of people at large to know these things; therefore we ought as much as possible to observe silence respecting them. Various evils may happen to our own selves, and to others, by such unnecessary talking. With some we may be led to pride, and with others we may be led to censoriousness, in discussing certain matters which the Society undertakes, and in all probability when those matters are discussed they are discussed without adequate knowledge; so that we are exposed to very great snares in talking over the affairs of the Society with strangers. And we are very liable, without intending it at the beginning, to convey a false impression with reference to this or that person; and it may sometimes be a very undesirable thing that any part of the work of the Society should be more known than is absolutely necessary. A little over-publicity may be extremely injurious to the work of a Mission society. We should therefore acquire a habit of reticence with reference to all concerns of the community.

The safeguard of a habit of reticence.

'*Great care must be taken not to quote Holy Scripture in any light or trivial manner.*'

<small>The care of reverence in quoting Holy Scripture.</small>
This, of course, is of the highest importance. We must form within ourselves a reverent regard of Holy Scripture, and if we allow ourselves to quote its words with levity or thoughtlessness, we must lose something of the spirit of reverence. The words of Holy Scripture should be specially dear to us, as we are entrusted with the administration of the word of God. The words of Holy Scripture should immediately recall our thoughts to Him whose we are and whom we serve. They should always be a sort of link between our minds and the mind of God. The words of Holy Scripture, as they are the form in which the word of God comes forth, should fit into our minds and fashion us according to the divine will. Not merely the more solemn words of Holy Scripture, but mere phrases of Holy Scripture which are immediately recognized as coming from Holy Scripture—all should have for us a living power. And the more we accustom ourselves to dwell upon the mystical meaning of Holy Scripture, the more we shall learn how even a casual reference touches upon the most sacred things. It is not merely that the words are sacred, because they are the words of inspiration; but, even though referring to some outward event, they have a spiritual meaning. We ought never to lose sight of that, and of the mysteries which are hidden behind the letter.

'*In the hour of recreation all shall assemble together, if*

OF CONVERSATION 309

possible; but any matters engendering controversy or party spirit must be avoided.

'*It is most desirable that the exposition and illustration of Holy Scripture and points of moral theology should frequently form the subject of conversation in common-room, and also when the brethren are out walking together.*'

The hour of recreation should bring us all together for the intercourse of mutual thought. In affectionate intercourse one with another we ought to find relaxation and repose. Not such excitement as to take us away from God, but such repose as to strengthen us more perfectly for the service of God, and such a sense of community, and community life, as will enable us to do the work of God more truly in the spirit of community. Our recreation should not be as the mere indifferent meeting of people in the world; our recreation should indeed be a gathering together of mutual fellowship and perfect confidence. Our recreation ought to tend to bind us all together in outer bonds, just as our devotion binds us together in the higher and spiritual bonds of divine grace. In our recreation each individual should seek as far as possible to contribute his own part to the common joy. {The hour of recreation is for mutual fellowship.}

Conversation need not always be definitely religious, but it should always be in the spirit of religion, and it should always be breathing with the life of religion. And therefore our recreation, as much as our devotion, should tend to cherish the religious spirit within us. Indeed our recreation is one great test of what our devotions are {Our conversation with one another tests our Religious character.}

doing for us. When we meet with more freedom of intercourse, we feel ourselves as we are more truly; our natural self comes out. The minor matters which are made the subject of conversation bring out the natural self without that guardedness which belongs to more solemn occasions, and so we see what we ourselves really are. Conversation shows what a man really is; conversation with many tends to bring out the special character of each one.

Avoidance of a controversial spirit necessary, as amongst brethren.
And we must take care that we take our part in recreation really in the Spirit of Jesus Christ, and so all 'matters engendering controversy or party spirit must be avoided.' Matters of doubt and difficulty may well be examined, and questions of interest may well be searched out. We must not seek to maintain our view, as a matter of controversy, for the overthrow of any one else. We must be careful in any matter to avoid anything that may bring forward the harsher side of our character. We must seek to speak in such ways as really tend to our mutual joy. We do not talk, like the brilliant talkers of the world, for the purpose of display, or for the purpose of victory, but for mutual joy. Controversy and party spirit must be avoided, for party spirit is the bane of conversation. It is difficult to enter upon conversation without party spirit, and so we must be very watchful to talk together on every matter as being really brethren, as having no personal predilection for, nor any antagonism to, some one else, but as seeking that which should be most for the joy and benefit of all.

So conversation will become a real matter of strength to us. Our recreation hour should not be a continuance of hard study, but that which we have learned by studying books may very well take root in our hearts by talking about it. It also becomes profitable to those with whom we talk. It would be well, then, to cherish a habit of bringing forward subjects of real interest which may lead to mutual discussion, and which would not engender any personal or party feeling. The more we know of divine truth, the more we are removed from party feeling. Just as in a large circle, the circle is as complete as in a small one, but the curvature is not so sharp; so the more the mind is enlarged, the less we have of the sharpness of conversation and party spirit about us. The more we accustom ourselves to talk about matters which really are of definite and spiritual instruction, and of gain and nourishment to the soul, the more we learn how much there is that is definite to live for, and in which to find our satisfaction—a satisfaction which is so much better than that which could be gained from those subject matters which from day to day are apt to form the great points of conversation.

The value of spiritual conversation.

'*Be very careful that conversation with externs shall be intelligent, spiritual, charitable, profitable, and not merely amusing.*

'*Say nothing which your companions would feel to be inconsistent with what they hear you say in the pulpit.*

'*Always be careful to say a prayer asking for divine*

control, as you go to recreation in the common-room, and upon every occasion of change in your work.'

In speaking with externs we must be very careful not to let them have a degraded idea of the Religious life. People often think that the Religious life is a surrender of intelligence, and that in taking up with a life of devotion we are laying aside the great faculties of our mind. But while we should never talk for the purpose of display, we ought always to be careful so to speak that it may be manifest that we are cultivating the powers of our intelligence. We must always present religion to others in such a form as shall make it commendable. The intelligence is one of God's great gifts; and much harm has been done to religion by many persons seeking to set it aside. We must show, therefore, that ours is no mere dilettante sentimental life; that we have really our reasons for doing what we do, and that these are of the highest kind, for they belong to the higher life.

<small>Conversation with externs must be intelligent.</small>

But if our conversation is to bear the mark of intelligence, then much more of spirituality. But we are not merely to say devout things for the sake of saying them. The great matter is for us to take care as to what we are to avoid. We cannot make our converse spiritual by saying so many spiritual things, but if we keep the atmosphere of our conversation clear from what is unspiritual, then its spirituality will shine out. To say spiritual things for the sake of an effect would be profane, but it is a great duty of charity to avoid saying

<small>Conversation with externs must bear the mark of spirituality.</small>

those things which may mar the spiritual effect of our intercourse.

And if our conversation is to be spiritual, so also it must be charitable. There can be no true spirituality without divine love, for that blessed Spirit who sanctifies our conversation, and is our life, is the very Spirit of love. Spirituality which seems to be wanting in love, or anything which seemed to be spirituality which was wanting in love, would be the spirituality of Satan. It might be austere, sublime, but not of God; for 'God is love' (1 *St. John* iv. 8). We must take care with all with whom we speak, that our Religious life does make us affectionate in the highest sense; not in outward demonstration—for we must be just the reverse—but in the intensity of love, with the wide-spreading reach of love, with the enduring, persevering patience of love. *[margin: Conversation must be charitable]*

Our conversation, then, must be manifest as being charitable and profitable. Better to be silent than to talk words to no profit. We may have to cheer the desponding, to encourage the disheartened, to enliven the saddened; we may have various things to do, but all our conversation should always tend to some definite profit. There never should be a saying of smart things just for the sake of saying things. As we look back upon our conversation, what a terrible thing it is to think of all the words one has spoken! How much injury there is that we have done to many, to set against so little good! And why so little good? Really because there has been so much evil. The Holy Spirit of God we may be sure would be ready *[margin: Conversation must be profitable.]*

to speak for much profit, for much good, by each one of us; but we stop up His utterance by saying that which is unworthy of Him, or antagonistic to Him. It is not because we are wanting in some great intellectual gifts that there is no profit; it is because we allow the world to get too great dominion over our words, and to rule our conversation more than it ought to do. Our conversations may be very clever and yet unprofitable, and they may be very profitable though lacking in cleverness.

The need of the grace of God. So we must be careful that the grace of God does indeed clothe our converse with its own sweetness, with its own solid instruction, with its own sentiment, with its own spiritual glory. We must be careful that the grace of God does indeed shine round about all our words, making manifest the divine life in them; while we speak, not as belonging to ourselves but as belonging to God, not in our own interests but in Jesus Christ's, not as having any heart but the heart of Jesus within us. In His heart we must love those with whom we speak for God's sake, and so love God as He deserves to be loved, for His own glory's sake.

The joy and strength of recreation, as we speak with one another in the fullness of divine love. The hour of recreation may be a season of great refreshment, of great delight, of great joy, of great brightness, of great renewal, of great elasticity, of great vigour; but the hour of recreation, on the other hand, may be a source of much mischief of every possible kind, just in proportion as we are careful to speak according to the fullness of divine love, or merely according to the impulse of the natural heart, merely in the way of ordinary men.

Meeting together day by day, there is but little new to talk about, but we must always meet in the freshness of the love of God. That love never grows old, never grows cold. It must be a power within our hearts, regulating our conversation; and we must rejoice, as we speak one with another, to take notice, each of the other, how we have been with Jesus. Coming from the privacy of our devotions to the things of the outer life, we must abide in the glory of the life of Jesus, and His word shall rule in our hearts, and our words shall be conformable thereto.

O Blessed Jesu, who art the Word of the Father, grant that in all our speaking one with another, and with those who are external to our Society, we may always speak in Thy power, and as by Thy gift of grace; so that Thy blessing may be upon our words, and the words we have spoken to man may not be a hindrance to those words of prayer which by Thy grace we speak unto the Father.

A prayer for God's blessing on our speech one with another.

www.ingramcontent.com/pod-product-compliance
Lightning Source LLC
Chambersburg PA
CBHW070233230426
43664CB00014B/2286